Treasure in the Sand

Tim Floyd

Xulon Press

Copyright © 2010 by Tim Floyd

Treasure in the Sand
by Tim Floyd

Printed in the United States of America

ISBN 9781609572556

All rights reserved solely by the author. The author guarantees all contents are original and do not infringe upon the legal rights of any other person or work. No part of this book may be reproduced in any form without the permission of the author. The views expressed in this book are not necessarily those of the publisher.

Unless otherwise indicated, Bible quotations are taken from The Holy Bible, New International Version. Copyright © 2001 by The Zondervan Corporation.

www.xulonpress.com

TABLE OF CONTENTS

Acknowledgments 7

Introduction 9

Week 1: An Appointment in the Desert 15

Week 2: The Power of a Disillusioned Life 37

Week 3: The Way God Works 53

Week 4: God- 10; Egypt-0 75

Week 5: The Truth will Set You Free 95

Week 6: Who's Watching My Back? 117

Week 7 What Every Leader Should Learn 139

Week 8 Loving God 161

Week 9 Loving Your Neighbor 181

Week 10: A Foundation that Endures 203

Week 11: Every Picture Tells a Story 225

Week 12: The Glory of the God Who Came Near 247

ACKNOWLEDGMENTS

Providence Baptist Church in McLean, Virginia, is the church I call home. This project is, in part, a reflection of their love, encouragement and support. I remain indebted to my church family for affording their pastor the space to grow and sometimes make mistakes, the freedom to think and write, and the kind of loyalty that is generally associated with family. Their hunger for truth and their enthusiasm for this project have been a powerful incentive for me to keep working.

I am also deeply grateful to other friends who have caught the vision and contributed to this process. Jerry Simmons edited the entire manuscript, and provided invaluable guidance. Pastor Hub Blankenship previewed an early version of this work and, likewise, offered practical feedback which has strengthened the work. Lynn Ashley of Good Shepherd Graphics jumped in with enthusiasm to create the wonderful graphics which brighten these pages. And Kelly Class has been an unlimited source of wisdom and strategy in developing the plan that has gotten this book off the shelves and into the hands of readers like you.

As always, my wife Jonnel has read chapters, conducted research, made phone calls, and offered encouragement that has kept the flame alive over nearly four years of development. She took care of extra details on the home front so that I could set aside time to study, pray and write.

Needless to say, I remain completely indebted to Jesus Christ, the Captain of our Salvation. His work and his character continually teach me about the transforming power of divine grace. And his timeless wisdom reminds me how small I am, and how much I have to learn.

Soli Deo gloria!

INTRODUCTION

There they shall offer sacrifices of righteousness; for they shall partake of the abundance of the seas, and of treasures hidden in the sand. -Moses[1]

Perhaps no other environment is more forbidding than a desert- or more instructive. Lost among the vast expanses of sand, wind and profound *waterlessness*, it becomes easier to focus on the things that matter most. That fiery blast of wind and sun has the power to strip away all that is non essential and superficial. Material wealth, trendy friends, cool clothes and plans for the week-end; all those things fall quickly away in the delicate balance of life and death. *What remains is what matters.*

In the same way, it is in the spiritual deserts of life where our thirst for the Father becomes most acute. Painful problems leave us feeling alone, isolated. Indecision and anxiety create the sensation of being stranded and hopeless. There seem to be no solutions on the horizon- *only more complications*. Our hearts cry out for the water of life. Our weary flesh craves the cool breeze of fleeting hope, if only for a momentary break in the tension. We are exhausted, floundering knee deep in an endless stretch of sand dunes. *Nobody but my heavenly Father can help me now.*

In times like these, our reactions can seem mechanical, borne of desperation. But God's responses are different. The Father replies from Eternity, and draws on heavenly reserves that belong to him alone. Without a doubt, God's involvement is far more urgent and more desirable than anything I might muster.

The timeless book of Exodus revolves around a man named Moses, and his epic relationship with the Almighty God. As we shall see, the life of Moses must have sometimes felt like walking through a furnace. He could have lived as a privileged Egyptian, but he chose to take his stand as an oppressed Hebrew. Scripture explains, "He thought it was better to suffer for the sake of Christ than to own the treasures of Egypt, for he was looking ahead to his own great reward."[2] The Greek word translated "great" is *megas*, which gives us our word "mega." Moses anticipated a mega reward at the end of his travail.

It's ironic that Moses had to leave the regal robes and the opulence of Egypt's royal palace in order to experience true riches. Forty years old and fleeing to Midian as a fugitive, he discovered something all the gold of Rameses could never afford him- *a sense of tribe*. The priest of Midian, a man called Jethro, offered him a home, a wife, a job and a community. Caring for herds in a merciless desert where the comforts were few, Moses took comfort in the give and take of tribal life.

Four decades later, he would finally have the heart and the wisdom to return to Egypt for his blood relatives. He actually set out wondering if any of them might still be alive. The good news was that they had survived their chains. The bad news was that they were broken in spirit; cynical, indecisive, impatient and shallow. Held hostage in a kingdom of pagan idols far from their own Land of Promise, they were open to change- *just not very much!* Where was that once proud Tribe of Israel?

Wherever they were is surely where many who call upon the name of Jesus are living comfortably today. We are nestled comfortably in a secular society, held hostage by our fears and our desires for respectability, seduced by a society which offers us consumer goods in exchange for our time- *our lives*. We constantly upgrade our smart phones and update our *Facebook* status because we value "connectivity." But we know nothing of "community." Research suggests we are lonelier and more friendless than ever before, because personal amusement and individualism are more convenient than authentic friendship. Often we have no clue about what we are missing, because we have never experienced a sense of tribe.

Just a few years ago in a place called Malindi on the coast of Kenya, I had the extreme joy of being part of the answer to one young man's prayers. In the course of a week of walking village to village, I saw his mother, his sister, his rebellious older brother, and his proud, distant father come to faith in Christ, something Christopher had been praying about for years. As a result, one afternoon his family, neighbors and relatives came together for a time of celebration. The young men scurried up tall palm trees, tossed down fresh coconuts and cracked them open. And in the shade of those towering palms, we drank coconut milk, scooped the white meat from the shells, and laughed together over what the Lord had done! It was all very spontaneous and natural for them.

For many of us in the States, things remotely like that only take place at weddings every now and then! We are too busy for real community, and can only afford it in very small doses and by appointment. My good friend Andy is one of those guys who love the Tribe of Christ. He will do anything for his friends- from giving them money or loaning his car, to helping them move or repairing a broken appliance. Andy is so tribal that he enjoys occasionally dropping by the house to consult briefly on a spiritual question or follow up on a problem. And for a long time, it drove most of us crazy! "What kind of friend drops in unexpectedly when I might be watching my favorite TV program or doing the laundry?" We never asked the larger question: "What kind of friend values a TV program or a load of laundry over a buddy who really cares about you?"

Exodus is the book that offers us the Ten Commandments. Later in the New Testament, Jesus will boil the ten down to only two: "Love the Lord your God with all your heart, soul, mind and strength, and your neighbor as yourself." Of course, those two are almost inseparable, because the most powerful expression of my love for God is the way in which I love his Tribe, my neighbors. Like Moses before him, Jesus is a pioneer in tribal faith. When he speaks of us as "blessed," one of the greatest assets he has in mind is our identity among His Tribe. Exodus painfully demonstrates that God will do whatever is required to build those sacred bonds.

Introduction

"As the deer pants for streams of water, so my soul pants for you, O God." David wrote those lyrical words. But does his experience sound familiar? "My soul thirsts for God, for the living God. When can I go and meet with God?"[3] History has shown us that God waits for us in life's most confusing, arid places.

The unforgettable, Old Testament book of Exodus is the story of trapped, hopeless people of faith who were called into the desert to meet with God. Their joyous day in the sun would arrive only after an entire generation of facing down one impossible giant after another. When Moses first arrived with an invitation from God, it must have seemed to the defeated Children of Israel that an unending desert of hopeless challenges and emotional sand dunes stood between them and the presence of the God of Abraham, Isaac and Jacob. Yet through supernatural faith and tireless community, with pitfalls of spiritual stupidity scattered along the way, they would taste victory.

What about you, dear friend? Are you thirsty? Have the sandstorms of despair and the heat of trial knocked you flat on your face recently? Has doubt or depression left you alone and defeated with the bitter taste of sand still in your mouth? Don't give up the fight! *Deserts happen to everyone.* But treasure happens to children of God who learn to rely on him.

The writer of Hebrews describes the early days of the church, when persecution was violent and constant. "So don't throw away this confident trust in the Lord. Remember the great reward it brings you. Patient endurance is needed now, so that you will continue to do God's will. Then you will receive all that he has promised."[4] Once again, we have found that promising Greek word *megas*.

This Bible Study is an exploration of the mega riches waiting in God's providence for you. Peter describes a share of that wealth as "pure, undefiled and beyond the reach of change or decay."[5] Yes, some of it's waiting for your arrival in Heaven. And that will be amazing.

But we have already seen there are treasures buried here on Earth as well. Take this promise, for example. "In Him, are hidden all the treasures of wisdom and knowledge,"[6] Paul told the Colossians. He was writing about Jesus, the one who shares with us in the fellowship of his suffering. In addition to Heaven, there are riches God makes available to us now when we are willing to endure with Him.

Treasure in the Sand
You are about to undertake a twelve week adventure based on the Book of Exodus. Our goal is to discover powerful lessons God wants to teach us; then to apply those principles to our lives. The plan is to prepare ourselves today for whatever trials and tribulations God may have calendared for tomorrow. When we enter the desert equipped, we are able to thrive and not simply survive. There are divine riches ahead for the faithful.

Before you begin, perhaps I should share some things you might want to know about making the most of this journey through the deserts of Exodus:

- Each week is broken up into four lessons. You can devote Monday through Thursday nights to the study and take the week-ends off; or you can study every other night and leave some time in between to think. *Find a plan that works for you.*

- Many lessons will conclude with a time of prayer and soul searching. Don't postpone this to some later date when it may be forgotten. Make time in your schedule to pause at that moment and be still before the Father. *We're looking for life change here; not just gathering information.*

- Each session contains a variety of basic scriptural texts you should read and process. The learning exercises that accompany each passage are designed to give you fresh insights and help you recall important truths. Don't be in a hurry! Make yourself slow down to fill in the blanks, etc. *Other readers have asked me to assure you that you'll be glad you did.*

- Whenever you read a familiar passage of Scripture in this study, try to see it through fresh eyes. Use a different translation or simply pause to ask very human questions about how you'd feel in situations like these.

- Scattered through each week's lessons, you'll find sidebars which contain interesting and often surprising facts about desert life. You'll also find occasional quotes from the desert fathers, men who fled the corruption of society and sought holiness and intimacy with Christ in the deserts of Egypt around AD 200. It's my hope that these will sharpen your understanding of the scriptural events, and encourage your efforts to relentlessly embody the truths of God's Word.

- Use margins to jot down additional thoughts and questions. If time permits, check out the details found in the end notes located at the conclusion of the book.

- Most importantly, consider working through *Treasure in the Sand* with a group of friends and fellow believers. By meeting together to discuss what you've learned each week, you will not only strengthen your learning experience, but will enjoy the benefits of tribe which are so fundamental in Exodus. Download the free *Leader's Guide* that accompanies the textbook at our website: **www.TreasureintheSand.org.**

Exodus is for people who are facing the desert, but it's not just about escaping. It's not merely about surviving. The God of the Exodus has designed the desert as a place where you and I can grow and flourish. *Thirst is a very good thing.* It means you have learned whom you require most. Let's go to him now.

Take a moment and make this prayer your own. Read it quietly to yourself, and then offer it aloud to your Heavenly Father.

Introduction

A Desert Prayer

Heavenly Father, no one understands me more than you. No one else can discern the deepest secrets of my heart like you can, because you created me, and you know the innermost workings of my soul. I need to be still now and draw strength from your company.

Gracious Lord, pour the water of life into my dry, empty soul today. Only you can anoint me with the oil of joy, and give me the peace to lie down and rest tonight. O Father, let my cup overflow.

The desert where I find myself today belongs to you. The trials and worries that frighten me seem small and insignificant to you. Give me the power to stand tall in this hour of trial, and show me the path that keeps me closest to your side. Thank you, Lord, for your presence, for your refreshing, and for your strength. Jesus, you are King of Kings and Lord of Lords. Amen.

WEEK ONE

AN APPOINTMENT IN THE DESERT

God descends to the humble as waters flow down from the hills into the valleys. -St. Tikhon of Voronezh, of the Desert Fathers

The ancient key that unlocks the book of Exodus is buried in the sands of Egypt near the end of Genesis. Following the death of his father Jacob, Joseph comforts his anxious brothers with this serene benediction: "You intended it for evil, but God used it for good."[7] Joseph acknowledges that his brothers were at their worst, and yet God was at his best.

One day history will tell the story of a nation of slaves who managed to defy the mightiest nation their world has ever seen. After years of bondage designed to break their spirit and suffocate their hopes, the Children of Israel will pack up their bedrolls and make their bid to escape this heart of darkness known as Egypt. A million Hebrews will bid farewell to ancestors lying in their graves in Goshen, even as grieving Egyptian fathers and uncles dig fresh graves for their own lost boys. And they will find life, hope and destiny waiting just ahead in the desert sands.

One day God will raise up a desert prophet named Moses. His leathery hands and countenance will be as parched and rough as the bark of a thorn tree. He will be feared for his blazing temper, but admired for a tenacious sort of faith. And neither the majesty of Pharaoh nor the scorching blast of the Arabian winds will be able to turn his face away from the call of the Almighty. Moses and his people will renounce the glories of Egypt to stake their claim on a promised land somewhere beyond the barren stretches of Sinai.

But before you shake the hand of the Great Liberator, may I introduce you to another astonishing Hebrew- a young visionary? You see, the Israelites did not arrive in Egypt looking for work as slaves. Nor did they invade to inflict God's judgment on pagan Egypt, although that would ultimately be the case. It was God's mercy that first beckoned them to Egypt.

The instrument of God's mysterious calling is this extraordinary young man with a name as common as Joe. By the grace of God, he will endure bondage and prison without ever sacrificing his character or his faith. He will face the treachery of family and the cruelty of strangers without ever seeming to complain. One glad day his spiritual nobility and his unquenchable faith in God's providence will be vindicated by a reversal of fortune like most of us have never seen or imagined. And no one will be able to miss the meaning behind all that misery!

Of course, you and I have faced moments like this one late in Joseph's life. Months or years after one particularly fiery trial or another, we look backwards, recognize how God sustained us, and confess we are glad that it happened; or that we are better people for it. But it's not that kind of confession so many years later that makes Joseph remarkable. Instead Joseph's life inspires us because he acts on the realization *before he knows how God will resolve his crisis*! Even on his way down as a slave, he role models impeccable surrender to God's purpose.

Why are you and I so slow to trust? It seems we have developed this aversion to pain even though we glibly speak of picking up the cross and following Jesus. So when we do experience the trials of life, our culture of grief counseling has programmed us that we must sit down and talk about our feelings. It's not "therapeutic" to claim idealistic Bible verses or behave like some Pollyanna by making a positive confession. Rather, we have this idea that healing only happens if we open up and verbalize all the fear, anxiety, bitterness and doubt hidden out of sight in the dusty corners of our minds.

But what are we supposed to do with all those retro Bible verses? Peter writes, "Dear friends, do not be surprised at the painful trial you are suffering, as though something strange were happening to you."[8] It is difficult to miss the obvious message of that statement: that painful trial is not strange or unusual. A New Testament worldview leaves no room for whimpering, "Why me?"

If we really believe that well known definition that faith is "being sure of what we hope for and certain of what we do not see,"[9] then isn't it evil to carp and whine until God actually does something visible? Can we agree that it's destructive to poison the lives and minds of our families and friends by confessing *unfaith* until we can actually see how things are going to work out?

Joseph's story is included in Genesis to accomplish more in your life and mine than merely giving us hope. Rather, he is set before us as a vivid picture of how faith is designed to bear up in times of pain and hardship. God hasn't gone to these lengths to merely inspire you and me; *he wants to change us*. And what happens in Genesis doesn't just stop there- it leads to further turmoil and greater challenge in the pages of Exodus. So before we join the children of Israel in their fiery trial in Egypt, it is important to pause for a moment and recall the human treachery and divine goodness that brought them here originally.

Three powerful ideas are interwoven into the fabric of the closing pages of Genesis and the unfolding chapters of Exodus.

- First, God convincingly demonstrates that *adversity is an asset*, not a liability. For people who live in the moment, personal trial feels very much like a painful interruption; a wasted moment in a brief life. But people of faith live in a continuum in which an eternal stretch of time is waiting for us just beyond this event horizon. If bearing up under trial now means something positive and precious in that future, then surely we can keep walking. *We can because it does.*

Week One   An Appointment in the Desert

- The second big idea involves *the power of healthy community*. Joseph begins his young life with the extreme favor of his father, but he finds himself sold down the river because his tribe is divided and diseased. Brothers who should be his defenders nearly become his executioners. By contrast, when they later find themselves on the threshold of starvation, their tribal bonds to a mighty man will save and sustain them. Sometimes there is no safety in numbers, but there is always strength within the Tribe.

- Finally, the story of Joseph, Moses, and Israel teaches us that *men and women are weighted with destiny*. The statesmen who wrote the U.S. Declaration of Independence took their cues from Scripture when they asserted that liberty is something God gives to us all. But even in the face of our freedom to choose, prophecy always comes to pass because the Creator God anticipates where we are going. His holy purposes and eternal power mean that certain things must take place, no matter what human beings may do to the contrary. And so Joseph's scheming brothers will never derail his dreams!

Before the opening verses of Exodus begin to rush past us, let's go back to the climax of Genesis and track the hand of God. Then by week's end we'll turn to Exodus and size up the situation that is developing as that saga opens.

Here are some of the questions we want to answer, as we explore how God uses desert experiences to energize and enrich the people he loves.
- Day 1: Do you believe that God is cruel when he allows an outstanding young man of faith and integrity to be wrongly accused, sold into slavery, and ultimately imprisoned for years? *Why or why not?*
- Day 2: Is Joseph being callous and vengeful when he frames his brother for stealing a gold cup, and places his family in such a terrifying situation?
- Day 3: How do you activate your faith when powerful people or painful circumstances are working against you?
- Day 4: What do we really mean when we say that God is "sovereign?" Can things ever spin out of his control for a moment? How does your life reflect that answer?

Day One: My Faith is Not a Fantasy
Read Genesis 37 and 40
As you read, highlight or underscore words or phrases that indicate or hint that God is somehow at work in this developing crisis.

37:3. Every child deserves the certainty of a parent's unconditional love. How would Jacob's parental devotion for his children stack up on a scale of unconditionality?

_____

_____

Has Joseph done anything negative that might justify his mistreatment? List the reasons you believe Joseph is or is not deserving of his brothers' resentment.

    1. _____

    2. _____

    3. _____

Genesis 37:5-11. Joseph's dreams are often overlooked as mere details, but they actually have huge significance in his story. The first dream finds the brothers all binding sheaves of grain in the field. Suddenly, Joseph's sheaf rises up and his brother's sheaves bow down before it. Later Joseph dreams of the sun, moon and eleven stars bowing down before him. His family clearly understands that the dream is a vision of Jacob's family bowing down before Joseph.

- Joseph's fourteen chapters in Genesis omit most of the details of his boyhood and adolescence, but include details of both dreams. What does this indicate about the importance of these dreams?

  _____

  _____

- Why should we conclude that Joseph sees these dreams as significant?

  _____

  _____

- *Genesis 37:11.* How do we know that Jacob believes these dreams may well prove to be important?

  _____

  _____

- Scripture never actually says these dreams are from God. How can we ultimately know that they are? *See Genesis 42:6.*

Week One   An Appointment in the Desert

_____

_____

God does not waste words in Scripture. Neither does he include extraneous, unimportant details. There is a reason why Joseph's dreams loom as the backdrop for his betrayal and eventual imprisonment, and it's not simply that they fuel his brother's jealousy. Rather, the two dreams give us vivid insight into Joseph's character and his response to apparent defeat later in his life.

Why does he accept slavery so blithely and treat his master with such courtesy and integrity? When he is framed by his master's lustful wife and is wrongly cast into prison, why does he remain so constant, so unshakeable? There's no doubt that he has extremely tenacious faith in the Almighty God. *But what does he trust God to do?* Among other things, he is relying on God to fulfill the vision that was planted in his mind while he was sleeping years earlier. Joseph believes that God can elevate him to a place of such power and influence that even people as unlikely as his brothers will be forced to respect him. He cannot possibly foresee the catastrophic crisis that will arise, but he senses that God's providence will position him to accomplish something positive on a massive scale.

Genesis 37: 12 – 25. The events described here become more plausible when we remember that this is not merely an aggravated case of sibling rivalry. While we usually speak of Joseph's young rivals as "brothers," all but Benjamin are actually half brothers living together in this "blended" family. Turn back to *Genesis 35: 23 – 26*, and match each man in Column A with his family status in Column B.

____ Joseph	A. Father of 12 sons by two legal wives and two maids
____ Jacob/Israel	B. Jacob's oldest son by his unbecoming wife Leah. He attempted to save young Joseph and return him safely to his father.
____ Reuben	C. Jacob's first of two sons by favorite wife Rachel.
____ Judah	D. Jacob's second son by Leah, the unloved.
____ Simeon	E. Jacob's second son by his favorite wife Rachel.
____ Benjamin	F. Fourth son from the less favored Leah. He persuaded his brothers to sell Joseph rather than murder him.

Important background: While you're thinking about this confused family situation, don't miss the irony of what happens next. After the ten half brothers toss Joseph into an empty cistern, a caravan of Ishmaelite traders arrives. *Do we know anything important about "Ishmaelites?"* We do indeed! These are the descendants of Abraham's less favored son, Ishmael.

As a boy and young man, young Ishmael had found himself sent away not just once, but several times, so that Isaac's status as favored son could be protected. While you and I can appreciate the high priority of Isaac's role as divinely ordained heir, it makes us cringe to observe the insensitive, heavy handed methods of Abraham and Sarah in dealing with the plight of young

Ishmael. (*See Genesis 16: 4-12; 21:8-10; 25:5-6.*) Ishmael will ultimately pass along his sense of rivalry to his descendants, some of whom become players in the story of Joseph.

Genesis 39:3. Now the story moves to Egypt, where Potiphar, Joseph's new master, soon recognizes that God has his hand on this young man. How can he possibly conclude such a thing in light of the harsh reality that Joseph has been sold into slavery by his own brothers? Explain below:

_____

_____

Genesis 39: 4, 21. Scripture teaches that God gives Joseph favor with Potiphar. Later, we learn that God gives him favor in the sight of the prison warden. The word translated "favor" is the Hebrew word *hen*. It denotes "grace, the moral quality of kindness." The same Hebrew root results in a similar word which is translated "without charge, without cost, in exchange for nothing, for no reason."

Which of the following statements do you believe best summarizes the work of God in these incidents? Check off the *one summary* that seems most accurate, based on the narrative:
- [ ] God's principles are so powerful that when Joseph lives by them, he becomes a more magnetic, more influential personality.
- [ ] God's Spirit uses circumstances to tenderize the hearts of these men who have power over Joseph's life, making them more receptive to his words and deeds.
- [ ] God gives Joseph a sort of "Midas touch," so that everything he touches leads to greater success and satisfaction.

In *chapter 40*, the dream scenario continues to play out in the life of Joseph. His brothers had plotted to kill him, adding "We'll see what comes of his dreams!" Now in prison, he correctly interprets the dreams of the Pharaoh's cup bearer and baker. Later, after the cup bearer is released and forgets about Joseph for a long time, Pharaoh loses sleep because of troubling dreams, and his servant remembers Joseph from prison. Consult *chapters 40 and 41*, and match each of the following dreams to the man it troubled.

40:9 _____ Cup Bearer		A. Baskets of bread intended for the king are eaten by wild birds.
40:16 _____ Baker		B. Healthy heads of grain consumed by withered heads of grain.
41:17 _____ Pharaoh		C. Branches of grapes produce a goblet of wine for the Pharaoh.
41:22 _____ Pharaoh		D. Fat, healthy cows emerge from the Nile to be eaten by some scrawny, skeletal cows.

Week One   An Appointment in the Desert

Briefly move forward to Genesis 41:41-49. Find this passage and fill in the blanks that follow:

"Pharaoh placed Joseph in charge of the whole land of Egypt. He placed his _____ on Joseph's hand. He dressed him in fine robes with a _____ around his neck. He made him ride in a chariot as his _____, and men shouted "Make way," as he passed. Joseph was _____ years old when he entered the service of Pharaoh."

Important background: Did you notice that Joseph will ultimately have two sons of his own while living in Egypt: Manasseh and Ephraim? When the Promised Land is distributed to the tribes of Israel following the Exodus, Joseph will actually receive two shares- *one for each of his sons*.[10] (See Joshua 16.)

Q: Do you believe that God is cruel when he allows an outstanding young man of faith and integrity to be wrongly accused, sold into slavery, and ultimately imprisoned for years? *Why or why not?*

_____

_____

_____

Christ in the Old Testament: The first thirty-nine books of the Bible constantly foreshadow the character and the truth of Jesus. Sometimes we find him in an Old Testament character, or in a person's response to an unusual situation. Where is Christ most visible in this segment of Joseph's story?

_____

_____

_____

One of the most overlooked facts in the Bible is found in Genesis 41:45. Along with everything else, the pagan ruler gives Joseph a new, Egyptian name. He calls him *Zaphenath-panea*. It means "God speaks and lives."

Day Two: Justice and Mercy Go Hand in Hand
Read Genesis 42 and 44
Review these three chapters and highlight or underscore each statement that refers back to Joseph's dreams from his youth or his betrayal by his brothers.

Genesis 42. The famine that has become such a boom for Joseph has been a complete bust for his family back home. Eventually Jacob hears rumors of surplus food in neighboring Egypt. When his sons arrive in Egypt asking permission to buy some grain they are referred to a government agency where Joseph recognizes them almost instantly! If he can spot them so quickly, why might they not recognize him?

_____

_____

Hints: Genesis 41:42; 42:13-b; 42:23

Complete *Genesis 42:6.* Now Joseph was the _____ of the land, the one who sold grain to all its people. So when Joseph's brothers arrived, they _____ to him with their faces on the ground.

In the words of Yogi Berra, "It's *déjà vu* all over again" as this chapter opens. Joseph discovers his brothers kneeling at his feet, exactly as he had foreseen in his dreams as a youth. Despite the indignation of his dad, and the opposition of his jealous siblings, Joseph's dreams are coming to pass. And more importantly, God's Word is being fulfilled- at several different levels.

One crucial element of a biblical worldview is the principle that choices always have consequences; that sinful decisions eventually result in unhappy outcomes. Jacob and his sons are keenly aware of that principle, and mention it time and again. Briefly summarize each of the following verses in your own words:

- 42:21. _____
  _____

- 42:22. _____
  _____

- 42:28-b. _____
  _____

Based on the *actual details* of the narrative, which of the following statements best characterizes this situation? *Choose only one:*

Week One An Appointment in the Desert

[ ] God is completely in charge, moving Joseph like a pawn on a chessboard.
[ ] Joseph is in completely in charge, taking advantage of his own good fortune and political power.
[ ] Joseph chooses to respond in faith to circumstances being orchestrated by his omnipotent God.
[ ] I would express it differently: _____

A New Testament perspective: Consult the following passages in the New Testament and complete the blanks below.
- *Galatians 5:7,8*. Do not be deceived. God cannot be _____. A man reaps what he _____.
- *2 Peter 3:8,9*. But do not forget this one thing, dear friends: with the Lord, one day is like _____... The Lord is not _____ in keeping his promise as some understand slowness..."

Take a moment and explain how those two New Testament ideas relate to Joseph and his mistreatment at the hands of his brothers.

_____

_____

Joseph knows his ten siblings are not spies. And he certainly knows they have spoken the truth about their two "missing" brothers. *What he doesn't know is the current state of their character!* Are they still the sort of self-centered thugs who would trade away a brother on a whim? Are they still so callous that they would break their aging father's heart again to save their necks? He creates a bit of drama to catch them off guard and test their mettle.

- *42:18*. Joseph requires that Simeon remain in prison until the brothers go home again and return with their youngest brother. What does Joseph hope to learn from this?

_____

- *42:27*. He has the silver they used to purchase grain secretly returned to their back packs. What does this accomplish?

_____

Chapter Summary: In *Exodus 43*, the brothers return to their father in Canaan and report of that a mysterious Egyptian has given them food, but is holding Simeon hostage until they return with Benjamin. Jacob refuses to let them return with Benjamin, even at the risk of losing Simeon, until their food supplies are once again exhausted.

- 44:2. When the brothers finally return with beloved Benjamin, Joseph has his servants frame the youth by placing a treasured silver cup in his bag. What does Joseph hope to learn from this?

  _____

  _____

- 44:17-34. After the planted cup is found on Benjamin, Joseph announces he will lock up the thief but allow the others to return home free men. What does he conclude from Judah's passionate appeal?

  _____

Now read Genesis 45: 1 - 6. We commonly assume that the climax of Joseph's story occurs when the Pharaoh exalts him to the role of Regent and places the royal seal around his neck. *Wrong!* The climax of Joseph's story-indeed, the climax of the entire book of Genesis- comes when he finally reveals his identity to his brothers.
- This is more than a grand family reunion.
- This is more than a chance for Joseph to show how far he's come.
- This is the literal fulfillment of Joseph's dreams from his boyhood, delivered by God!

True to life, even this emotional moment is marked by dramatic turns and twists. Concluding that his brothers are now godly men, Joseph divulges his true identity and asks about his father. Even though tears are streaming down his face, Joseph's brothers are suddenly more terrified than ever! All along they have assumed they've been dealing with a cynical stranger. Suddenly, they discover this powerful Egyptian is actually their long lost brother whom they trapped in a pit, threatened to kill, and ultimately sold as a slave!

The horrified siblings are surely thinking, "At least we had a chance of success with a stranger. After all we've done to Joseph, he is sure to have us executed!" But the men are in for yet one further surprise. Joseph repeats that he is the brother whom they sold into slavery. Then he adds, "And now, do not be distressed. And do not be angry with yourselves for sending me here, because it was to *save lives* that God sent me here."

There's so much drama and emotion coiled into this scene, that it's easy to miss the underlying point. So let's take a moment and reflect. Not only is Joseph *not* angry or vengeful, but he tells his unworthy former assailants not to be distressed either. Come on, even if Joseph has put this foul deed behind him, why should he comfort his brothers instead of leaving them to twist in the wind? *Don't miss the answer.* Nobody should be angry here because this is the best thing that could have happened! Of course it looked bad at the time, but this was simply God's way of sending Joseph ahead to save his people! Had this not happened, everyone in this story might have died of malnutrition by now!

Week One An Appointment in the Desert

If this was a good thing, not a bad thing, why should anyone be angry or upset? That's the point! That's why Joseph is so gracious. Good has prevailed! God has reaped the victory.

Consult *Genesis 45:8* and fill in the blanks that follow. "So then, it was not you who sent me here, but _____. He made me _____ to Pharaoh, _____ of his entire household, and _____ of Egypt."

Note: Don't overlook that powerful observation in *verse 8*; "God made me father to Pharaoh." Although Joseph is most likely younger than the king and is actually a foreigner who was summoned from prison, the ruler of mighty Egypt has come to regard him with the trust and respect a son offers his father. This is clearly a supernatural turn of events.

Genesis 45:14-20 describes yet another amazing moment! Joseph throws his arms around his brother Benjamin and weeps. Then he embraces the ten others, and weeps over them as well. The scene is so astonishing that aides and officials began to whisper excitedly, and news of this extraordinary event soon reaches the courts of the Pharaoh. The Pharaoh sends the family of Jacob an invitation that is almost beyond belief:
- They should come immediately to live in the prosperity of Egypt;
- They should leave all their possessions behind and allow the king to provide everything they will need for a new life;
- He will give them the best of the land of Egypt.

Compare this to what might have happened had Joseph been a different sort of man. *Use your imagination here.* Project what would have been the likely outcome had Joseph demanded justice rather than showing mercy. What would have happened to the brothers, to Jacob, to the budding new nation of Israel?

1. The ten brothers would have _____

2. Their father Jacob would have _____

3. The budding nation of Israel would have _____

Christ in the Old Testament: Where do you see the character or principles of Jesus Christ in this incident from the life of Joseph?

_____

_____

Day Three: The Moment of Decision
Read Genesis 46, 47, 50
To enjoy chapter 50 in context, you will need to begin with 49:29. Highlight or underscore words or phrases that relate to times of change or uncertainty.

Have you ever found yourself so torn between two possible choices that you become paralyzed by indecision and ultimately do nothing? Most of us know exactly how that feels. It's very human to wait... until the future becomes less cloudy... until some pivotal event happens... until we are in a more secure situation... until we are forced to choose. Tragically, our unwillingness to take necessary action can cost us opportunities and produce a life of mediocrity.

On our road to the book of Exodus, we find Joseph's father Jacob in just one of those anxious moments of decision. His grown sons have returned from Egypt with the most unlikely story- his long lost son Joseph is allegedly the Governor of Egypt and has invited the entire family to come and join him! But should he trust them and move to a foreign land?

- There are good reasons to refuse. They have, after all, lied to him before. And besides, the family is already living in the Land of Promise, and the idea of Joseph ruling in distant Egypt sounds far-fetched!
- Nevertheless, the boys have brought wagonloads of clothing and supplies to support their story. Even Benjamin insists this story is true. And realizing what an impact Joseph's dreams had on the family so many years earlier, there's one additional factor:
    ✓ Joseph had always dreamed his family would bow down to him.
    ✓ It must have occurred to Jacob by now that the story his sons have brought home sounds a great deal like Joseph's boyhood dreams!

Genesis 46: 1 - 7. Despite the obvious uncertainty, Jacob's heart is revived by the news and the evidence piled in all the carts and wagons the brothers have brought home. So he takes a big step of faith and sets out for Egypt. When he arrives at Beersheba, Canaan's southernmost city before the border of Egypt, Israel stops to offer a sacrifice to God.

- What does this sacrifice before crossing into Egypt say to you about Israel's attitude and emotions at this moment?

_____

_____

_____

- God comforts the aging patriarch with a vision filled with promises. Consult *46: 3-4* and complete the four promises below:
    ✓ I am God, the God of your Father.
    ✓ Do not be afraid to go down to Egypt for _____
    ✓ I will _____

Week One   An Appointment in the Desert

- ✓ And I will surely_____
- ✓ And Joseph's own hand _____

- Like his grandfather Abraham two generations earlier, Israel is comforted in this anxious moment by God's reassurance about his Tribe. Look at the promises again and explain how each relates to the Tribe of Israel.
    - ✓ "I will make you into a great nation in Egypt..."

    _____

    _____

    - ✓ "I will surely bring you back again..." [See 47:30]

    _____

    _____

    - ✓ "Joseph's own hand will close your eyes."

    _____

    _____

Did you take note that Jacob actually made his decision and began the journey to Egypt *(45:25)* before receiving confirmation from God *(46:2)*? Obviously, this is not the first time that Jacob has been called to trust the Father through a treacherous and uncertain situation. As a young man, Jacob had deceived his brother Esau, and was forced to flee for his life. On the run, he found himself in the home of Uncle Laban who was a master of the old bait-and-switch con.

It is no accident that Joseph becomes the kind of man who clings tirelessly to his divinely ordained purpose. He must have learned that lesson as a boy from his passionate, unrelenting dad. It's easy to miss the significance of the fact God's people were called the children of Israel/Jacob, rather than the children of Abraham.

Genesis 46:26,27. The future nation of Israel will begin their stay in Egypt with a tiny population of less than 100. Who is included among those seventy people?

_____

_____

Genesis 46: 28 – 34. Jacob's emotional reunion with the son he once thought was dead is one of scripture's unforgettable moments. Use your imagination here. Try to visualize the scene in your mind.

- Jacob is a retired shepherd, 130 years old. How would he look?

- Joseph has spent perhaps 20 years in Egypt, many of them in the palace. How would he appear?

- Joseph is riding an ornate chariot. How would Jacob be traveling?

- After the long, tearful embrace, what might have been the first words on their lips?

> **SECRETS OF THE DESERT**
>
> Herding sheep was not respectable in Egypt, but eating sheep was commonplace. Meats in the Egyptian diet also tended to include cattle, goats, and hedgehogs. Egyptians typically did not eat pork, but they did enjoy mice. It is believed that, like the Romans, they force fed mice with raisins, and other fruits and spices to add flavor to the meat.

Genesis 47. Jacob and his descendants arrive in Egypt after the second year of the Great Famine. There is food here in abundance, but the tribe will have to acclimate to a different culture, different standards and a different diet. Joseph gives them an occasional word to the wise.

Old Testament background: Joseph coaches his family about how to behave when they meet the Pharaoh. Most important, when asked about their occupation, they should reply that they are in the livestock business. The narrative explains that livestock farming is respectable in Egypt, but herding sheep is a disgusting occupation in the eyes of the Egyptians! They are strangers in an afflicted land, but God uses Joseph's influence to win them the royal treatment.

Review the details of this chapter. *Then read each outcome on the left and draw a line to the correct group of the right.*

FAMINE OUTCOME	RECIPIENTS
In charge of Pharaoh's livestock *v6*	
Traded all their livestock for food *v17*	
Awarded the best land in Egypt *v5*	Family of Jacob
Exchanged land ownership for seed *v19*	
Were fruitful and grew in number *v27*	People of Egypt
Exchanged their freedom for slavery *v25*	

Week One   An Appointment in the Desert

Things go so well for the descendants of Jacob that you almost feel sorry for those poor Egyptians, don't you? Didn't they actually contribute some of their surplus grain during the famine years? If that's true, why are they now paying dearly to retrieve it? In truth, there's a lot we don't know here. For instance, we don't know if they were compelled to freely contribute part of the seven year surplus, or if the government purchased it from them. Genesis explains only that Joseph "collected" the surplus grain and stored it in each city. Whether it was purchased or simply contributed in the name of national security, we do not know.

Now read Genesis 49: 29 - 50: 1 – 14. When Israel passes away, he wants to be buried in the tribal burial plot near Mamre. Who is already buried there?

1. _____ and _____
2. _____ and _____
3. _____

Why isn't his favorite wife Rachel buried there? *See Genesis 35: 16 – 19.*
- While traveling many years earlier, she had died while giving birth to _____.
- Because the family was on the road, Rachel was buried where she died, near _____.

Genesis 50: 15 – 20. Israel's death is a heartbreak for Joseph, but it is doubly tragic for his brothers. They have apparently worried for some time that Joseph has been kind to them only out of respect for Father Jacob. If that's true, now that Old Dad is no longer on the scene, Joseph may finally seek the vengeance he has denied himself for so long.
- *v16.* They send messengers to Joseph with advice _____ had given them in advance;
- *v18.* They go to him in person and _____
  _____
- They offer themselves up as his _____

v17. Why do you suppose Joseph weeps when he receives their message? *Choose [x] only one answer which you believe is most accurate.*
- [ ] He has been planning to kill them, but now concludes he must honor his father's wishes.
- [ ] He is filled with sorrow that his brothers have lived in fear because they have doubted his sincerity.
- [ ] He recalls all the anxiety and misery he endured as a young man trapped first as a slave and then as a prisoner.

[ ] He is overjoyed at the opportunity again demonstrate grace to his brothers and bring healing to the tribe.

[ ] Other _____

v19. Joseph responds to his brothers with a question: "Am I God?" What does this imply about the role of revenge and retribution?

_____

v21. What promise does Joseph make to his extended family, his tribe?

_____

_____

Think about the elements of faith in the lives of Jacob and his son Joseph which kept them moving forward through bleak, frightening times. In just a sentence or two, summarize the role of the following factors in a believer's life:

- A clear vision of God and his purpose for your life

_____

_____

_____

- Fervent Prayer

_____

_____

_____

- Basing one's choices and behavior on the principles of God rather than the circumstances of the moment

_____

_____

Day Four: Servants of the Most High God
Read Exodus 1

As you read this opening chapter, highlight or underscore phrases or sentences that indicate God is working behind the scenes to bless his people.

Exodus opens with a summary statement that Israel's sons and all their family members comprised a population of seventy people. Much earlier, God had promised Abram that if he would follow in faith to a new land that would be shown to him, God would make him the father of nations. His descendants would number like the stars in the sky. [11]

- By the time Abram died, he had one supernaturally conceived heir, but certainly not a nation full of descendants.
- As Exodus turns the page, several generations have passed, but still the descendants of Abraham (through son Isaac and grandson Jacob) number only 70.

Exodus 1:7. One sentence changes everything. In a short time, God has enabled his people to turn the tide, and scripture observes the number of the Hebrews has multiplied so dramatically that "the land is full of them!" Why do you think the writer doesn't just come right out and explain that God caused this to happen?

_____

Exodus 1:8. "Then a new king who did not know Joseph came to power in Egypt." In all honesty, no one knows the identity of Joseph's Pharaoh. What's more, we tend to wonder how someone with political connections could rise to power without being aware of Joseph's historic role. But look at the text again.
- It could be that the incoming ruler knows little about Joseph's leadership.
- But more likely, the text indicates the new Pharaoh doesn't know Joseph personally.
- Perhaps he wants to make major course corrections and prefers to forget about what has happened under previous administrations.

Exodus 1: 9 - 11. The Pharaoh complains that something must be done about the Israelites. They have become so numerous that they could be a massive threat to national defense should a war break out with a nation with ties to their tribe.

Because we focus so quickly on the aspect of bondage, we overlook what is truly notable here. Take a moment and recall *verse 5*. Now, what is truly remarkable about the conditions cited in *verse 7*, and again by Pharaoh in *verse 9*?

_____

There's more! Look again at *verse 11*, which describes how cruel bondage is deliberately imposed in order to discourage population growth. Then return to *Exodus 1:12*. What is the point here? Check the one possibility below that is most likely the one in the writer's mind.

[ ] Under such cruel, hopeless circumstances, the Israelites conclude that bearing children for the future is their only hope.

[ ] Although fatigue and hopelessness would normally limit population growth, God is working behind the scenes to bless his chosen people and keep his promise to make them a nation.

[ ] The Egyptians are just unlucky because they have settled on a strategy of population control that doesn't work.

[ ] Other _____

_____

Imagine the situation from an Egyptian perspective. *Verse 9* can legitimately be translated, "The people of Israel are more numerous and mightier than we are."

- Even a rapidly growing nation across the border can be intimidating and unsettling, but imagine the dread one might experience upon realizing the rapidly growing nation of strangers is already inside your borders

- Harsh measures and mistreatment cannot derail the Israelites. Their wealth may be affected, but their epidemic reproduction goes on unabated!

- No wonder *verse 12* indicates that the Egyptians came to loathe and despise the Israelites. Nothing could stop them- or at least, nothing could stop God from blessing them!

Exodus 1:14. Fill in the blanks. The Egyptians made the Israelites lives bitter with hard labor in

_____ and _____; and with all kinds of work in the _____; in all their

hard labor the Egyptians used them _____.

While neglecting to mention the name of one of the mightiest rulers in the world, God fondly recalls the names of two "insignificant" women who have stood tall and had a huge impact on the history of their world. Have you noticed the tendency of the Bible to include names and lists of names? Take a moment to locate these nearby texts and write what you discover.

- *Exodus 6: 14 – 27* features a _____. How many names

  found here do you recognize? _____

- *Genesis 46: 8 – 25* lists the _____ of _____ and their

  _____.

Week One   An Appointment in the Desert

Why do you think God is so intentional about listing names, clans and tribes?

_____

_____

_____

It's a fact that the history and chronology of the Bible are dramatically more accurate than the history and chronologies of ancient Egypt. This is so evident that whenever possible, archaeologists actually date Egyptian rulers by comparing them to their Israelite contemporaries catalogued in the Bible.

Based on what you've learned thus far, can you think of any reasons why the history of Israel might be more detailed and reliable than that of Egypt? *Check any of the following statements that might apply:*
- [ ] The people of Israel are better educated than the Egyptians.
- [ ] God wants the stories of redemption passed along to future generations.
- [ ] The people of Israel have a longer history than the Egyptians.
- [ ] Even people who seem insignificant to us today are all part of a great tribe that is beloved of God.
- [ ] God loves the names of his family.

- [ ] I'd also add _____

_____

Beloved saint, whenever you find yourself standing alone against something you know is completely wrong, never worry that you will be crushed and forgotten. To the contrary, be sure of three great truths:
1. *Matthew 28:20-b.* God is always _____ you.
2. *Romans 8:28.* God is at work behind the scenes to bring _____ into your life.
3. *Genesis 5:22.* God knows you by _____.

We know very little about Shiphrah (*pronounced shif-rah*) and Puah. They are apparently Hebrew women who oversee the work of a group of midwives. When Pharaoh tries to enlist them in his scheme to annihilate the Hebrew boys, their reverence for God will not allow them to take part. Later, they explain to the king that no boys have died thus far because the Hebrew women are so hardy and capable that they give birth before help can arrive! In fairness, this may not be a dishonest statement. The women may have directed other midwives to dawdle along the way so that boys could be born in safety whenever possible!

Verses 20-22: The midwives' allegiance to God brings two divine blessings; one to the nation of Israel, and one to the women. Summarize them below:

33

- God blessed the Israelites by _____

- God blessed the two women by _____

Once again the forces of darkness respond to God's revealed mercies. The Pharaoh enlarges his deadly initiative and orders all Egyptians to drown newborn Hebrew boys whenever they discover one. Just imagine what this will mean to unfortunate Hebrew boys, to their shattered families, and to the hearts of ordinary citizens who participate in this barbarous behavior.

But step back and recover your perspective. What is the singular golden thread that has been winding through the narrative of Jacob, Joseph, and the Children of Israel thus far? *Check the singular most accurate summary below:*
- [ ] Life is tragic because God cannot fix every problem.
- [ ] Random chance dictates that pain and suffering will eventually crop up in every life.
- [ ] God is constantly working behind the scenes to shape history and bring good to people who trust him.

Read *Romans 8: 28 – 39*. Then answer the questions that follow?
- *v28*. How can I know that that God is at work in the painful things that are happening to me?

- *v31*. If God is on my side, how significant is anyone who could be working against me?

- *v32*. As Jesus was suffering and bleeding on the cross, would it have appeared to average bystanders that his God was in control or out of control?

Week One   An Appointment in the Desert

- *v35-38*. If this victorious text does not guarantee that we will never suffer trouble, hardship or persecution, what does it promise us?

  _____

  _____

Take a moment now to reflect back on your own lifetime. Can you remember the singularly most painful trial you have endured thus far? Summarize it in a few sentences below. What do you now realize God was doing then on your behalf?

What were you experiencing?

What was your Heavenly Father doing behind the scenes?

Based on the promise of Scripture and the lessons of human experience, when is the ideal time to begin praising God? Check the biblical answer:
- [ ] When you finally realize how he has brought good from evil?
- [ ] When you finally see light at the end of the tunnel?
- [ ] While you are facing a painful trial in which you cannot sense what God is doing?

Perhaps you, like most of us, have made resolutions like this before. "I will focus on the cross of Christ, and will praise God even when it hurts." However, when fiery trials return to my life, it's amazing how fear and insecurity can conjure up the most compelling reasons why, in this special circumstance, I must link my behavior to the situation and not the cross. Which of these excuses have you used before in order to rationalize not being like Christ? Choose as many as applicable.
- [ ] If I don't do something decisive right now, later it will be too late!
- [ ] God isn't behind this. Evil people are!
- [ ] I need to act quickly, or they'll think I'm weak.
- [ ] I can't take any more!
- [ ] He/she is never going to change.
- [ ] I don't deserve this.
- [ ] This has gone on long enough!
- [ ] Your personal favorite: _____

In which area of your life must you trust God today even though you cannot sense what he is doing to resolve a thorny situation?

_____

_____

_____

WEEK TWO

THE POWER OF A DISILLUSIONED LIFE

If the soul is vigilant and withdraws from all distraction and abandons its own will, then the spirit of God invades it and it can conceive because it is free to do so.
-Abba Cronius of the Desert Fathers

That childhood fable, The Emperor's New Clothes, only becomes more humorous and more instructive as we become adults. That's because human experience continually underscores our ability to deceive ourselves. Like the naïve ruler who walked naked down the street, clothed only in a ludicrous idea, most of us have a great capacity to be misled by our vanity and our fears.

A woman named Rita first visited our church after the death of her godly mother. Over the months that followed, it became clear that Rita had been left scarred and extremely angry by a turbulent childhood. Her father had been cruel, explosive and criminally abusive. Before he finally abandoned them all, his treatment of his wife and five children had gone beyond the pale. Sadly, although that wretched man had been absent for years, Rita was still haunted by ghosts of the past. On one hand, she had been amazed by her mother's faith and character, and the serenity and peace that had marked her death and her funeral. But on the other hand, this searching wife and mother had come to associate her father's behavior as typically male. What's more, the idea of God the Father was absolutely revolting to her, because her only experience with a father was heartless and brutal.

We found that Rita needed to be disillusioned. She had developed an untrue image of God as being harsh and vindictive. She imagined him lurking behind every corner, watching for one misstep in order to fire off another cruel lightning bolt of vengeance! She had completely adopted the old comic slogan, "God will get you for that!" As a result, she could not trust her Heavenly Father to forgive her or work behind the scenes to bring good into her life. Only when she finally released that lie from her past could she begin to move toward the tranquil life of faith she'd seen in her godly mom.

We've all entertained ideas about God which were not based on scripture or truth. During most of their three years with Jesus of Nazareth, his apostles were convinced that his most important role was as a revolutionary, a liberator, or a political ruler who could free Israel from Roman occupation. The truth, that Christ had come as the Suffering Servant of the Most High God, was completely unthinkable. They were sure that all they needed was a new prince and a new regime. Of course, the cross completely shattered that illusion.

In his first letter, Peter has this to say about life's trials and tribulations: "These have come so that your faith- of greater worth than gold, which perishes even though refined by fire- may be proved genuine and may result in praise, glory and honor when Jesus Christ is revealed."[12] He reminds us that gold is refined by fire (or acid today) in order to melt away the impurities that diminish its value. Likewise, faith is tried by fire to blast away false ideas and misguided convictions that have become a part of our thinking.

Years ago, a buddy from South Africa walked into my office and placed a small bottle filled with beautiful gold dust on my desk. A label indicated it was ore from a gold mine there on the southern tip of Africa. I was surprised and delighted until my friend started to laugh. This was a part of the ore alright- *the part that had been removed by acid.* It was gold colored. It was mingled in the ore with the real stuff. It had retained the color of gold, and even made an attractive souvenir. *But it was virtually worthless!*

Some of the ideas about God which you and I have picked up from our life and experiences are equally lacking in value. They have the appearance of Christian ideas, but they are simply dross which weaken our faith and make it more likely to fail. They have to go.

You're no doubt familiar with some of these *un-beliefs*:
- Some people are convinced God wants every Christian to be healthy, wealthy and successful in the eyes of the world. If you come up short of cash or find yourself in the hospital, it's only because your faith is weak. These folks believe that God has no choice but to make you well if your faith is the real thing!
- Others teach that God is angry all the time: furious at pathetic, floundering sinners, and eager to zap them with bolts of rage. Of course, that hardly sounds like the carpenter born in Bethlehem who went around forgiving wicked people, does it?
- There are church members who believe that simply by tacking on the name of Jesus at the end of a prayer, they can obligate God to give them whatever they request.
- I've known lots of church members who supposed that if they kept their lives clean and above reproach, everything would go well and God would never allow them to suffer pain, loss or humiliation. Clearly, Paul and Silas were faith-challenged! Right?

When I base an important decision on a wrong idea about God, then see that decision go south, what happens? It's very easy in moments like that to conclude that God cannot be trusted. Or even worse, I can go into denial and pretend nothing has changed, but my family and friends watching from nearby draw negative conclusions about faith. *What a mess!*

That's why God sends heat and pressure into our lives on a regular basis. The fire melts away the false ideas we've been trusting. And the pressure allows fellow Christians and bystanders to see what my faith is really made of. They are able to discern how fully I can be trusted as a brother in Christ. What's more, even I come to understand how much stress my faith can withstand. These are good things to know.

Week Two The Power of a Disillusioned Life

That brings us back to Egypt where the Pharaoh has orchestrated some back breaking labor to discourage the Israelites and depress their birthrate. An order has gone out that all newborn Hebrew boys should be thrown into the Nile as soon as they are discovered by Egyptian neighbors. A pregnant woman who loves the Lord is about to find herself standing in the face of rising heat and mounting pressure.

This week, we'll be examining the things we believe about God. Do we ever rely on wrong notions in attempting to win God's support for a pet project?
- Day 1: Do you have any misconceptions about God that can weaken and pollute your faith?
- Day 2: Do you base your decisions on changing circumstances or the unchanging Word of God?
- Day 3: What does God reveal about himself when he first appears to Moses at Sinai?
- Day 4: What can we learn from the conversation between God and Moses that can help us deal with passive disobedience?

Day One: The Birth of a Bright Idea
Read Exodus 2: 1 – 10
Go back and review this very brief text, highlighting or underscoring words or events that suggest God's hand or his providential work. Pause and try to personalize these events by imagining the circumstances being described and the emotional responses of the main characters.

Chapter two begins with the marriage of a man and a woman, both of whom are from the tribe of Levi. Realizing that these two people are about to become the parents of one of history's most amazing and unforgettable heroes, it's useful to know something of their background. What is the significance of their ancestry in Levi?
- Read *Genesis 34: 1 – 31*. How do Simeon and Levi earn their reputation for deception and violence?

- Read *Genesis 49: 5 – 7*. When Jacob offers a final blessing to each of his sons, what quality does he describe as most prominent in Simeon and Levi?

In the eyes of countrymen from the other tribes, the Levites must seem blighted and inferior. Only God knows what they can become, however. And long before anyone else could possibly have guessed the lofty role the Levites will ultimately inherit, God shows his favor by entrusting

39

them with the life and upbringing of a rare and anointed man of God. The Levites will surface again near the end of Exodus.

Exodus 2: 2 – 4. Only later[13] will we discover the woman's name is Jochebed, meaning "The Lord is glory." (*Her husband's name is Amram, but the Hebrew meaning is unclear.*) The couple have already given birth to two children; a son Aaron, and a daughter whose name is Miriam.

Although the imminent birth of a child is almost always a time of celebration in the ancient Hebrew culture, Jochebed's third child will arrive in a very painful time. Take a moment to recall the conditions into which this child is about to be born:

- Living conditions. *Exodus 1:11.* To control the population, the Israelites have been forced into _____.
- Working conditions. *Exodus 1:13-14.* When this proves insufficient to discourage population growth, the Egyptians work the Israelites _____ with _____ labor.
- Brutal government. *Exodus 1:22.* When all else fails, the Pharaoh orders the people of Egypt to search out newborn Hebrew boys and _____ them in the Nile.

Jochebed suddenly finds herself alone and confronted with an agonizing decision: to obey the new law and sacrifice her newborn son, or risk the lives of her other children in attempting to save him. Scripture does not explain the whereabouts of her husband, but Egyptian history offers us insight. Slaves assigned to massive building projects were commonly transported to distant sites far from home. In these remote locations, they were housed with other slaves and laborers for extended periods until either they died or the project was completed, in which case they were returned to their homes. With the new Pharaoh attempting to use bondage and hard labor as a means to disrupt reproduction among the Hebrews, it's a safe bet that Amram and many other married men have been dispatched to some distant slave labor camp.

How do you reason through a miserable decision when the choices are so limited? The Bible doesn't reveal how Jochebed worked through the options available to her, but we can guess. *Draw a line to match each choice on the left with the likely outcome on the right:*

OPTIONS	OUTCOMES
1. Take the child and flee	Neighbors will notice and drown him
2. Do nothing	There's a chance he won't be discovered
3. Hide the baby	A mother and infant won't survive the desert

After only ninety days of attempting to hide a healthy, growing baby and muffle the sounds of his crying in the still of the night, it becomes clear that the plan is doomed. No doubt, Jochebed has been hoping God would intervene to muffle the baby's cries, or harden the neighbor's ears, or even reverse the Pharaoh's evil decree. But nothing changes. Why does God remain silent? Why does he seem so far away?

Week Two   The Power of a Disillusioned Life

Can you recall an unusually difficult time in your life when it seemed at the moment that God was not paying attention? Summarize it here in a few sentences:

_____

_____

_____

_____

_____

Exodus 2:3. Finally Jochebed is forced to find a Plan B. She racks her brain trying to deduce some way in which she can save her beautiful child from being drowned due to Pharaoh's wrath. Finally, at her wit's end, she recalls a true story of faith she's heard time and again since childhood. She remembers another occasion when God spared an entire family from being drowned! There actually is a way she can place her child in the Nile, as required by the Law, and yet offer him one final shot at somehow being rescued by God.

- What epic story from Genesis must have come to Jochebed's mind as she wondered how God might save her son from drowning?

  _____

- Of course, drowning is not the only danger facing little Moses. The shallow edges of the Nile are frequented by crocodiles, hippo, water buffalo, and other herds seeking water. Apart from drowning, what other possible hazards await this child in the dark water of the Nile?

  _____

  _____

  _____

Think about it: How much does Jochebed trust the Almighty? Even if the small basket does not capsize, little Moses will be resting in a river famous for its hungry population of combative crocodiles! Ironically, in a land where the Pharaoh, the Nile and the Sun were all considered divine, one of the most feared and powerful figures of all was Sobek, the crocodile god. Inscriptions on tomb walls and in the *Book of the Dead* depict him as the familiar man with a crocodile head. He was considered to be the embodiment of life and rebirth, and was seen as the source of Pharaoh's power. In fact, in hieroglyphics, his name was expressed as two small crocodiles followed by the bird which represented Pharaoh.

Treasure in the Sand

But Jochebed is not intimidated by myth and legend. In taking her bold course of faith, Jochebed believes that her child will be rescued by the one true God who is all powerful. She believes that the God of Abraham, Isaac and Jacob can overrule all the false gods of Egypt!

Exodus 2:4. What kind of outcome does Jochebed expect, considering that she leaves her young daughter to bear witness and bring back a report?

_____

Exodus 2:5. The basket is still safely bobbing in the water when the daughter of Pharaoh arrives for her bath, accompanied by an entourage of royal attendants. She notices the strange object floating among the reeds, and asks one of her attendants to retrieve it. Peering inside, she spots the infant. Immediately, she recognizes that this is one of the outlawed Hebrew infants! *Try to imagine this real life situation.* What are the young woman's options? List them in the spaces below:

1. _____

2. _____

3. _____

4. Keep the child and recruit a village woman to nurse him for her.

Q: *What's your opinion?* Do you think the Egyptian princess suspects that Miriam is related to the baby in the basket? *Why or why not?*

_____

_____

_____

_____

Exodus 2:8-10. So the Pharaoh's daughter dispatches Miriam to find a Hebrew woman who can nurse this infant for her. Needless to say, Miriam returns with her mother. And that's how it comes to pass that the princess hires Jochebed to take Moses home and raise him until he's old enough to be cared for in the palace! Just imagine that:
- This Hebrew mother gives her son up to God.
- God returns him to her care and her household, along with a royal salary from the Egyptian treasury to take care of him.

Week Two The Power of a Disillusioned Life

The princess gives the baby a Hebrew name in keeping with his heritage. He will be called Moses, which sounds like the Hebrew word for "draw out" or "lift up" because Moses was lifted up from the water.

This chapter begins with a desperate mother hoping that God will somehow enable her to hide her child from her neighbors who are under orders to drown all Hebrew baby boys. God does not follow through, does he? And it's not because he can't possibly engineer a way to mute a baby's cries. Rather, God has merely waited because he has a *much more incredible* plan in mind. Far from burying this child in the corner of a slave hut, God desires to prominently display this baby boy in the very palace of the Pharaoh! Moses will grow up with all the advantages of a world-class Egyptian education.

And even as his adoptive mother, the princess, will point him to the wisdom of the Nile, his real mother will always be nearby to remind him of his true heritage of faith. The Egyptian education will be a blessing, but his faith in the God of Abraham, Isaac and Jacob will direct the course of his life.

Read *Isaiah 55:8-9*. Then fill in the blanks in the translation below.
"For my thoughts are not your thoughts, neither are your ways my ways. For as the _____ are higher than the _____, so are my ways higher than your ways, and my thoughts than your thoughts."

Take a few moments to mentally process how those words from Isaiah's prophecy interface with the story of Moses. *Then answer these questions.*
1. Why is it often so difficult to anticipate what God will do next?

    _____

    _____

2. Would it really be more comforting to you if God were less complex and more limited so that you could easily figure him out? Why?

    _____

    _____

3. Are you already aware of a wrong idea about God that's been polluting your faith and requires removal?

    _____

    _____

Day Two: Never Late, Always on Time
Read Exodus 2: 11 - 25
If time permits, review this brief text. Underline or underscore words or phrases the give hints to the character and temperament of Moses. What would you identify as his most prominent trait thus far?

Moses spends his boyhood and adolescence in the privileged environment of the royal palace of the King of Egypt. Scripture says little about the assets and advantages available to him there. *Acts 7:20-36* sheds some light on this period in the life of the great man. Read this passage and record the answers to these questions.

- *v22*. As Pharaoh's grandson, Moses receives a world class education, becoming powerful in _____ and _____.
- *v23*. How old is Moses when he kills the Egyptian to defend a slave? _____
- *v30*. Based on that number, how old is Moses when God calls him from Midian to return to Egypt? _____
- *v36*. Based on that number, how old is Moses when he dies after leading his people through the wilderness? _____

Another of the Bible's few hints is found in *Hebrews 11: 25-26*. Read that text now and fill in these blanks:

- *v25*. Moses chooses to suffer with his own people rather than to enjoy the _____ of _____ for a moment.
- *v25*. He regards disgrace in the name of God to be of greater value than the _____ of _____.

We can only guess the subjects in which young Moses receives training during his palace days. For example, the design of the pyramids demonstrates Egyptian knowledge of geometry and astronomy. Their proficiency in embalming the dead suggests keen insights into the processes of the human body. The ability of Egyptians to produce gold leaf even finer than we can manufacture today reflects their advanced mastery of ancient technologies.

As Moses becomes a man, his intellect has been developed by some of the greatest scholars in Egypt, but his heart has been cultivated by his Jewish mother who has learned to trust God completely. The product of two competing cultures, the young man soon finds himself torn between the two. Like most young adults, he finds himself re-examining all the things he's been taught, and choosing which truths he will carry with him.

Exodus 2: 11 – 15. It may be this quest for truth and identity which one day leads Moses beyond the palace to one of the slave quarters. In describing the event, *verse twelve* twice uses the phrase "his own people." The point here is that despite his royal privileges, the young man's sympathies are clearly drawn to the Jews. He sees an Egyptian beating up a Hebrew, and decides to intervene.

Week Two   The Power of a Disillusioned Life

v12. One phrase in this sentence tips us off that killing the Egyptian is not simply an *impulsive* act of passion. Write that phrase here: _____

_____

Let's dig deeper here. It's tempting to excuse the crime that Moses commits here. On one hand, God has not yet delivered the Ten Commandments, one of which forbids murder. And on the other hand, we recall that Hebrews 11 seems to cast this decisive moment in a positive light. Before moving ahead, let's pause and get our theological bearings here.
- Read *Genesis 9: 1 – 6.* Is murder a sin or a merely a gray area for the people of God?
  _____
- Refer to *Hebrews 11:25-26* once again. Verse 25 indicates Moses chooses ____ _____ with his people, and verse 26 indicates he chooses _____ with his people. Hence, God applauds the priorities Moses chooses, not the crime he commits.
- **Faith requires that we base our choices on God's unchanging Word, rather than our changing circumstances.**

2:13. A day after the murder, Moses is once again walking among his own people when he finds two of them scuffling. He questions the practical wisdom of two enslaved men fighting one another. Their insolent reply suggests that the crime Moses committed a day earlier is no longer a secret.

Think about it. If the two angry slaves are aware that Moses rescued a fellow Hebrew just the day before, why do you suppose they are so resentful? Read *Exodus 2:14* once again and explain.

_____

_____

_____

When the Pharaoh issues a warrant for his arrest and execution, Moses flees for his life. To reach the distant land of Midian, he will need to leave Egypt, cross the entire Sinai Peninsula, and then continue eastward. Apparently, he travels this great distance in hopes of escaping the influence of the furious Egyptian ruler.

Exodus 2: 15 – 23. At a well in Midian, he encounters a young woman whose father is a priest there. What can we learn about this mysterious priest whose name is "Reuel," or Jethro?
- Consult *Genesis 25:1.*
- Who was Midian's father? _____
- Which God would Midian have been taught by his dad to worship?
  _____
- Several generations later, it seems most likely this priest of Midian would be a follower of the same God his famous ancestor worshipped.

- Reuel means "friend of God." Jethro [3:1] is probably a title that means "excellent."
- We do not know if Moses chooses this refuge because of stories he heard as a youth, or because God's Spirit leads him here. In either case, spending this next era of his life in the company of a priest who worships the one true God will be a huge advantage for this young man schooled in pagan Egypt.

Moses calls attention to himself by rescuing some of Reuel's seven daughters from overbearing shepherds who have stolen their place at the watering hole. When the priest hears the accounts of this 'Egyptian' hero, he sends the girls back to the watering hole to invite the man home for dinner. Moses shares dinner with the family, agreeing to live with the family and work as a shepherd.

SECRETS OF THE DESERT

Midian lies on the edge of the Arabian Desert, amid mountain ranges, lava beds, and some of the deepest and most massive sand dunes in the world. The air is so hot by day and yet so cold by night that the austere silence is often broken by sudden "gunshots." This happens when dramatically shifting temperatures cause rocks to explode and shatter.

Ultimately, he marries Reuel's daughter Zipporah. They give birth to a son and name him Gershom, because it sounds like the Hebrew for "an alien there."

Interesting Note: Among ancient Hebrews, offspring are often given names which memorialize their parents' situation at the time of their birth. Hence, Moses acknowledges his condition as an alien in the strange land by naming his firstborn son Gershom. Other Old Testament children are given equally heavy names which mean "sorrowful" or "the glory is gone." [14]

The name Moses gives his son denotes, "I have become an alien in a foreign land." Does this indicate to you that Moses plans to remain here for life, or does it suggest he anticipates someday returning to Egypt? *Write your answer below and explain your reasoning.*

_____

_____

_____

Whatever Moses' short term plans may be, God clearly has a long term strategy in mind. As a shepherd under the authority of his father-in-law, Moses will spend a generation learning the secrets of the desert. He will train himself in navigation by the stars, the principles of finding water, the art of identifying edible plants, the ways to survive in unbearable heat. After forty years, he will be fully capable of helping his people survive their life journey through the Sinai.

v25. The chapter concludes with a fascinating statement. The NIV reads, "God looked upon the Israelites and was concerned about them." The NLT expresses this verse, "God looked down on the Israelites and knew it was time to act." The Hebrew text literally explains, "God looked upon the Israelites and knew them." He *knew* them. That Hebrew word is so broad and so powerful, that its definition can literally range from knowing someone's name to knowing someone intimately and sexually.

God knows you. And more than simply knowing your name, God knows your emotional responses, your deepest needs, and your destiny. Realizing how intimately God knows you, what do you think must be some of the factors that determine when he will rescue you from a life crisis and turn the tide for you? *Write two or three of his possible criteria below:*

1.

2.

Day Three: Greetings from the Great I Am
Read Exodus 3

Pause and read Exodus 3 once again. Use a marker or pen to indicate words or phrases which indicate Moses' emotional response to this revelation of God. Can you think of one word or term which would describe this experience?

Exodus 3: 1 – 5. One of the true breakthrough moments in the Bible comes out of the blue on an otherwise ordinary day. We have no indication that Moses has done anything out of the ordinary in seeking God or pursuing his destiny. Rather, he is routinely tending his father-in-law's flocks near Mount Horeb when the supernatural power of God interrupts the natural order of things. It's just another hot day in the desert until the shepherd sees something unusual and inexplicable.

- *v2.* What causes this manifestation? _____

- *v3.* Why does it arouse Moses' curiosity? _____

- *v4.* Approaching the site, whose voice does Moses hear? _____

Pause and do some detective work here.
Moses quite suddenly finds himself standing on holy ground. And it's more than the fact that God is manifesting Himself here at the moment. Rather, we are informed by the text that this is the "Mountain of God." So where is this place?
- Moses has escaped to _____, so we know this mountain is near that region.
- *v1*. This particular mountain is identified as Mount _____.
- Skip ahead for just a moment. In *Exodus 3:12*, God indicates that Moses will ultimately bring his people to worship Him on "_____ _____."
- Now move ahead once again to *Exodus 19: 1 – 10*. When the people of Israel finally arrive at their destination to meet God, the mountain is also known as (*v10*) Mount _____.

- *What are the practical implications of this?* This place where Moses has spent 40 years mastering desert survival will comprise the general area where he will help the Israelites survive for the next 40 years. The map on page 108 indicates the site of Mount Sinai according to tradition. However, the location of Midian suggests the mountain might be found more to the north and east, where Moses could have reached it with his flocks.

Imagine the complexity and the mystery of what is unfolding here. An angel is creating this unworldly spectacle to divert Moses from a familiar path and into the very presence of God. But the angel is not speaking. What Moses hears is the truly awesome voice of God.
- He calls out the name of Moses.
- He directs him to approach no farther.
- Then Moses is commanded to remove his sandals because he's standing on holy ground.

Think about it. What advantage or benefit do sandals afford a shepherd walking across desert sands? _____
- Can you think of a modern day custom of respect that is similar to Moses removing his shoes? _____
- Removing one's sandals on holy ground would denote what sort of attitude towards the Almighty? _____

Exodus 3: 6 – 10. God reveals his identity to Moses: the God of his father; of Abraham, Isaac and Jacob. In other words, although this is an unprecedented moment for Moses, his people have a long history with this deity. *Refer to the text to fill in the blanks below*:
- *v7*. God has seen the _____ of his people, and is _____ about their suffering.
- The Hebrew text literally explains "for I know their sorrows."
- *v8*. He has determined to _____ them from the Egyptians, and brings them to a spacious land flowing with milk and honey.
- "Milk and honey" is a figure of speech. It describes a well watered region so fertile and lush with vegetation that grazing cattle produce an abundance of milk, and hard working bees generate a wealth of honey.

3:10. God concludes his initial comments with a charge: "So I am sending you to Pharaoh to bring my people out of Egypt." There is a lot more irony here than just the matter of an eternal God speaking to an insignificant shepherd in the middle of nowhere! Think about the dynamics that are in play here.
- Based on what you've read so far, how would you characterize the power and military might of the Pharaoh? _____

- How much influence would you suppose Moses, the condemned fugitive, currently enjoys back in Egypt? _____

- Thinking merely in human, political terms, what are the chances that a mission like this could result in success? _____

Exodus 3: 11 – 15. Moses is fully aware the Pharaoh will be surrounded by the trappings of authority over Egypt. He will be surrounded by servants, will be guarded by elite warriors, and will be seated on a massive, golden throne. He will wear a royal signet around his neck, a gold encrusted miter on his head, and will hold a golden staff in his hand. All these things are tokens of the authority he wields over the wealth and power of Egypt.
- Moses is <u>not</u> merely trying to weasel out of this job. There can be no doubt this man is passionate about combating injustice and rescuing the oppressed. *Think about it:*

  ✓ Why did he murder that Egyptian? _____

  ✓ What was he doing when he learned that crime was no longer a secret? _____

  ✓ How did he originally gain the attention of the Priest of Midian? _____

- Rather, he is simply asking, *"By what authority* will I stand before the most powerful ruler on Earth and make such a demand?" *That is a reasonable question.*

If Pharaoh wears a signet around his neck, giving him the authority to issue decrees, tax people, and dispatch the army, what will be the signet certifying Moses has authority to make his demand? Check out *3:12.* God replies, "This will be your sign that I have sent you: you will receive what you demand!" In other words, in spite of the odds against him, Moses will succeed in leading the Jews out of bondage in Egypt and across the Sinai Peninsula to the Mountain of God, where they will worship the God of Abraham, Isaac and Jacob. Moses will need to overcome the Pharaoh, the Egyptian Army, the Red Sea, even many of his own people. By the grace of God, he will surmount every challenge!

v13-15. God has already indicated he is the God of Abraham, Isaac and Jacob, so Moses knows the identity behind this voice. Nevertheless, he is certainly reeling from the suddenness and the strangeness of this encounter with God. He is no doubt staggered by the scope of this divine mission about which he's just been informed. Not cowardly, but quite humanly, he struggles to wrap his mind around what is being asked of him.
- *v13.* He wonders how he will explain this to the _____.
- They might expect him to offer proof of his calling. Perhaps they'll ask the _____ of the one who has sent him.
- *v14.* God replies, "Tell them _____ has sent you."

God is identified by several different names of titles in this brief, compelling passage. Let's identify and learn from them. *Read the following references and fill in the blanks.*
- *v1.* When Mount Horeb/Sinai is characterized as the "Mountain of God," the Hebrew word for God is Elohim.
    - ✓ This word is the plural version of El, the singular word for God. (i.e. "Bethel" means house of God.) The plural denotes God's eternal majesty.
    - ✓ Refer to *Genesis 1: 1-8*. This name captures God's powerful role as _____ of the cosmos, the one who spoke everything into being.

- *v2.* When scripture speaks of the angel of the Lord, the word translated Lord is YHWH. The same word is included in *3:4*.
    - ✓ Spelled with only consonants and no vowels, this name of God could never be _____. Today, we insert vowels to vocalize it as either "Yahweh" or "Jehovah." The NIV is one of several translations which always render this name "the LORD." Some translations use all caps to denote the sacred nature of the term.
    - ✓ This title reflects the authority God wields over his world and his people. The term "lord" indicates an owner, master or king who has sovereign power.

- *v14.* When Moses suggests the Israelites might ask the name of the God who has commissioned him, God offers yet another name: "I AM."
    - ✓ The Hebrew word is very common in the Old Testament and is extremely dynamic. It can mean to be, to become, to exist, to happen, to come to pass, to be done.
    - ✓ Because Hebrew verb tenses are not as precise as English tenses, the name "I am that I am" can also be accurately translated "I am whom I have been" or even "I shall be what I have been."

Week Two   The Power of a Disillusioned Life

- ✓ Jesus Christ uses a similar expression to introduce himself in John's Revelation. *Read Revelation 1:4 and write the phrase which describes Christ in that brief text:* _____

- v15. "This is my name _____, the name by which I am to be remembered from _____ to _____. No wonder Christ cites it once again to introduce The End in John's Revelation!

Practice your theological thinking: This encounter between Moses and the Almighty God is saturated with eternal truth. It teaches us that certain things are true about God, and that other popular ideas are not valid. Take some time to review the account of Exodus 3 and infer what we can and cannot learn about God from the text. *For each quality or idea listed below, indicate either T/True; F/False; or NA/Not Applicable.*

1. ____ Universalism: all gods are actually the same, as are all religions.
2. ____ Grace: God is loving and merciful.
3. ____ Pantheism: God inhabits every person and every thing.
4. ____ Election: God selected Israel in advance and favored them over others.
5. ____ Holiness: God reserves his power for select purposes.
6. ____ Deism: God does not interfere in the affairs of men.
7. ____ Omnipotence: God is not only eternal, but is all-powerful.
8. ____ Creationism: God made the world and everything in it.
9. ____ Sovereignty: God makes all things work according to his plan.
10. ____ Millennialism: Someday God will reign bodily on the Earth.

Exodus 3: 16 – 22. Moses is directed by God to return to Egypt, assemble the Elders of Israel, and describe what he has experienced at Sinai. In the name of the Lord, he is to promise that they will be set free from bondage, and delivered to a new land so green and lush that it will be an agricultural dream come true. God promises the Elders will heed the message, and will accompany Moses to confront the Pharaoh with this demand from God: "Let my people go."
When Moses finally reaches Egypt and asks permission for a three day pilgrimage into the wilderness to worship the God of Abraham, Isaac and Jacob, he is assured that the proud king will flatly refuse. When that happens, Moses can stand on three promises from the Almighty. *Read the statements below and use an X to indicate each statement that is actually promised in this text*:

- [ ] God will stretch out his hand and perform terrifying signs.
- [ ] Pharaoh's sons and likely heirs will all die.
- [ ] The Pharaoh will change his mind and release the people of Israel.
- [ ] At first, the Israelites will refuse to leave.
- [ ] The Israelites will make their exit eagerly but face misery and death in the desert.
- [ ] The Egyptians will look with favor on the Jews, and will give them gold and silver for their journey, as well as clothing for their children..

Day Four: A Forecast of the Coming Storm
Read Exodus 4: 1 – 17
Go back and read these verses once again. Underline or highlight every word or phrase that reflects God's supernatural power to intervene and change circumstances.

Although Moses has spent the last four decades in small rural community far from Egypt, he is not out of touch with the realities of the situation there. He knows that the Pharaoh is powerful and proud, and that slavery has become a large share of the Egyptian economy. "Let my people go," will not be an easy sell! In addition, Moses understands that the spirit of Israel has been broken by generations of bondage. The Jews will not accept change easily, and neither are they great candidates for surviving the brutal life of the desert.

But there's more. Moses is aware of his own limitations. Even as a prince back in Egypt, he'd never met much success in helping his own people. What kind of success is likely to achieve now with such a huge rescue effort and with absolutely no royal influence on which to draw? He's an ordinary shepherd given to brooding and emotional extremes. He has grown comfortable spending days on end in solitude and silence. He's impatient and he's getting old, and he has this seemingly logical idea that God will definitely require a more powerful figure to accomplish a feat of this magnitude. *Clearly, Moses needs to be disillusioned!*

Exodus 4: 1 – 9. The Great I AM meets the great "I AM UNABLE!" Moses has not yet made the discovery that Paul would make many centuries later: "When I am weak, then I am strong!"[15] When Moses worries that the people of Israel might reject his message, God gives him three signs of divine authority which will convince them. List the three signs:

1. *v3-4.* _____

   _____

2. *v6-7.* _____

   _____

3. *v9.* _____

   _____

The first sign from God is jam packed with meaning. The staff was not only a tool of Hebrew shepherds, but was a prominent symbol of royal power back in Egypt. Pharaohs were commonly depicted with their arms crossed, holding a flail (whip) in one hand, and a striped shepherd's staff in the other. (The golden sarcophagus of King Tutankhamen is a classic example.) The staff, or "crook," reflected the Pharaoh's authority in leading his people, and was always carried by a new ruler during his coronation. Similarly, the snake was closely associated with Egyptian throne. The most familiar piece of clothing worn by the Pharaohs was the *nemes* headdress bearing the head of a cobra, *Wadjet,* front and center. Tomb drawings routinely depict cobras guarding the king.

Week Two   The Power of a Disillusioned Life

When God transforms the staff of Moses into a snake, most likely a cobra, and enables him to safely pick it up, the message is clear. The authority, responsibility, and protection God affords Moses are far, greater than that of the Pharaoh. God will enable this shepherd to master that king.

Why will this sign encourage and comfort fearful Hebrew slaves? Explain:

_____

_____

_____

_____

Now think about the second sign (4:6) and imagine how you'd respond to the idea of having your hand suddenly infected with leprosy! Moses must feel the blood draining from his face when he lifts his hand from his cloak and realizes how God has changed everything! In Moses' world, leprosy brings two words to mind: "incurable" and "separation." Short of a divine miracle, leprosy guarantees a lifetime of discomfort and decay. And even more painful, its violently contagious nature requires that victims leave the comfort of their families and live on the outskirts of town in isolation with other lepers.

The second sign for Moses communicates that God can "heal" and "restore." He can heal the spiritual and physical damage of centuries in harsh bondage; he can restore the exiled Moses to the hearts of his own people; he can restore the Israelites to their destiny in the Land of Promise.

What kind of emotional response would this sign create among the Hebrews?

_____

_____

_____

The third sign may seem obscure to you and me, but it speaks volumes to people who depend on the ancient Egyptian economy. Moses is well aware that the Nile not only waters the surrounding lands, but actually fertilizes the land as well when it spills over its banks during the flood seasons. In the mind of ancient Egyptians, the Nile is a major source of life for them, and power for the king. In sharp contrast, the sight of blood spilled on the ground would be alarming to ancient people, denoting injury, destruction and possibly death.

Think about it. When Moses takes water from the Nile and pours it on the ground where it morphs into blood, what will this communicate to the Israelites about the power of their God? *Use this space to record your ideas.*

_____

_____

_____

_____

Exodus 4: 10 – 17. Moses realizes these signs will certainly give him credibility in the eyes of his skeptical Hebrew countrymen. He's still not ready to enlist, though. He confesses, "Lord, I was not eloquent before you appeared to me today, and it doesn't feel like anything has changed now. I'm still stumbling over my words, 'cause I'm just not much of a talker!"

What's really going on in the mind of Moses right now? Consider all the possibilities. *Then select the single best explanation from the choices below or add your own.*
- [ ] He is probably just afraid. It's a dangerous undertaking.
- [ ] He's become a very private, brooding man and doesn't want to leave his family and flock for a return to the glare of public life.
- [ ] He's eighty years old, and is exhausted from life.
- [ ] He honestly feels inadequate for this assignment.
- [ ] Other: _____

_____

Take a moment here to explain your rationale. _____

_____

_____

_____

_____

v11-12. Don't gloss over God's reply too quickly. The Lord explains that Moses' lack of eloquence is not a problem. *"Who gave man his mouth? Who makes him deaf or mute? Who gives him sight or makes him blind? Is it not I the Lord? Now go: I will help you speak and teach you what to say."*
- The God who formed Moses' tongue can correct any deficiencies.
- Moses won't need to write a speech. God will tell him what to say.

Week Two The Power of a Disillusioned Life

But notice that God is taking credit for things we'd prefer to consider accidents of nature. We're comfortable asserting that our God is sovereign, but we're very uncomfortable with the idea that God might literally make someone mute or blind. *Consult these additional references and match each text on the left with its key idea on the right:*

TEXT	MESSAGE
A. Isaiah 45:7	_____ God has good reasons for our infirmities.
B. John 9:3	_____ God is responsible for prosperity & misfortune.
C. 2 Corinthians 12:7	_____ Some bad things occur so that God can be glorified when he fixes them.

v13. Moses offers up one final plea: "Oh, Lord, please get someone else to do this!" It seems like Moses has considered how unyielding the Pharaoh will be, and how cynical and critical the Hebrews will be. Perhaps he hasn't considered how angry God is going to be if this procrastination goes on!
- God's anger burns against his chosen vessel.
- He consents to anoint Aaron, the brother of Moses, as the spokesman for the undertaking. Moses will speak to Aaron, and Aaron will deliver his words to the appropriate audience.
- God apparently improves the speaking abilities of Moses as well. Don't forget that Acts describes Moses as "powerful in speech."[16] God doesn't need Aaron, but he adds him to the team.

v17. "Take this staff in your hand so you can perform miraculous signs with it."
Like all shepherds, Moses has come to depend on his staff for an entire range of tasks which are central to his occupation. And like most men, it is in the work he does with his hands that Moses finds much of his identity and his satisfaction.
- He has laid down his staff at God's direction, has seen what God can do with it, and has picked it up again.
- Now he will lay his life and his life's work down in the desert, will discover how God can change and equip him, and will pick up his new identity and head for Egypt. He is no longer a sheep herder. He is a prophet and the leader of a nation.

Is there an area in your life in which you have heard the call of God, but continue to postpone and procrastinate because you feel inadequate? Describe that situation briefly:

_____

_____

_____

Which description most accurately summarizes this situation in your life? Check only one, the most accurate.

[ ] I'm not 100% sure it's God's Will.
[ ] I'm afraid I will fail.
[ ] It's hard for me to break out of my comfort zone.
[ ] I honestly believe I don't have what it takes.
[ ] I've never taken a step of faith this large before.
[ ] I don't think I can financially afford to do this.
[ ] I don't have enough time to take care of this.
[ ] I'm afraid of how my loved ones will respond.
[ ] I worry that God may disappoint me.

Think about the summary statement you just affirmed. What must you do to resolve this problem of life and faith? More than one of these alternatives may be in order.

[ ] Search the Scriptures, fast and pray for confirmation.
[ ] Take a spiritual gifts test and seek confirmation from God.
[ ] Consult a godly person you respect and ask for counsel and prayer.
[ ] Re-evaluate and re-prioritize your schedule and/or your finances.
[ ] Chart the spiritual turning points in your life and look for a trend line or a direction suggested by what God's already done.
[ ] Confess your lack of faith and ask for forgiveness.
[ ] Stop wavering and step out into the water of obedience.

Review the options you just selected for yourself. Take a moment now and commit this path to God. As a token that you will indeed follow through with these actions, sign your name below.

Signature _____

Date _____

WEEK THREE

THE WAY GOD WORKS

Suffer me to become the food of wild beasts, through whom I may attain to God. I am God's grain, and I am ground by the teeth of wild beasts, that I may be found the pure bread of Christ.-
Ignatius the God Bearer, martyred AD 117

Like the vast, trackless desert, God challenges the imagination, even as he defies the mind of man. For every fact we know about Him, there must be ten thousand mysteries and unseen truths. No doubt that's largely because there's a great deal about an eternal God that you and I could not possibly understand with our *byte-sized* earthly minds, even if it were engraved in stone or spray painted on the sky. There are still other powerful truths recorded in Scripture that you and I haven't read or applied yet. And finally, there are insights about God that we discover through experience, as we walk with Christ and observe the way he works.

Surely, that's one of the things Paul has in mind when he writes to the Ephesians, "I pray also that the eyes of your heart may be enlightened in order that you may know him better."[17] There are endless veins of wisdom and truth we can mine simply by reading the Word of God, but there's another share that is experienced as we embody the truths of God and follow Jesus.

A good friend of mine works with the US State Department. Not so long ago, he found himself in what seemed like a season of *spiritual springtime*. He was dealing successfully with some personal sins that had long plagued him. He had come into a growth period in his marriage. He and his wife were putting down roots deep in our local church ministries. And quite suddenly, out of the blue, he found himself being dispatched to a remote and dangerous area overseas to which his family could not accompany him. Not only did the pending assignment run counter to standard department practice, but it felt like a door in Heaven slamming shut! Frankly, both he and his wife were thrown for a loop! *What was God doing?* They had been making real progress on several spiritual fronts! This seemed frustrating and random… and arbitrary.

My buddy did the year solo overseas. Unexpectedly, he was able to fly home on several occasions for joyful two week stays. The other months of isolation and boredom passed. And much to his surprise, the time away drew his family even closer, strengthened his marriage, and intensified his own spiritual growth. He came home a different man, stronger in his faith, and more passionate about carrying his cross. *But who would have suspected this kind of outcome when the unexpected assignment first came through?*

Quite often there's this huge disconnect between what we infer from sermons or best-selling books, and what Scripture actually teaches. That is, we have this wildly popular idea that when we're being obedient and doing God's Will, everything must operate smoothly and there can be no difficult moments or loose ends. We cite notable examples like Joshua and his Army seeing Jericho fall after they march around those impregnable walls seven times. We look fondly on David's victory over Goliath, courtesy of one well aimed stone.

But we utterly gloss over Joseph's journey of destiny that required thirteen years in slavery and imprisonment. God was in it every step of the way, but that did not preclude long dark nights and days of being wronged and mistreated. Of course this was the right path for Joseph: God-ordained. *But was it a joy ride? Not likely.*

This week, we travel with Moses back to the Land of the Nile. Despite the fact that he feels completely inadequate for the task, he will undertake a long, harrowing journey of faith. And once he arrives on the scene, the most amazing thing happens: *everything seems to fall apart!*

We will stand with Moses as he faces down the Pharaoh, the most powerful man in the world. And we'll be asking questions like these:
- Day 1: Moses begins his journey but strange things occur. What can we learn from one of the most mysterious texts in the Bible?
- Day 2: Moses goes west and things go south! Why does God allow this to happen?
- Day 3: Abraham was the father of faith. Jacob gave his name, Israel, to the people of God. Yet God reveals things to Moses than the patriarchs never saw. What does this later generation learn about God?
- Day 4: Moses and Aaron boldly draw a line in the sand. Is it okay to be afraid when you're taking a stand for God?

Can you remember a time in your life when you walked in faith as far as the light God had given you, and then you boldly took one more step? Did a rainbow suddenly appear? Or was your immediate experience more like the ground suddenly giving way beneath your feet?

Like Paul, I've been praying for those of you who will take this journey of faith with me. I'm praying that the eyes of your heart will be enlightened, so that you will know Christ better. It's my prayer that you will gain new insights into how God works, so that you will be more comfortable every day in walking through life's deserts with Him.

Week Three   The Way God Works

Day 1: God Doesn't Call Perfect People
Read Exodus 4: 18 – 29

Read carefully and imagine the circumstances. As you review the text, underscore or highlight words or phrases that speak of emotional frustration or physical hardship.

Exodus 4: 18 – 23. When you read what Moses says to his father-in-law, don't fail to notice what he *doesn't* say. He doesn't mention his visitation from God in the burning bush! He doesn't mention that he's returning to Egypt on a divinely ordained mission. And he doesn't hint that there is any danger or hardship in store for his family.

Why doesn't Moses disclose any of those details to Reuel? *What do you think?*

[ ] Perhaps he does, but scripture simply omits that part of the
    conversation.
[ ] He realizes there are dangers in store for Zipporah and the boys,
    and he fears Reuel won't approve or give his blessing.
[ ] Moses is a very quiet, private man who is still conflicted by his
    fears that he is not qualified for this assignment.
[ ] Other: _____

I suspect Moses is simply unable to talk about his experience and his mission because he's still so fearful of the outcome. On the one hand, he is clearly depicted in the Old Testament as a brooding man inclined to silence. And on the other hand, while Moses is obedient and respectful in returning to Egypt, he doesn't do it with much joy or confidence. Skip ahead for just a moment to the following texts:

- Read *Exodus 5:22-23*. If Moses responds this way to the very first obstacle, what does it say about his expectation for success?

  _____

  _____

- Read *Exodus 6:12*. Is Moses merely rehashing this same old argument simply as an excuse, or does it seem he truly worries about this disability, whatever it is?

  _____

  _____

I would venture that most of us are not accustomed to thinking about personality quirks and character flaws in the life of such a powerful, prophetic figure. We are probably more inclined to project all kinds of virtues and capabilities onto Moses, rendering him far above average in looks, leadership and ability. But that's not really useful. Not only is it dishonest to diminish quirks and weaknesses which are included in the Bible for a reason, but it also detracts from the breath taking power of the Almighty God.

Pause and reflect: God selects a silent, brooding man who lacks confidence, then immediately sends him to defy the mightiest government in the world, and liberate Israel from the slave economy of Egypt. What does that indicate about God's supernatural ability?

_____

_____

v19-20. Moses will not be haunted by complications from the past. The men who wanted to see him charged with murder are dead. He packs up his family, loads up a donkey with some essentials, and returns to Egypt. Notice the sentence: "And he took the staff of God with him."

Q: This is apparently the same staff he's carried routinely for years. What now makes it "the staff of God?" [See 4:1-5] *Choose the best answer:*
- [ ] The staff is now infused with supernatural power.
- [ ] When he cast it down, Moses surrendered it to God as a gift.
- [ ] God has designated it as a token of Moses' divine authority.
- [ ] Moses no longer needs the staff as he is no longer a shepherd.
- [ ] I'd express it differently. _____

v21 – 23. Take another look at these verses. *Then firm up your understanding by labeling each of the following statements as T/True or F/False.*
- _____ Moses will perform wonders to demonstrate God's authority over the pagan land of Egypt.
- _____ The miracles will serve to soften Pharaoh's heart toward Israel.
- _____ God must have a purpose for the Pharaoh's unwillingness.
- _____ God compares his special love for Israel to the Pharaoh's love for his first-born son who is in line to succeed him.
- _____ The Lord assures Moses that everything will go smoothly.
- _____ God provides Moses with a timetable with deadlines.
- _____ God will use the first meeting to demand that Israel must be permanently liberated to build a new homeland in Canaan.
- _____ The fact that Pharaoh refuses permission even for a three day trip suggests that the Egyptian government now depends on the Hebrew slaves.

Exodus 4:24-26. On the surface, this surely seems like one of the strangest texts in the Bible. It revolves around the Hebrew ritual of circumcision. *For a clearer understanding of this very Hebrew situation, read the text that follows, and then fill in the blanks.*

Genesis 17: 1 – 14.
- *v1.* Abram is still childless, though he is _____ years old.
- *v2.* The covenant requires that Abram will walk with God, who will in turn give him many _____.

Week Three The Way God Works

- v8. God will also turn over the entire land of _____ as a home for Abram's descendants.
- v10. The sign of God's authority in this covenant will be male _____.

As Moses and his family begin their journey to Egypt, a crisis arises at a clearing commonly used by long distance travelers. In some way, the Lord comes close to striking Moses dead. Since no words of God are recorded in the text, we can only surmise that Moses is stricken with a virulent, life threatening illness. In some way, the man and his wife determine that God is angry because their sons have not been circumcised.

While this seems trivial and almost insignificant to you or me, it's a serious violation of the Old Covenant. Just like the shepherd's staff carried by Moses, the rod of God, circumcision was a seal of God's authority. By maintaining this sign commanded by God, the Jewish nation demonstrated their reliance on God's authority.
- Lifting the designated shepherd's staff would demonstrate that God, *not Moses*, had authority over the Red Sea.
- Circumcision of the male reproductive organ was a confession that the many descendants promised by God would come about not through male potency, but through divine sovereignty.

Think about it: Why were children and posterity considered such a huge blessing in the world of Moses?

_____

_____

_____

Has this emphasis on future generations changed among people of God today? *Explain your answer.*

_____

_____

_____

We can only speculate about the spiritual intensity of Moses before the burning bush. Prior to that visitation by God, we have no hint of his spiritual disciplines while living in Midian, for it's obvious that the burning bush was a surprising event and a new work of God. Perhaps the Midianites, descendants of Abraham but not Isaac, no longer practiced circumcision. Or maybe

Moses has simply been distracted by desert life and the cares of survival. He may well have felt completely cut off from the people and the covenant of God

But when God speaks from the burning bush, it becomes apparent that Moses is once again front and center in the covenant, and well on his way to being a spiritual leader for the people of God.
- 3:6. God identifies himself as the God of Abraham, Isaac and Jacob.
- Whatever his past attitudes, regardless of his personality quirks and character flaws, Moses has now been recalled to the Covenant of Abraham.
- *From this moment, he knows that every male in his family must be circumcised.* For some mysterious reason, he delays and begins his long journey of obedience without acknowledging this important sign of God's authority.

4:25-26. It is an event veiled by the mists of time, distance and culture. God is angry and Moses is ill. Firm up the details in your mind by completing these blanks.
- But Zipporah took a _____ _____ and cut off her son's foreskin, and touched Moses' _____ with it.
- "Surely, you are a bride groom of _____ to me."

Suffering this near disaster on the road to such a moment of destiny must be alarming and discouraging to Zipporah. With Moses sidelined in the throes of his near-death experience, his wife circumcises Gershom. Hoping that God will transfer her obedience to Moses because she has acted on his behalf, she touches the foreskin to her ailing husband's leg. The blood of the son rubs off on the life of his father. In calling Moses her "bridegroom of blood," Zipporah must mean that her marriage to Moses has been restored through the blood (circumcision) of their son, Gershom.

Personal Inventory: It's easy to get distracted and drift away from God's authority. Is there any area in your life in which you have been careless in your walk with Christ?
    [ ] Yes [ ] No Do you worship Him consistently and wholeheartedly?
    [ ] Yes [ ] No Do you read His Word and apply it on a regular basis?
    [ ] Yes [ ] No Have you removed all false gods and idols from your life?
    [ ] Yes [ ] No Do you bring tithes and offerings back to Him?
    [ ] Yes [ ] No Do you practice forgiveness when others hurt or offend you?
    [ ] Yes [ ] No Are you devoted to the discipline of prayer?
    [ ] Yes [ ] No Are you intentional in attempting to win your world to Christ?
    [ ] Yes [ ] No Do you confess your sins and flee temptation?
    [ ] Yes [ ] No Do you make every effort to walk in the Spirit?

Exodus 4: 27 – 31. Moses has been careless, but God has been faithful. The men who once sought the life of Moses have been removed. His brother Aaron, whom Moses has not seen in four decades, is not only alive and well, but has been summoned by God.
- v27. Where does God arrange for the brothers to meet?

_____

- *v28.* What does Moses divulge to Aaron?

- *v29.* When the duo returns to Egypt, who speaks to the Elders?

- *v30.* Who performs the signs for the Elders and other leaders?

- *v31.* When the Hebrews learn that God is concerned about their plight, what is their response to Him?

> **SECRETS OF THE DESERT**
>
> Pharaohs often wore ornamental golden sandals which were decorated with images of Egypt's enemies on the soles. In this way, the Pharaoh symbolically crushed his enemies underneath his feet each time he took a step.

Day Two: Moses Goes West, Things Go South
Read Exodus 5
Review chapter five once again. Use a pen or marker to mark each verse in which the earthly king moves to resist the God of Heaven and Earth. Exodus 5: 1 – 5.

Moses and Aaron are granted an audience with the Pharaoh, with whom they share the commands of God. The God of Israel says, "Let my people go, so that they may hold a festival to me in the desert. The word translated "hold a festival" (or "feast") is the Hebrew verb, *hagag*. To appreciate the dynamics of such an activity, consult each of the following verses. *Then describe what happens in each of those contexts*:

- *Deuteronomy 16:13-15. Hagag* is translated *(v15)* "celebrate the feast." What attitudes must accompany such a feast?

- *Psalm 42:4. Hagag* is translated "those going to the festival" or "festive throng." How do those people behave?

  _____

- *1 Samuel 30:16. Hagag* is translated "dancing." What other actions accompany this festive form of dancing before the Lord?

  _____

When the people of Israel ultimately arrive at Mount Sinai, what sort of celebration does God anticipate?

_____

_____

How does Pharaoh respond to the message from God's servants?
- *v2.* _____ is the Lord that I should obey him?
- I do not _____ him, and I won't let Israel go!
- *v4.* You are distracting the people from their _____.

Exodus 5: 6-18. In order to nip this rebellion in the bud, the Pharaoh makes the work of the Hebrews even more difficult. *What is his command?*

_____

_____

_____

v11. The slave drivers command the Hebrews, "Go and get your own straw, wherever you can find it, but your work will not be _____ at all."
v12. "So the people scattered _____ _____ _____ to gather stubble used for straw."

v17. When the Israelite foremen complain to the Pharaoh about the new work load, what is his reply?

_____

Exodus 5: 19 – 23. We've all seen too many old Westerns in which a drifter arrives in an endangered town, offering to help them fight off an approaching band of outlaws.

Unfortunately, though the townspeople find the idea appealing, they tuck their tails and head for the hills at the first sign of difficulty. It's too bad that the citizens of Goshen feel exactly the same way!

Learning the Pharaoh's decision, they return to Moses and Aaron with anger and scorn. "May God punish you for what you've done! We've become a stench in Pharaoh's nostrils!"

v22-23. Moses, in turn, goes to God! "Is this why you sent me?" he asks the Lord. "You have not _____ your people at all!"

Put yourself in their sandals. Imagine yourself and your family as victims of cruel slavery. You hate it, but you've grown accustomed to it over time. Suddenly a man of God arrives, performing miracles to prove his divine credentials. So you believe him and prepare for deliverance. But instead of being set free, you suddenly find your conditions have worsened? How would you feel?

_____

_____

_____

Q: Why might Moses logically feel betrayed by God at this moment?

_____

_____

_____

_____

Q: Why has God allowed events to take this turn for the worse?

_____

_____

_____

_____

Character Study: Ironically, the experience of the Israelites is not a fluke. To the contrary, this is a pattern that is commonly found in Scripture. *Take a moment and research another example of delayed deliverance. Read each of the very brief texts in the chain that follows, and answer the related question.*

- *1 Samuel 17: 50-58.* David proves that God's hand is on him when he _____ _____.
- *1 Samuel 18:6-7.* David's fame is so great that he is celebrated as a _____ in Israel.
- *1 Samuel 19:1.* Saul becomes so jealous that he orders his son and other men around the palace to _____ David.
- *1 Samuel 20:1.* David is forced to flee for his life. "What _____ have I committed?" he asks.
- *1 Samuel 22:6-18.* Saul orders the murder of _____ priests because they assisted David by feeding his men.

It hardly sounds like instant success for David, does it? He's been anointed by God. He performs feats so amazing that there's no doubt God's hand is upon him. Even the king recognizes his power. And yet even after slaying Goliath and inspiring the defeat of the Philistines, David spends at least 15 years in hiding before ascending to the throne of his nation!

What distinction sets Moses and David apart from other heroes of faith in the Old Testament?

_____

_____

_____

Hint: Exodus 33:11; 1 Samuel 13:14

When God delays the results that Moses and David are ordained to achieve, is he punishing sin in their lives, or is he magnifying the impact each will achieve?

_____

_____

_____

Take the truth to heart. Joseph was apparently anointed for the job of rescuing Israel when God gave him dreams of his parents and siblings bowing down at his feet. Of course, he was in store for years of hardship before realizing those dreams of destiny. Moses was anointed to lead his people out of bondage when God appeared to him in the form of a burning bush at Sinai. Despite his ability to do signs and wonders, things would get worse before getting better. David was anointed as the next king and even killed Goliath years before actually ascending to the throne. And for much of the interim, his living conditions were anything but royal!

What about you, dear friend? Has there been any kind of anointing experience in your life, when God supernaturally placed a vision in your heart?

    [ ] YES   [ ] NO   [ ] I'M NOT SURE

If you answered "Yes," describe the experience and explain the vision or the calling you were granted.

_____

_____

_____

_____

God's anointing is never merely experience for the sake of experience. It is always related to a task. What work or accomplishment did God set before you?

_____

_____

What is the status of that work in your life? *Check only one*:
    [ ] I have finally accomplished it.
    [ ] I have begun the work for which I was anointed.
    [ ] I have postponed this assignment.
    [ ] There are conditions which must change before I can begin.

If you checked **"I have postponed the assignment,"** explain why:

_____

If you checked **"There are conditions which must change…"** explain those conditions:

_____

_____

Who must change those particular conditions? Is this a choice you must make, or does it require intervention from God?
    [ ] I must choose to make the changes.
    [ ] I must wait for supernatural intervention.

Set aside a few moments now to be still before the Lord. Sit or kneel quietly. Turn the palms of your hands facing upward, as a token of your willingness to receive whatever God has in store for you.

- Ask the Heavenly Father to speak to you and recharge your spiritual batteries.
- Read a psalm of praise and thanksgiving aloud to Him.
- Commit your current circumstances to him and, even though they may be difficult, praise him in the midst of your life.
- Write down anything the Holy Spirit impresses upon you, and tuck the sheet into your Bible.

Day Three: Experiencing God
Read Exodus 6

Read Exodus 6, paying attention to details. Then use a pen or marker to indicate each phrase indicating either that God is speaking or someone is speaking for Him.

Exodus 6: 1 – 12. God does a lot with promises. He promises Joseph that a time will come when his parents and siblings will kneel to honor him. He promises Moses that he will successfully stand against the Pharaoh and win the release of all the Hebrew slaves. Needless to say, people of faith are moved to action by promises like these. *That's why experiencing God becomes so important.* When we hear His promises, we step out in faith. But at some point, it's important that we experience the divine fulfillment of those promises that motivated us.

v1. This chapter begins with a promise: God says to Moses, "You will _____ what I do to Pharaoh. Because of my mighty _____, he will let them go: he will _____ them out of his country.

v 2-3. God [*Elohim*] also said to Moses, 'I am the Lord [*Yahweh*.] I appeared to Abraham, to Isaac, and to Jacob as God Almighty [*El Shaddai*,] but by my name the Lord [*Yahweh*] I did not make myself known to them."

We're familiar with the names Elohim and Yahweh [*Jehovah*,] but this is the first instance of El Shaddai in Exodus. In fact, God is called El Shaddai only forty-eight times in Scripture, and thirty-one of those are found in the book of Job. Check out the following texts in which this name usually translated God Almighty is used.

- *Genesis 17:1 – 8.* El Shaddai reflects God's power to _____

- *Ezekiel 10:1 – 5.* El Shaddai speaks of God's _____

- *Job 37:23-24.* El Shaddai is _____

Week Three The Way God Works

Based on those examples, what aspects of God's power are associated with the name El Shaddai?

_____

_____

God discloses that He appeared to the Patriarchs, but that they did not "know" him [*v3*] as Yahweh, the Lord. At first this seems strange, because it's clear that he used this name in identifying Himself to Abraham, Isaac and Jacob! At second glance, however, the distinction probably comes in the Hebrew word *yada*, which is translated "to know." It means much more than just to hold an idea in your head.

Later, when the Exodus experience is drawing to a close, Moses will recall some of the ways in which God has demonstrated his love. Deuteronomy details what the Israelites have witnessed. Read this excerpt and answer the questions that follow:

Deuteronomy 29:2-9. "Moses summoned all the Israelites and said to them: 'Your eyes have seen all that the Lord did in Egypt to Pharaoh, to all his officials, and to all his land. With your own eyes you saw those great trials, those miraculous signs and great wonders. But to this day the Lord has not given you a mind that understands or eyes that see or ears that hear. During the forty years that I led you through the desert, your clothes did not wear out, nor did the sandals on your feet. You ate no bread and drank no wine or other fermented drink. I did this so that you might know that I am the Lord your God.'"

- What was miraculous about their clothing?

  _____

- What was extraordinary about the Jews' diet in the desert?

  _____

- *v6.* Why did God do all these wonders?

  _____

When God says his people have not previously known him as the Lord, his message is that they have not known it or experienced it in the way that he is about to work. Granted, they have seen miracles:

- Abraham and Sarah conceived their first child when they were very old.

- Jacob received a vision from God at Bethel, and was able to miraculously assemble a herd for himself despite his father-in-law's treachery.

- Joseph saw God use slavery and prison to bring him to a position of unprecedented power in Egypt.

What they have not experienced is the sort of overwhelming, shock-and-awe supernatural warfare that they are about to experience. Clearly, what happens next in Egypt will constitute a divine line in the sand for centuries to come.

The Red Sea will become a new reference point for how much Israel can trust the God of Abraham.

v6-12. Take note of God's promises to his people. Then review the following summary and fill in the blanks:

God promises to bring Israel out from the yoke of _____ and free them from _____. He will take them as _____ _____, and will give them to a land he has promised to _____ to give. Moses shared this message with the Hebrews but they refused to believe because of _____ and _____.

v6. "I will **redeem** you with an outstretched arm." Circle the word "redeemed" in your text. This is the first occasion on which this powerful term has been used in the Bible.

- The Hebrew word is *gaal*.

- It means to buy back a person from slavery or to reclaim anything from the ownership of another. It can denote a payment, an action, or someone who makes such a payment or takes such an action.

- *Note: Today in the Sudan, there is a Christian ministry which literally buys back followers of Jesus who have been captured by Muslim terrorists and sold on the slave market. The ministry raises funds to redeem men and women forced into bondage at gunpoint.*

Let's make this our desert oasis for a few moments, and explore the biblical dynamic of this concept: "I will redeem you." The term redeem applies to a variety of situations in God's Word.

- *Leviticus 25:25.* When a poor Jew is forced to sell the land God has given him, his nearest relative must redeem the land if possible.

- *Think about that for a moment.*

Q: What would happen to a family who lost their land forever?

Week Three The Way God Works

- *Micah 4:10*. God promises His people that even though they will be carried away to Babylon during the captivity of Israel, He will ultimately redeem them from the hands of their enemies.

    Q: What will this redemption mean to the captive Jews living in Babylon so far from their homeland?

    _____

Now, take a look at how God uses the term "redeem" as an expression of his ministry to his people:
- *Job 19:25*. What future event does Job ascribe to his living redeemer?

    _____

- *Isaiah 44:21-22*. Isaiah expresses joy and relief because of his redeemer's work. What has God done for him?

    _____

- *Isaiah 49: 25-26*. What will God's redemption of his people make evident to the watching world?

    _____
    _____

The way in which God will redeem Israel from slavery becomes a powerful picture of what Jesus Christ does for us who follow him. With this Old Testament backdrop, summarize what it means to call Jesus Christ "my redeemer."

_____
_____

Exodus 6: 13 – 27. Don't miss something important that is a part of this section of verses. This is not just a genealogy- one of those long, winding lists of names that are hard to unfamiliar and often unpronounceable! *I wonder why God has included these insignificant people.*

The answer is that this is more than another list of names: *this is a love letter.* The reason God scatters lists like this throughout the Bible is because he loves names. Names represent the faces, lives, achievements of people he loves. When you and I love somebody, we'll occasionally find

67

ourselves writing their names idly on a piece of paper, a prayer list, a gift. We write those names with fondness because each name has a story, a love story.

This list reminds you and me that God loves us deeply. Our names are close to his heart. And he knows our destinies long before we ever have a clue. Read the genealogy outlined in this text. Take note that the sons of Aaron will be ordained by God to serve with their father as priests. By contrast, the sons of Levi will be set apart as helpers in maintaining the Tabernacle.

Take a moment and take pleasure in the details that God enjoys. Consult Numbers 3 and learn more about the descendants of Aaron. *Read the brief texts that follow and draw a straight line to match each name at left with its matching fact at right.*

Nadab & Abihu	*Numbers 3:2-4.* These sons of Aaron will serve as priests during his lifetime.
Sons of Merari	*Psalms 42,44,45.* Will become worship leaders and composers of worship songs
Eliezer & Ithamar	*Numbers 3:21-26.* Cared for the tent, curtains and coverings of the Tabernacle
Sons of Korah	*Numbers 3:27-32.* Will care for the Ark, tables, lamp stand, and altars of the Tabernacle
Sons of Kohath	*Numbers 3:4.* Sons of Aaron who will be struck dead for offering unholy fire in the Tabernacle
Sons of Gershon	*Numbers 3:36.* Will care for the frames, crossbars and support structures of the Tabernacle

Personal Reflection: Look back over your walk with Jesus Christ, and write down your honest answer to the two questions that follow.
1. At this point in your journey, what is your experience in knowing Christ?
   [ ] I don't know much about Jesus.
   [ ] I mostly know him through my family and/or friends who are believers.
   [ ] Primarily, my knowledge of Christ is intellectual, based on what I've read and heard.

Week Three   The Way God Works

[ ] Some of my knowledge of Christ is now based on my experience in walking with him and discovering how he works.

2. Use the space that follows to describe how Jesus Christ has redeemed you.

</br>

Day Four: Standing before the Throne
Read Exodus 7
Read this chapter twice more. Wherever Moses and Aaron are mentioned, circle or highlight the verb describing their activity.

Exodus 7: 1 – 6. As you probably recall, the Egyptians worshipped hundreds of gods and goddesses, many of whom were represented by cattle, crocodiles, gnats, snakes and dozens of other creatures. Pharaoh himself was regarded as one of the most important gods. We'll deal with many of these popular idols next week. For now, simply notice God's comment in verse one: "See, I have made you like a god to Pharaoh, and your brother Aaron will be your prophet."

Explain this idea. In what way would Moses assume the stature of a god before the king of Egypt?

_____

v2-5. Moses and Aaron are to repeat God's message to Pharaoh in its entirety. They are to complete each step of the assignment God sets before them. Still, the Pharaoh will not surrender because God has promised "to harden his heart." Why does God play both sides of the field by causing the Pharaoh to refuse? *How can one justify this strategy?*

- *v3.* Pharaoh's resistance will allow God to _____
  _____

- *v5.* When God is done, the Egyptians will know _____
  _____

v4. The Lord promises, "Then I will lay my hand on Egypt and with mighty acts of judgment, I will bring out my divisions, my people the Israelites." The Hebrew grammar literally speaks of "great judgment."

- This kind of judgment is always from a holy God, and may include all kinds of catastrophes ranging from warfare and the sword to fire or wild beasts[18].
- Judgment is God's righteous response to particular unrighteousness on the part of a nation. It is applied both to Israel[19] in other eras, as well as to Egypt at this moment in history.

v8. It is no accident that Exodus reminds us of our heroes' ages. Moses is _____ years old, and his brother Aaron is _____.

- Pharaohs often died at relatively young ages.
- Thutmose III (ca. 1450 BC) died somewhere in the range of 70 years of age. Rameses the Great (ca. 1280 BC) died at the advanced age of 90, although the average Egyptian lifespan of this era was around 40-50 years of age.
- There's a good chance that Moses and his brother would have seemed much older and, therefore, much wiser than a typical Pharaoh. *Remember that age, not youth, conveys status in the ancient world.*

Exodus 7: 8 – 13. Finally, the two sons of Amram and Jochebed find themselves standing before the golden throne of Egypt, facing down one of the most powerful and brutal men on earth.

- Clearly, Pharaoh is unimpressed. As was the custom, he asks for some sign of authority.
- Moses passes his rod to Aaron who casts it on the ground. It becomes a snake, coiling on the palace floor.
- Pharaoh's magicians manage a counterfeit miracle. It has been suggested that they were snake charmers who were able to put cobras into a trance and then release them.
- *v12.* Even when the snake under Aaron's power swallows up the snakes from the magicians, Pharaoh is unmoved. As promised, God has hardened his heart because so much judgment is waiting in the pipeline.

Exodus 7:16 – 24. The next morning, Moses and Aaron wait for the Pharaoh to emerge from the palace and prepare for his bath in the Nile. *Review these verses and fill in the blanks that follow:*

[*v16*] God commands that Pharaoh should set the Israelites free to _____ him in the desert. [*v17*] God will _____ the Nile and change the water to blood. [*v18*] The _____ will die, and the river will _____. [*v20*] Aaron raised the _____ with Pharaoh and court looking on, and the Nile turned to blood

To appreciate the seismic impact of what God does here, you must understand how this historic river impacts virtually every aspect of life in Egypt.

- The Nile is the longest river in the world, flowing 4,000 miles south to north from the high ground of Burundi downward to the delta of Egypt. Although it touches nine

Week Three The Way God Works

- nations altogether and drains three million square miles of Africa, it is almost exclusively associated with Egypt.
- The ancient Egyptian calendar containing twelve months of thirty days each, is divided into three seasons, corresponding to the three stages of the Nile.
- Each year the flood waters of the Nile inundate adjacent lands, dumping 140 million tons of rich top soil along the way to make farms more fertile and productive. The river and its god Hapy are considered the source of life and wealth in Egypt.
- Transportation on the Nile is so central to Egyptian life that the sun god, Ra, is depicted traveling across the sky in a boat. This is in sharp contrast to other pagan nations who generally imagine the sun god traveling in a chariot or cart made of fire.
- Creatures of the Nile elevated to the status of gods include the Hippopotamus [Tawaret,] the crocodile [Sobek,] the frog [Heqet,] and the ibis [Thoth.]
- The river even contributes to education and culture due to the fact that papyrus, the universal writing material of the age, is produced from reeds along the Nile.

With that backdrop, imagine what kinds of messages God intends to send when his first plague on Egypt turns that prominent body of water to blood. *Read the following possibilities. Check off those which are most likely intended as parts of the message God is sending Egypt.*

____ The Good Old Days of Prosperity are over.
____ Hapy, the god of the Nile, is not in control, and cannot provide the necessities of life.
____ Egypt is bleeding.
____ The God of Abraham Isaac and Jacob is above all other gods.
____ People who resist the One True God are always at risk.
____ Gods like Tawaret, Heqet and Sobek are all defenseless against the God of Israel.
____ Rejection of the God of Israel results in desperation and death.
____ If you believe freeing the slaves will cost too much, wait until you realize what it will cost you to keep them.

Now that we understand what God intends to say to Egypt, be sure that you don't miss the exclamation point at the end of his sentence. According to *verse 19-b*, this is not simply a matter of the Nile turning to blood. Even more dramatically, every drop of water in Egypt turns to blood: streams, ponds and reservoirs; even water stored in buckets and stone jars!

- How does this particular fact mesh with recurring theories that the plagues were simply a chain of natural events that began with some sort of "red tide" or natural pollution of the Nile?

_____

_____

_____

- *Personalize this.* How severely would you be affected if *without warning*, all the water in your city, your well, your refrigerator, and even water stored or sold in bottles suddenly turned to blood?

  _____

  _____

  _____

  _____

- In addition to being unable to drink or bathe, how would ordinary people respond to the constant sight of blood throughout the land, and the oppressive smell of dead fish floating in that polluted body of water?

  _____

  _____

  _____

- List the reasons Egyptians must realize this event is from God:

  ✓ _____

  ✓ _____

  ✓ _____

  ✓ _____

Thinking about Judgment: Are the plagues of Egypt unique, or does God punish all pagan nations? For example, someone has said "If God doesn't punish America, he will have to apologize to Sodom and Gomorrah." What is the role of God's judgment?
- Read *Romans 1: 18 – 23.*

- Does this passage apply to Egypt?
  [ ] YES   [ ] NO

- What do you believe determines when God brings judgment on a nation, and when he relents and delays in the interest of mercy?

  _____

Week Three   The Way God Works

_____

_____

_____

I don't think Moses ever feared that God would fail him in this mission. *But I do believe Moses was afraid that he would fail God.* The task seemed monumental and Moses knew that he had feet of clay.

Have you ever been afraid that way? Has there been a task so intimidating or a standard so high, that you just knew you were doomed to disappoint?

Q: What was it like, and what happened?

_____

_____

_____

_____

_____

_____

Be Still and Know: Find a quiet place where you can draw aside and be still before the Lord right now. Kneel before him, and thank him for the work he has called you to do with your life right now. Tell him the places where you're afraid or anxious. Confess all your fears. Then commit your path to Him. Selah.

WEEK FOUR

GOD - 10, EGYPT - 0

When God wishes to take pity on a soul and it rebels, not suffering anything and doing its own will, He permits it to suffer things it does not want, in order that it may seek Him again. Abba Isaiah

If you really think about it, you can feel like you're watching the God of Heaven carpet bombing the civilian population of Egypt in the chapters we're about to read. I think most of us tend to deal with the unpleasant thought by focusing on the special effects. It's amazing when the Nile turns to blood! It's mysterious and awe inspiring when hail pummels the Land of the Nile, sparks flying as each hailstone strikes the earth! It is more difficult for comfortable, sensitized Americans to imagine Egyptian boys and girls who have nothing to drink, who are being swarmed by flies and gnats, who suffer hunger pangs when many of the cattle get sick and die. We're slightly more put off by the death of all the first-born children, although it's easy to lose sight of that in all the details of the Exodus.

God gets a pass here from most of us only because we marvel at the miracles and don't think about real people facing these consequences. *There are other places in Scripture that we find much more unsettling.*
- We are offended later when God punishes Moses for striking the rock to obtain water, rather than speaking to it as commanded. One little mistake and this godly man is denied the Promised Land? What's that all about?[20] We cringe when God orders King Saul to destroy all the Amalekites- not only the army, but the women and children as well.[21]
- And we can hardly watch as Jesus describes the plight of the rich man in Hell. From that flaming pit of despair, he cries out for just a drop of water. But he's told that he wasted all the good things in his earthly life, and now this is his fate![22]

These acts of God trouble us because we live in a pampered age with an ever expanding list of civil rights, and we because we don't grasp the meaning of one English word- *sovereign*. The Bible teaches that our God is sovereign.
- There are more than three hundred instances in which the Word of God states directly that God is sovereign.

- Daniel uses an Aramaic word, *soltan*[23], which gives us our word "sultan." It means that God has absolute control over everything that is. And in the case of God, his dominion is never ending!
- This is the connotation of the Hebrew word *adonai*, translated "Lord" throughout the Old Testament. God is in absolute control of the cosmos.

You and I have been instructed with axioms like "Power corrupts, and absolute power corrupts absolutely." So we are ill at ease with the concept of anyone having that kind of power. In the case of God, however, absolute power rests easily on His shoulders. As Psalm 139 reminds us, our eternal God is all-wise, all- powerful, and present everywhere at the same time. Besides all that, His nature is unchanging, so He cannot be corrupted.

This brings us back to the stand off between the God of Israel and the gods and goddesses of Egypt. Is it good policy for the only true God to devastate the population of Egypt in order to teach them their religion is false?

In a book filled with powerful, vivid words and expressions, some biblical promises and observations are particularly incisive. One of my favorites is God's assurance, "They sow the wind, and reap the whirlwind!"[24] Our universe operates according to foundational laws and principles. In the physical realm, there are the laws of gravity, motion and energy. In the spiritual realm, there is the law of reciprocity: whatever a man reaps, that also will he sow. Nations that play deadly games reap fatal consequences. *God doesn't have to send them.* They are built in to the universe as surely as electrical current comes through a wall outlet, whether summoned by a plug in the hand of a parent or a fork in the hands of a toddler.

But in Exodus 8-10, God is extremely intentional. There is a proud tyrant who hails himself as god and must be humbled. There is a misguided land of idol worshipers who must be instructed. And there is a nation of slaves, beloved of the Father, who must be redeemed. Let's learn about the sovereign power of the Most High God as he rains down terror onto Egypt, and calls his chosen people out of bondage.

Along the way, we'll be answering questions like these this week:
- Day 1: How do spiritual impurities creep into our lives, and how do we remove them?
- Day 2: When God sends trial and hardship into your life, what is your most common response?
- Day 3: Pharaoh thought he was on the throne for one purpose, but in reality had been placed there for a different reason. Is this a common experience among human beings?
- Day 4: Why are sin and spiritual ignorance so frequently compared by God to living in darkness?

Week Four God – 10, Egypt – 0

Day 1: Amphibians and Insects
Read Exodus 8: 1 - 19
Read this short section of scripture a couple of times. Use a pen or highlighter to mark specific promises; those kept by God, and those broken by the Pharaoh.

Exodus 8: 1 – 7. In his first plague, God turned the Nile to blood. And as evidence that this was not simply some unpleasant natural phenomenon, even water already collected in buckets and jars becomes bloody as well. There was no clean water in the land of Egypt. Now seven days later, the Almighty God prepares to unleash a second calamity on Egypt.

v1-4. God makes a promise, not a threat. Summarize His message to Pharaoh in your own words:

_____

_____

_____

_____

Once again, the Lord God issues a powerful indictment of yet another beloved Egyptian deity. Heqet, the frog goddess, is associated with fertility, life and death. Egyptian women of this period commonly wear small frog-shaped amulets intended to invoke Heqet's protection during pregnancy. Egyptians believe that this goddess gives breath to children, whose bodies are formed by her husband. She is often depicted holding the familiar Ankh symbol as she performs her work.

Think about it: If God can transform this trusted deity into a troublesome, uncomfortable and smelly source of anguish, what does this reveal about the powers of Heqet? *Read the following conclusions and mark all those you believe apply here:*
- [ ] The birth rate of the frogs is determined by the God of Israel, not by the frog goddess.
- [ ] If Heqet cannot control the multiplication of frogs, why should one assume she can affect the birth rate of humans?
- [ ] Frogs lead to death rather than life.
- [ ] The priests of Egypt are mistaken and not reliable.
- [ ] Frogs are stupid pests rather than intelligent creatures.
- [ ] Heqet is no match for the real Lord of Life.

v6-7. Aaron stretches out his hand and frogs soon cover the land. Scripture adds, "But the Egyptians did the same things by their secret arts; they also made frogs come up on the land of Egypt.
- It's clear that the Egyptian priests are merely producing a small facsimile of what God has done. How do we know this?

- *Simple.* The Pharaoh does not call on his trusted magicians to remove the frogs from the land. He must rely on Moses because the problem is clearly under the control of Yahweh, not Heqet!

Think about it: What do you think the Egyptian magicians might have done to give the impression of calling forth frogs?

_____

_____

_____

_____

v8-9. Fill in the blanks: So Pharaoh summoned _____ and _____, and said "_____ to the Lord to take the frogs away from me and my people, and I will let the people go to offer _____ to the Lord." Moses said to Pharaoh, "I will leave you the _____ of setting the time for me to _____ for you..."

- Did you notice the pagan ruler's choice of words?

- He does not refer to God as "your god" or "your lord." Rather, he asks Moses to pray to "the Lord."

v10-12. Pharaoh asks that Moses pray for the frogs to be gone the very next day. Moses agrees, explaining that certain conditions will enable the Pharaoh and his people to know there is no one else like the God of Israel. What will those conditions be?

_____

_____

_____

_____

v13. What happens after Moses prays?

_____

_____

_____

Week Four God – 10, Egypt - 0

v14. What will remain for the people of Egypt to do?

_____

v15. While the mountains of dead frogs remain for many days as a testimony to the power of God, the Pharaoh changes his mind again. He refuses to allow Israel to leave. How do you explain his behavior? *(Choose only one summary that best explains it.)*
    [ ] Pharaoh concludes this has all been bad luck, and it will be safe to deny Moses
        request once again.
    [ ] God's spirit provokes Pharaoh to be defiant in order to give God more time to
        perform his miracles and reach out to the Egyptians.
    [ ] Pharaoh believes he can rely on his magicians to protect him.
    [ ] God overrules the will of Pharaoh in order to humble this proud, pagan nation.
    [ ] I'd put it this way: _____

_____

8:16 – 19. When Pharaoh once again declines God's offer, Aaron stretches forth his hand and strikes the ground with the rod of God. Before long, the sky is black with gnats, dive bombing into eyes, food, mouths, noses and open wounds.

- This time, Pharaoh's magicians cannot even manage the semblance of this miracle.
- They explain, "This is the _____ of God."
- In this plague, God completely humiliates the pagan priests paid to support the Pharaoh and honor the gods. They were apparently able to produce a few frogs from the sleeves of their robes, but they cannot begin to touch this feat with swarms of tiny gnats!
- *Note*: The Egyptians word *ken* which is translated "gnats" in this passage may also be translated "lice." When William Tyndale produced the first English translation of Exodus, he preferred the word "lice." This would create an even more serious crisis for the priests, as being infected with lice would render them ceremonially unclean. They would be unable to lead worship in the temples until the epidemic had ended.

At first glance, it might seem that God is punishing the Egyptians for their paganism and for their Pharaoh's stubbornness. But in fact, this is only one of many instances in Scripture where God uses trial and even curses to instruct people and purify their faith. He does this not only to enemies, but to his own people as well.

Page forward through your Old Testament to *Isaiah 1: 21 – 26*. Write your observations below.
- *v22.* What does God mean when he says, "Your silver has become dross?"

_____

- Is it a positive or negative that the choice wines have been diluted with water?
    [ ] It's a good thing.   [ ] It's a sign of disgrace.

- *v25*. What does God mean by his expression, "I will turn my hand against you?"

  _____

- What is the benefit whenever dross is purged (refined) out of the silver?

  _____
  _____

Even people who follow the One True God occasionally require that our faith is refined and the dross is removed. Is there anything in your life of faith that might be characterized as "dross" or "alloys?" If the answer is yes, what must be done about it?

_____
_____

Day Two: Pests Fly and Cows Die
Read Exodus 8:20 – 9:12
Read this passage three times. Use a marker to highlight phrases and sentences that explain why these plagues are different from the previous curses inflicted on Egypt.

The wrath of God falls upon Egypt in three cycles of three plagues each. Phase One turns the Nile to blood, sends an epidemic of frogs infesting the land, and then inundates the Egyptians in either gnats or lice. With Phase Two, the tragedy escalates.

Disease bearing flies are obviously a more serious hazard than gnats or even lice. But one limitation will set this plague apart from the previous three. Explain the difference below. *(If you didn't catch it, refer to v22-23.)*

_____
_____

v20. This is the second time Moses has been directed to meet Pharaoh in the morning on his way to the river (also *7:15*.) Why would you expect Pharaoh to walk out to the Nile each morning?

_____

Week Four   God – 10, Egypt – 0

Once again, God demands that the Pharaoh release his people to participate in worship in the deserts beyond Egypt. Clearly, God is working for a permanent end to slavery. Why do you believe he continues to speak in terms of worship rather than establishing a new homeland? *Select the one best answer.*

[ ] God is cleverly attempting to deceive the Pharaoh.
[ ] The Lord God will soon raise the stakes from worship to permanent freedom as this poker game continues.
[ ] By focusing on the aspect of worship, God is contrasting his own divine right to worship with the Pharaoh's counterfeit role of god.
[ ] The Almighty is simply affirming the true role of his nation Israel- to worship Him.
[ ] Worship is what God's people will ultimately learn in the desert.
[ ] Other _____

_____

The Hebrew word translated "flies" in this passage is a very broad term that can actually be used to describe any number of very common insects. For this reason, it's difficult to determine which Egyptian god is in the crosshairs of God's supernatural shotgun.

- The scarab beetle (prominent in the motion picture *Curse of the Mummy's Tomb,*) was the symbol for Khepri, the god whom Egyptians believed caused the sun to rise each morning. Khepri was sometimes depicted as a man with a beetle's head.
- A plague of flies may have pointed up the inadequacy of Nut, the goddess of the sky. The pests would have come pouring in from the sky which was purportedly under her control.
- Some writers have suggested that an inundation of flies would challenge the authority of Apshai, an evil god who was perhaps represented by flies.

v24. God's Word comes to pass, and insects pummel the land, filling the Pharaoh's palace, the corridors of the temples, the huts and houses of ordinary Egyptians. Only the Hebrews in the Land of Goshen are spared the ordeal.

v25. Pharaoh summons Moses and grants permission for the Israelites to go and worship God, but with one stipulation. What's the stipulation?

_____

_____

v26-28. Moses declines, explaining the Egyptians would be offended at the sight of Hebrews worshiping Yahweh, and would _____ them. Pharaoh grants permission to go into the desert with another stipulation. What is the stipulation this time?

_____

v29-32. Match the figures at left with the corresponding result at right.
   ____ Moses & Aaron   A. Sudden Disappearance
   ____ The swarms of flies B. Change of Mind
   ____ Pharaoh   C. Prayer is answered

9: 1 – 7. Now God threatens to raise his hand against the livestock of Egypt: donkeys, horses, camels, cattle, sheep and goats. Stop and think about it. *Why would this crisis be far more catastrophic for the people, their health and their economy than flies bearing germs and bacteria?*

_____

_____

_____

_____

Fill in the Blanks. *v4.* No animal belonging to the Israelites will _____.
v5. God sets a time and promises this will occur _____. *v7.* So Pharaoh dispatches men on the following day to investigate. Everywhere they find diseased and _____ livestock- except in _____.

9: 8 – 12. With Pharaoh once again hedging on his promise to release the Israelites, God dials up the pain and suffering once again. Moses and Aaron throw soot into the air and illness strikes the population. To appreciate the sixth calamity, you need only to decipher three Hebrew words used here:
- *Sehiyn* = a serious skin condition resulting in painful boils and sores.
- *Parah* = to blossom. While this word most commonly refers to flowers, it can also denote sores "blossoming" and running over with disgusting fluids and infections.
- *Ababuot* = blisters which erupt on the skin of people or animals

That's right. Although the Hebrew language is very spare, the text actually includes three different words to characterize a condition of painful, running sores which spread across the body creating blisters that erupt with misery that goes on 24/7.

Can you think of another well-known case of agonizing boils in Scripture?

How did Job respond to a similar condition? Consult *Job 2:8* and summarize it here.

_____

_____

_____

Week Four   God – 10, Egypt - 0

v11. How did these boils affect the work of the magicians in standing before Pharaoh or in being ceremonially clean to lead worship in the temples?

_____

_____

_____

v12. Imagine how Pharaoh must appear to his own people when he is unable to counter God's awesome power, but will not surrender in order to bring this calamity to an end. In a few words, characterize each of the following situations in Egypt at this moment:

- The health of ordinary people: _____
- The supply of meat and food: _____
- Supply of transport animals: _____
- Economic conditions in Egypt: _____
- State of religion in Egypt: _____

The Greeks will later coin the term "Pyrrhic victory" to describe a military accomplishment which was so costly that it was unbearable. By now, one would think that any victory Pharaoh might hope for could be an extremely bitter one. But even a Pyrrhic victory is not in the cards for Egypt.

Think about it. God uses profound pain and suffering to set off warning bells and flashing lights for the people of Egypt. They are an extremely religious people, but their devotion is misplaced. Not only are their gods imaginary and powerless, but their religion is not even working at the mythical, motivational level. Their form of worship cannot make things better: it is making them worse.

Does God still use personal trial as a means to faith? Read *1 Peter 1: 3 – 9*.
Review the text again, marking key words. *Then answer these questions.*

- *v5.* Peter assures his readers they are "shielded by faith," and yet they are suffering. If a "shield of faith" cannot preclude persecution and suffering, what would you suppose it achieves for us?

_____

_____

_____

- *v6.* What kind of trials would you guess these Christians are enduring?

  _____

- *v7.* Trial has the same effect on immature faith that fire/acid have on unrefined gold. What is that result?

  _____

  _____

- *What do you think?* Does God love Christians like you and me more than he loves pagans like the ancient Egyptians? *Explain your answer.*

  _____

  _____

  _____

When God sends trial and hardship into your life, what is your most common response?
    [ ] Doubt: It makes me question God.
    [ ] Complaint: I rant about how this is so unfair.
    [ ] Compromise: I cut corners to alleviate my suffering.
    [ ] Unfaithfulness: I rebel and do things to demonstrate my displeasure.
    [ ] Calm confidence: I remain resolute in my determination to be holy.
    [ ] Praise: I change the subject and praise God for his blessings.
    [ ] Other _____

In a word, how do you want to respond *the next time* God refines your faith?

_____

_____

Week Four   God – 10, Egypt - 0

Day Three: A Harvest of Despair
Read Exodus 9: 13 – 10:20
Read this passage carefully, noting details. Use a marker to highlight phrases and words which indicate these calamities are somehow different from ordinary storms and locust swarms which have occurred in the past.

9: 13 – 22. As a prelude to the seventh plague, God reveals a bit more of his rationale. He warns Pharaoh to relent and release the Israelites lest all his plagues come to pass.
- Either outcome will prove there is no one else like him in all the Earth.
- *v16. For I have raised you up for this very purpose…* In other words, this Pharaoh came to the throne for a very specific purpose. And it was not through the power of Amun or Ra; it was through the power of the one true God.

It can be hard for us to understand why God would ordain that some rulers ever come to the throne. However, Scripture is clear that the Almighty is the force that brings individuals to positions of power. *Consult these two New Testament texts and express them below in your own words.*
- *John 19:11 records Christ's comments to Pilate.*

_____

_____

- *Romans 13:1 was written during the reign of Nero.*

_____

_____

For this very purpose: Consult the text [*9:16*] in order to complete this sentence.
"But I have raised you up for this very purpose: that I might show you my _____ and that my _____ might be proclaimed in all the Earth."

Three qualities that distinguish a supernatural miracle from a freak act of nature:
- *Timing*: God foretells in advance when it will occur.
  v18. The hailstorm will happen _____.
- *Intensity*: Unprecedented power fulfills an unusual purpose.
  Rank the severity of this hailstorm compared to others: _____

- *Limitations*: While acts of nature are random, this event will take place within arbitrary geographical limits set in advance by God.
  Where does this hailstorm strike? _____

v19. What do we learn about God from this comment that people should be warned to keep their families and their animals in on the following day?

_____

_____

_____

v20-21. After the preceding six plagues, why would anyone ignore the warnings and leave their livestock in the field?

_____

_____

9:22-31. Moses lifts his staff to the sky, as directed by God, eliciting thunder and lightning that shred the sky. Hail stones strike everywhere except the Land of Goshen, destroying crops just before the harvest, and stripping trees bare.
- *v27*. Pharaoh again summons Moses and Aaron.
- What's different about his attitude on this occasion?

_____

_____

v29-30. Moses agrees to pray for an end to the hail, even though he knows that the king and his officials do not yet truly fear the Lord. If Moses knows they aren't sincere, why bring this plague to an end so soon? *Select the single best answer.*
- [ ] Moses is tender hearted and merciful.
- [ ] The crops have all been destroyed already.
- [ ] The wheat has not yet been destroyed and people will need bread.
- [ ] God plans to orchestrate all ten plagues as a reflection of his supernatural majesty and power.
- [ ] Other _____

v31-32. Can you guess why Scripture injects this explanation that the barley and flax, being in bloom, are destroyed, while the wheat and spelt survive this plague?

_____

If you're stumped, look ahead to 10:5.

Week Four   God – 10, Egypt - 0

v35. There are additional miracles here in Exodus even beyond the escalating plagues. For example, consider the fact that Pharaoh continues to change his mind, withdraw his promise, and harden his heart. Despite all the devastation that is spiraling out of control, he continues to reject God's offer- just as God promised Moses! Is this miraculous? Explain?

_____

_____

10: 1 – 6. This section begins with an explanation from God, detailing why he continues to negatively charge the Pharaoh's heart. *What is the Lord's rationale? Choose the best answer.*
- [ ] He does this to cripple the Egyptian slave economy.
- [ ] He performs these miracles so that future generations of Israelites can tell the stories to their grand-children and great grand children.
- [ ] He strikes Egypt because the Pharaoh is haughty and blasphemous.
- [ ] Other _____

SECRETS OF THE DESERT

A desert locust can eat the equivalent of its own body weight every day. As a result, in only one day a swarm of 50 million locusts can consume vegetation that would have fed over 180,000 people. And entomologists insist that 50 million locusts would be a small infestation!

v3-4. Once again God's message for Egypt is simple. Either the Pharaoh keeps his word to allow the Israelites to leave the country and worship him, or God will bring locusts into the land to devour the crops. Ordinary locusts are a well-known scourge to farmers in this ancient kingdom. How much more terrible would be the result of divinely superheated locusts? Well, here's how much more terrible: Moses and Aaron explain that the next day's swarm will:
1. *[v5]* Cover the surface of the ground until it can't be _____.
2. Devour all the _____ that have escaped the hail storm;
3. *[v6]* Fill the _____ of all the Egyptians;
4. Be more numerous and destructive than any other locust swarms in _____!

v7. Inside the palace, resistance suddenly bubbles to the surface. The king's aides and courtiers suddenly wake up and smell the coffee. They must be wondering what Pharaoh can possibly be thinking. Read their counsel once again. *Then record your impressions of what's happening inside the palace at this moment:*

_____

_____

_____

_____

_____

v8-11. Once again, the ruler of Egypt grants permission for the Children of Israel to leave. Yet again, he adds a stipulation that is not acceptable to God. He approves the departure of the Jews, but adds: *(select the one correct answer.)*
- _____ You must return within seven days.
- _____ You must be accompanied by Egyptian soldiers.
- _____ You must take only the men, without the women and children.
- _____ You may only go as far as the Red Sea.

v12. Moses and Aaron are expelled from the throne room without even being given a chance to respond. But of course, God's response is already in the pipeline. Moses is directed to lift his hands over Egypt and summon the Great Swarm.

v13-17. Notice once again how God uses natural forces to accomplish supernatural purposes. It is the timing, intensity and limitations that distinguish miracles from other natural phenomena.
- A strong east wind blows all day and all night.
- The next morning, the wind brings millions of hungry locusts across the borders and into Egypt.
- The ground is black with insects and everything green in sight is devoured.

Joel 2: 1 – 11. How devastating is a locust infestation? For a more personal perspective on how the people of Egypt must be reeling, check out a similar event that happens much later in the Bible. Read the account of approaching locusts in *Joel 2, and then answer these questions:*
- *v2-a.* To what huge natural event does Joel compare the spread of the swarm that is approaching?

    _____

- *v3.* Joel compares the hordes to _____ consuming the Garden of _____.

- *v10.* A swarm of locusts can't literally shake the earth or darken the moon. What is Joel's point with this hyperbolic imagery?

    _____

    _____

    _____

Week Four God – 10, Egypt - 0

Exodus 10:18-19. When Pharaoh repents and Moses prays, how does God engineer the removal of all the locusts from Egypt?

_____

_____

Personal Application: One of the haunting lessons from today's session involves the divine purpose that brought Pharaoh to power. In his own mind, it must have seemed he had come to the throne to lead Egypt to a new era, or at least to make his name great. Tragically, the era awaiting Egypt was a time of profound hardship, and we can only refer to this ruler as "Pharaoh" because his name has been lost to us.

Do you have a clear sense of life purpose? That is, do you know at least some of the outcomes you were designed by God to achieve? Just because it's your destiny doesn't mean it has to be easy, even for a person of faith.

Don't forget Queen Esther's dilemma in Persia centuries later. She had been informed that her own people were in danger of genocide, but palace rules only permitted a queen to enter the king's presence when summoned by him. She wondered should she take the risk. And that's when Uncle Mordecai replied with a timeless truth. *If you don't recall this affirmation, refer to Esther 4:13, and write Mordecai's comment below.*

_____

_____

What are some of God's obvious purposes in your life for the coming year? Identify the ones you know for certain, and write them below.
   1.

   2.

   3.

   4.

   5.

Psalms 37:5,6. Commit your way to the Lord; trust in him and he will do this: He will make your righteousness shine like the dawn, the justice of your cause like the noonday sun.

Take a moment right now and find a quiet place to kneel before the Lord, or even prostrate yourself before him. Commit to achieve the purposes he has ordained for you. Ask him to anoint you with power and bring it all to pass in your life.

Day Four: The Heart of Darkness
Read Exodus 10: 21 - 29
Read this brief passage several times. Pause and reflect on other biblical events which last for three days. Notice a mysterious promise and ponder what it means.

In response to yet another flip flop from Pharaoh, Moses stretches his hand toward the sky, and three days of total darkness descend upon Egypt. *Rather than rushing through the third plague in the third cycle, let's slow down and explore this heavy blackness.* Why does this incident last for three days? And what makes this particular darkness so deep?

The Three Day Cycle: read the following texts from Scripture and summarize what how the number three plays a role in each.

- *Jonah 1: 11 – 17.* _____

- *Matthew 17:17 - 23.* _____

- *Acts 9: 1 – 9.* _____

- *1 John 5:6-11.* _____

In the ancient Hebrew world, some numbers had particular significance. *Seven* was the number of perfection; *six* was the number of man; *five* was the number of grace; and *three* was the number of God. With this fact and the preceding texts in mind, what do you believe is the significance of the number of days the darkness over Egypt lasted?

_____

_____

_____

Notice that this ninth plague represents a break with the preceding pattern. As the previous eight curses have been decreed, each has been more catastrophic and extensive than the one before. Test your memory by listing these first nine plagues. *Consult the previous texts only if your memory fails.*

Plague #1: _____

Plague #2: _____

Plague #3: _____

Plague #4: _____

Plague #5: _____

Plague #6 _____

Plague #7: _____

Plague #8: _____

Plague #9: The Days of Darkness

Ordinary Egyptians must be terrified when the darkness suddenly descends on their land. Even smaller anomalies in the sky are seen as signs of ominous events. Imagine how threatening a heavenly sign of this magnitude must be! But as the days wear on, the darkness becomes less frightening. No one is dying because of it. Nothing is being destroyed. It's simply a matter of being unable to work or travel. Everyone is forced to stay indoors and be still.

*10:21.*What do you think is intended by the expression "darkness that can be felt?" The Hebrew word in question is *masas*, which literally means "to touch or grope." It alludes to the nearly blind Isaac [25] when he gropes with his hands to feel his son's skin and determine if this is Esau, or if it's actually Jacob.

Use your imagination: what would you expect to experience in darkness that can be touched? *Write your impressions here*:

_____

_____

Scripture records yet another historic time of darkness just before another earth shaking event. It lasted hours, not days. Then something historically unprecedented occurred! Can you recall it?

Read *Matthew 27:45 – 50*. The sudden darkness on this occasion sets the stage for what ultimate event? _____

- What would you suppose is the significance of three hours?_____

_____

- What sort of emotional response would this darkness have created in the minds of ordinary people? _____
_____

This seems to mesh with the fact that the forces of nature are sometimes programmed to provide a brief calm before the storm. It's almost as though there is time built in to prepare or at least to consider the ordeal that is about to descend. Unable to get out of their houses for three days because of the uninterrupted night, the Egyptians can only cling to their families and anticipate the final wonder of God that is yet to unfold.

v23-b. But notice the limitations set on this miracle. In the midst of this 72 hour midnight, the people of Israel enjoy sunlight in Goshen. Life goes on uninterrupted in this city of faith.

v24. Yes and No once Again: Again the Pharaoh pretends to submit to God's command, but with one small stipulation. "You can go and worship your God," he decrees, "Only…" *Complete the Pharaoh's exception clause below*:

"Go worship the Lord- even your women and children may go with you. Only _____
_____"

v25. What reason does Moses offer in refusing to leave the herds behind? *Check only one correct answer*.
[ ] We will need the animals to offer as sacrifices to God.
[ ] We will need meat and milk to survive in the desert.
[ ] Animals are our livelihood.
[ ] You're not big enough to bargain with the Almighty.

v27-29. Pharaoh insists on keeping the animals. Angrily, he orders Moses out of his presence. "Make sure you do not appear before me again, for on the day that you do, you will die!"

What are the final words of Moses to the Egyptian king? _____
_____

There's no doubt that the ninth plague is directed against one of Egypt's most popular god figures. Ra, the sun god, had a variety of names and activities, but he was best known for purportedly giving life and empowering the noon day sun. In Egyptian thought, Ra did battle each day with creatures from the underworld who wanted to swallow up the sun. The rising of the sun was therefore welcomed each day at a token that Ra had again won his battles.

Week Four God – 10, Egypt - 0

When the God of Israel snuffs out the sun for three days, He clearly demonstrates that the legendary Ra has no power to protect the sun or give life. But at a more foundational level, God is making a devastating comment on the spiritual conditions in Egypt. In a nation that celebrates the sun disk as a source of light, the people of this land are living in darkness and death.

The Bible is chock full of statements from God about the darkness and hopelessness of spiritual night. Consider these brief excerpts from three of the most notable texts. *(Consult each text and fill in the blanks.)*

- *Psalm 107:10-11.* Some sat in darkness and _____ _____, prisoners suffering in iron chains, for they had rebelled against the words of God, and despised the counsel of the Most High.

- *Isaiah 9:2.* The people walking in _____ have seen a great light; on those living in the land of the _____, a light has dawned.

- *1 John 2:9.* Anyone who claims to be in the light but _____ _____ _____ is still living in darkness.

For personal reflection: Think about the last time you found yourself in complete darkness. Perhaps your electrical power failed in the middle of the night, or you woke up and couldn't find a lamp or light switch.

- How did you feel about the darkness?

  _____

  _____

- Why are you so vulnerable in a complete darkness, even if the room is familiar?

  _____

  _____

- Why do you think God so frequently refers to sin as "living in darkness?"

  _____

  _____

  _____

  _____

Peter warns us to beware Satan who is walking around like a roaring lion, looking for someone to devour. [26] *When are lions most active?*

_____

Paul thanks God who has "rescued us from the dominion of darkness and brought us into the kingdom of the Son he loves, in whom we have redemption and the forgiveness of sins."[27]

What are some of the practical benefits the light of Christ brings into your life on a regular basis? *List a few of those very practical assets below*:

    1.

    2.

    3.

    4.

    5.

Take a few moments right now just to be still and thank God for becoming the light of your life. Talk to him about what a difference it has made for you to be living in light and filled with truth.

WEEK FIVE

THE TRUTH WILL SET YOU FREE

Why do you trouble yourself in a house that is not your own? Let the sight of a dead man be a teacher for you concerning your departure from hence. St. Isaac the Syrian

Years ago I had the heartbreaking task of assisting in the funeral service for an eleven year old who had been struck by lightning while playing outside with his friends. I will never forget that moment when I entered our usually joyful, energized worship center on the occasion of the little boy's funeral. The floor and balcony were packed with worshipers and the atmosphere was nearly suffocating with grim despair. You could almost touch the sorrow. I had never experienced this kind of unyielding grief in a church building before, and never have since. Two thoughts were cycling and recycling unmistakably through every mind in that crowded room:
- "Did God do this?"
- "This could have been my child!"

Had the victim been struck by a drunk driver, we could have blamed the monster behind the wheel. Had he drowned after falling into a dangerous stretch of river, we could have blamed negligent bureaucrats for failing to erect a barrier and warning signs. But the child was destroyed by a random bolt of lightning, meaning there was no one to blame but- *well, God*. And everyone in that crowded funeral was having a terrible time with that grim prospect.

Of course we know that death, like life, is in his hands. We even understand that our body clocks are set by him in Eternity; that your life span and mine are determined in advance. But we prefer to keep as much distance as possible between God and the death of children. Face it: putting those inconvenient ideas together - God and infanticide - would force us to confess that our pat answers and pop psychology cannot even begin to explain the One we know as God.
That's why we so commonly imagine the events of the Passover as a cartoon rather than an historic event written in flesh and blood The characters all seem as one dimensional as the figures on those colorful Bible story posters we enjoyed in Sunday School as kids. The blood over the doorposts of Hebrew houses is so bright red it could have been lifted straight from the pages of a Batman comic. That's because it can feel ominous to treat the Passover as real life. If we unpack the details as three dimensional realities, what in the world will we do with all those first born children struck down by an angel from the Lord? *Too often, our God isn't big enough because we're afraid of what that might mean.*

From his throne room in Heaven, the Ancient of Days makes decisions that impact life on earth for generations, centuries, and millennia. He undoubtedly weighs the impact of individual pain and suffering, but he weighs them against actions that will positively change the destiny of nations. In Egypt, some children will die. But in contrast, multitudes of other children will escape from bondage, and will grow up to bear children of their own in a land of freedom. Some parents will be devastated by the loss of a first-born child, but a countless multitude of parents will rejoice through the centuries because their children have been able to be born again into a kingdom where they will never die. Our Heavenly Father is timeless, looking beyond the centuries to discern purposes and priorities that are invisible to us.

Don't confuse God's redemptive strategy with the human rationalization that "the end justifies the means." Just as the Pharaoh ordered that Israelite baby boys should be drowned to keep the population under control, power crazed dictators have rushed to similar extremes in more recent history. Hitler slaughtered the Jews of Europe under the pretext of producing a Super Race of Germans. Stalin starved millions of Ukrainian peasants in a massive governmental land grab. In these and other historic atrocities, the means were "justified" as the only way of reaching an ideal ending. In fact, those profoundly empty goals neither required nor justified such mayhem.

It's useful to pause here and allow yourself a few minutes to differentiate the holy work of the Almighty from the wretched schemes of notorious totalitarians. The Psalmist would write "Selah." *Pause here and think.*
- Are God's motives ever selfish or self-centered? Who benefits from the liberation of Israel?
- Do God's plans ultimately come to pass? Do the Israelites embrace freedom and ultimately reach a new homeland, or do they all expire in the desert?
- Is God seizing control of things that belong to others, or does his creation already belong to him? Are his methods unjust, or is God simply continuing his original work of design, creation and management?

Scripture says our God is the Lord of Life; that his life is the light of men, shining into our darkness even when we don't understand it. A few years ago I was surprised to learn that the earth's shifting tectonic plates, which create deadly earthquakes, also contribute to conditions that make life possible on this planet. Yes, a proportionately small number of people are tragically lost to earthquakes each year, but without the forces that make deadly fault lines possible life on this planet would be completely impossible for anyone. God has a merciful purpose even for earthquakes.

For every insight we have into the benefits of forces like earthquakes, there must be ten thousand other hidden blessings yet to be discovered. Our perspective is too small and our minds are too limited. And our God is simply too vast, too wise, too powerful.

This week, you and I will watch as our Heavenly Father dips his paint brush into a very dark pigment to create his masterpiece of redemption. There will be deep, deep sorrow on the seismic evening we call the Passover. But there will be joy in the morning and for generations to come. So we'll watch for God's mercies even in this night of tragedy. And along the way we'll answer questions like these:

Week Five   The Truth Will Set You Free

- Day One: What are the lessons of Passover for the Pharaoh and for people of faith like you and me?
- Day Two: How does Passover preview the cross of Christ?
- Day Three: When God gives a command, shouldn't you first count the cost?
- Day Four: How does one ensure the works of God will be recalled by the next generation?

Day 1: The Ultimate Curse
Read Exodus 11: 1 – 12:11

Read this short passage carefully, imagining yourself in the story. Although the plot is familiar, there are probably details that will catch you by surprise. Use a marker to highlight facts that surprise you, and ironies that would not normally be expected.

11:1. God explains to Moses that one final, crushing plague remains to fall upon Egypt. After this final judgment, Pharaoh will not simply allow the Israelites to depart; he will drive them out of the land.

How do you explain the radical reversal from stubborn rejection to his angry insistence that all the Israelites must depart immediately?

_____

_____

_____

_____

11:2. At the appropriate time, the Israelites will ask the Egyptians for articles of silver and gold. Looking ahead to the desert journeys, what do you think God has in mind here? *(If you can't guess, skip ahead to Exodus 25:1.)*

_____

_____

11:3. The people of Egypt are favorably disposed toward Moses. How could this possibly be? *Select the single best answer from the following:*
- [ ] The Egyptians do not blame Moses for their misfortunes; they blame God.
- [ ] The Egyptians do not blame Moses for their misfortune; they blame their own Pharaoh.
- [ ] God has providentially done a work in the hearts of the Egyptians.
- [ ] Moses has charisma and an appeal that is hard to resist.

11:4-5. The plague of total darkness is still in effect and has not yet ended when God's prophet makes his way back to the palace. We can infer this because:
- 10:29. Moses promises that Pharaoh will never see his face again.
- 11:4. Only four verses later, Moses is in the palace again with yet another message. This occurs so quickly that it cannot be an oversight.
- The only solution must be that the penetrating darkness continues and Pharaoh literally cannot see the man of God's countenance!

Shrouded in darkness, Moses begins to speak in verse four. When God goes through the land at midnight, exactly who or what will die?
- Every firstborn _____ from the palace of Pharaoh to the home of a slave girl;
- Every firstborn male of _____ as well.

11:6-8. A loud wailing will drift from house to house, street to street throughout the land of Egypt. Only in one region of Egypt will there be no moaning, no sobbing, no howling of dogs or lowing of cattle. Which area will be exempted from the plague?

_____

According to God's plan, what will the Pharaoh learn from this particular experience?

_____

_____

v8. What is the irony of Pharaoh's assistants and palace leaders bowing down before Moses?

_____

_____

_____

Moses is furious as he exits the royal court and the palace. The actual Hebrew text uses two words to describe the emotions of Moses: the word for anger, plus an adjective which means "blazing" or "burning." Take a moment to review the history surrounding this event. Why do you believe Moses is so furious when the end of this ordeal is finally in sight?
- [ ] He is high strung and naturally inclined to anger.
- [ ] The Pharaoh's arrogance and pride are simply too much to bear.
- [ ] Moses is enraged by the way this religious government deceives and abuses the trusting people of Egypt.
- [ ] Moses is angry at God.
- [ ] His anger has been escalating throughout the entire series of events.
- [ ] I'd put it this way: _____

Week Five   The Truth Will Set You Free

v9-10. Whatever the cause of Moses' anger, we know it is not disappointment. God had already made it clear that Pharaoh would refuse to release the Hebrews. There is still one final scene to be played out on the stage of Egypt. For yet another moment, the king's heart will remain hardened for the purposes of God.

Exodus 12: 1 – 11. How pivotal is the Exodus in the life and history of Israel? It is so central and significant that God decrees the Jews must reset their calendars and begin measuring time differently because of this event.
- *v1,2.* "This month is to be for you the _____ month…"
- What's the name of this month? (*Exodus 13:4* notes this is the month of _____. It will later be renamed Nisan.)
- The Hebrew year is slightly shorter than our own solar year, so dates shift in relationship to our calendar. This month roughly corresponds to our late March- April period.
- *12:3.* The Hebrews must be told that on the _____ day of this month, each family must prepare a lamb to be roasted."

The value of the sacred: Notice how God directs his people to take care that the Passover lamb should be treated with respect, and nothing wasted.

- *v4.* What should be done if a family is too small to consume an entire lamb?

- *v4.* How should a family calculate the size of a lamb that is required?

- *v9.* What should be done if a portion of the roasted lamb remains until morning?

- In your opinion, what value is derived from handling sacred symbols with care and respect? _____

- What does your handling of sacred things reveal about your attitudes toward God?

Can you see how the Passover demonstrates our confidence in God's ability to set his people free?
- *v7.* When yeast is included in a recipe for bread, several additional hours are required for the bread to rise before it can be baked. Why might God require this ingredient be omitted?

_____

_____

_____

- *v11.* The practice of lifting the robe and tucking it into ones belt is called "girding your loins." In preparing to work or travel, girding the loins ensures the robe is out of the way so that it cannot be soiled or hinder ones movements. If a man eats the Passover with his robe tucked into his belt, what is the expectation?

_____

_____

- *v11.* One would assume that a sacred meal should be eaten in a leisurely, contemplative manner. What is implied by God's command that this meal should be eaten *hurriedly*?

_____

_____

The Passover visually depicts the work of Christ. Christ will not be an alternate plan designed by God at the last moment. Rather, his life and passion were already in God's mind long before the Exodus. Take a few moments to match up the following Passover elements on the left with their fulfillment in Christ on the right. *Write the letter at left in the corresponding blank at right.*

    A. A male animal without any defect   _____ Matthew 27: 50 - 57
    B. A lamb was acceptable   _____ Revelation 5:9
    C. Slaughtered late but before dark   _____ John 1:29
    D. The blood leads to salvation   _____ 2 Corinthians 5:21

In *1 Corinthians 5: 6 – 8*, Paul uses some of the principles underlying the Passover to address sexual immorality and indifference within the church at Corinth. *Read that passage and, after a few moments of reflection, answer the questions that follow.*

1. How do the qualities of yeast apply to the inner, spiritual life?

_____

_____

_____

Week Five The Truth Will Set You Free

2. When God directs Moses that yeast not be used in the Passover bread, what spiritual insight is he offering his people?

   _____

   _____

   _____

3. When Paul writes [v7] that believers should "get rid of the old yeast," what is he explaining we should remove from our lives?

   _____

   _____

4. What title does Paul attribute to Christ?

   _____

   _____

5. What is Paul's message here? If the original Passover freed the Israelites from bondage in Egypt, from what sort of bondage does the ultimate Passover of Christ deliver us?

   _____

   _____

   _____

   _____

Day 2: A Lasting Reminder
Read Exodus 12: 12 – 30
Read this brief text thoughtfully. Then underscore or highlight words or expressions that indicate this ritual is created as an ongoing teaching tool for future generations.

Complete the thought: v12. On that night I will strike down every _____ male.-28
- Both men and _____-
- And I will bring _____ on the gods of Egypt.
- I am _____ _____.

God promises to execute judgment against the gods of Egypt. The Hebrew term *sepet*, translated judgment, literally casts God in the role of a judge who is required to impose a sentence against a law breaker.
- A skeptic might observe that most of the Egyptian gods are legends and fantasies. Even the Pharaoh is not really divine. Why does the One True God of the Universe even bother thinking about them?
- How would you explain God's concern in imposing justice?

_____

_____

_____

_____

_____

When God affirms his identity here at the end of *verse 12*, he uses the name Yahweh [or Jehovah.] It's important to remember the message behind that name. Return to Week 2; Day 3 for just a moment, and refresh your memory. Complete *these statements from that section:*
> "This title reflects the _____ God wields over his world and his people. The term "Lord" indicates an _____, _____, or king who has sovereign power."

v13. The blood will be a _____ for you on the houses where you are, for when I see the blood, I will pass over you. No destructive plague will touch you when I strike Egypt.

The Hebrew term translated "sign" is the word *'ot*. It denotes a signal or a miracle that verifies God's message.

Think about it. The Almighty God knows his people individually and by name. He hears their prayers and knows where they live. If that's true, then this requirement that all Jews identify their houses with blood stains can only be a teaching exercise. *What is the lesson (or lessons)*

Yahweh has in mind when he orders the blood be painted on the sides and tops of the doorways where they live?

_____

_____

Will God use any of these other well known symbols to teach that same lesson, that each Jewish family is part of a unique community? *Check the ones that do.*

    _____ Circumcision
    _____ The Ten Commandments
    _____ Dietary rituals that forbid eating pork, shrimp, etc.
    _____ No intermarriage with pagan people
    _____ No divorce
    _____ The Sabbath
    _____ Other _____

v14. The Jews are commanded to _____ the Passover for generations to come, and to _____ it as a festival. When God designates this as a lasting ordinance, he uses the word *'olam*. It denotes an extremely long time, and often means "everlasting."[29]

- What will be the positive impact of making this a national act of remembrance? Does your nation have a commemoration similar to the Passover?

_____

_____

- How does our New Testament ordinance of the Lord's Supper/Eucharist compare to the Passover? *Read Luke 22: 7 – 30. Then respond to each of the following questions with T/True;*
- *F/False; or I/Insufficient Information.*
    _____ Jesus obviously associates the Lord's Supper with Passover.
    _____ The Lord's Supper is the NT equivalent of the OT Passover.
    _____ The Lord's Supper is celebrated with elements of Passover.
    _____ Christ's body replaces the Passover lamb.
    _____ The blood of Christ fulfills the role of the lamb's blood.
    _____ There is a command to celebrate this act.
    _____ The Lord's Supper should be a solemn commemoration.
    _____ The Lord's Supper should be a joyful celebration.
    _____ Unbelievers should not be included in the meal.

v15-20. Take note of the very specific commands regarding yeast:
- The bread must be baked without yeast.

- The Jews are to avoid yeast for seven days.
- During those seven days, yeast is not even permissible in the house.
- Anyone who consumes yeast during those seven days is to be cut off from the community of Israel!

For reflection: Why does the forbidden nature of yeast figure so prominently in the Passover, and why is any violation of this ban punished so severely? Clues can be found in the way yeast is regarded throughout the Bible. *Consult the references that follow, and summarize each in a brief phrase or sentence*:

- *Leviticus 6:14-16.* _____

- *Matthew 13:33* _____

- *Luke 12:1* _____

- *1 Corinthians 5:6* _____

Note: The history of yeast in food preparation is quite revealing. Scholars believe that the use of yeast for baking bread and making beer actually originated in Egypt more than three thousand years before the birth of Christ. If that is true, it would explain why the Jews might have uniquely associated yeast with the arrogance and pretense of Egyptian culture.

What is the quality (or qualities) associated with yeast that is dangerous and completely unacceptable in a life of faith?

How can "spiritual yeast" cause you or me to be cut off from God and from the community of faith?

Personal Inventory: are there places in your thought life or your routine in which spiritual yeast has become habitual and acceptable? Intentionally pause here, and take a few minutes to prayerfully reflect on your life. *Then work through the following list, checking areas where you may be infected, briefly explaining why you think this is true:*

1. ____ Manner of dress: _____
2. ____ Ideas about appearance: _____
3. ____ Motives for success: _____
4. ____ House or automobile: _____
5. ____ Attitudes about family: _____
6. ____ Status at church: _____
7. ____ Spiritual disciplines: _____
8. ____ Attitudes toward the lost: _____
9. ____ Habits at work: _____
10. ____ Personal social status: _____
11. ____ Recreational priorities: _____
12. ____ Decision making: _____
13. ____ Tithes and offerings: _____
14. ____ Responses to sin/temptation: _____
15. ____ Attitudes about spending: _____
16. ____ Conversation topics: _____
17. ____ Other: _____
18. ____ Other: _____

Personal repentance: Don't smooth this over by rushing ahead. Stop here and talk to your Heavenly Father about yeast qualities in your spiritual life. Make your confession personal and specific. Ask for forgiveness and grace.

Exodus 12: 21 – 30. For the most part, the final verses in this section simply reiterate what we have already come to expect.
- At the appointed moment, Moses dispatches the men to begin their preparations for the first Passover.
- Blood on the doorposts will be God's sign that the destroyer may not enter a house.
- This is the beginning of a lasting ordinance.

v25. Why will the Passover ceremony become more essential after the Jews have a land of their own?

_____

v26. How will the Passover serve as a practical teaching aid in passing along truth to future generations?

_____

v29,30. God moves at midnight, and there's scarcely a pagan home in Egypt where cries of mourning are not heard. Think about the scope of this plague:
- "Firstborn" includes all firstborn males, humans and animals.
- Not only does a large share of families have a firstborn son, but the father himself may also be a firstborn.
- One household could suddenly lose a child, a parent, and a variety of firstborn livestock. *Exodus 12:30-b* reflects the wide scope of the plague.

Christ, our Passover Lamb, is our only effective remedy for sin. The Passover reminds us not only of the power of our redemption, but also of the essential nature of humankind. Sin is not only deeply rooted, but incredibly complex. It entraps and destroys individuals, families, and societies in a variety of ways. But as diverse as the mechanisms are, the bottom line is always very uniform: death and grief.

Day 3: Deliverance- Next Exit
Read Exodus 12: 31- 50
It has taken us several weeks to arrive here. It took the Jews 430 years to reach this point. So don't rush. Quietly read this passage several times and let the images sink deep into your mind. Underscore or highlight the objects and possessions the Hebrews carry with them. (A complete inventory requires that you also consult Exodus 13:19.)

Exodus 12: 31,32. Pharaoh's release of the Israelite slaves is so dramatic that the news generally overshadows another jolting revelation: all of Egypt, even the Pharaoh, concedes the superiority of the God of Israel.
- Pharaoh directs Moses to take his people to worship God; to take their _____ as well.

- The Egyptians urge the Hebrews to get out of town quickly because they are afraid _____.

- What is Pharaoh's last poignant request [*v32*]?

  _____.

Week Five   The Truth Will Set You Free

Despite the acknowledgement that their pagan gods were no match for the true God of the universe, the Egyptians apparently continue their traditional religion after the Hebrews depart. How can you explain their eventual failure to respond positively to what they have experienced?

___

Consult Jonah 3: 1 – 10. When Jonah simply appears in the pagan nation of Assyrian, he sees a much more dramatic response, despite the fact that supernatural fireworks are not at his disposal. *How would you account for the difference in the reactions of these two very different pagan nations?*

___

SECRETS OF THE DESERT

Many scholars date the exodus around 1445 BC. (This estimate is based on the construction of the first temple which took place 480 years after Israel's departure from Egypt.) It's interesting that less than a century after the exodus, a pharaoh named Akhenaten declared there was only one true god. The Pharaoh decreed that this god named Aten should be worshipped in the bright sunlight, rather than in the dark, shadowy temples required by the other gods. Akhenaten attempted to compel all of Egypt to follow this one supreme god, but his reforms resulted in chaos and ultimately failed. *Were the seeds for this radical experiment first planted in the minds of his ancestors during God's historic and unforgettable deliverance of Israel?*

12:34. The unleavened dough has both a theological and a practical significance.
- See *12:19* and explain the theological significance: _____

___

- See *12:39* and explain the practical significance: _____

___

12:35,36. Scripture teaches that the Jews are directed by God to ask their Egyptian neighbors for gold, silver and articles of clothing. Despite the terrors they have endured, the Egyptians respond generously. *Among the following factors, check the one which best explains this:*
   ___ The Egyptians are relieved the Jews are leaving.
   ___ The Egyptian majority has always opposed slavery.
   ___ God has caused the Egyptians to look favorably on the Jews.
   ___ The Jews have always behaved with kindness and consideration
       toward the Egyptians.

The Journey Out of Egypt

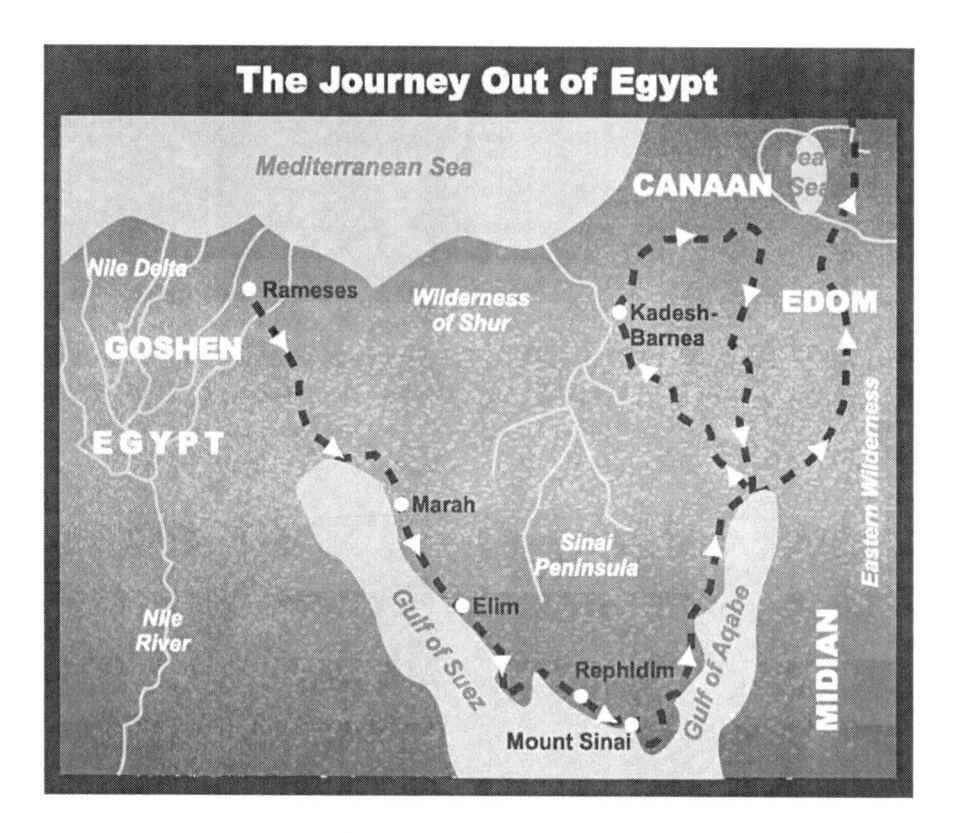

THE JOURNEY BEGINS

12:37 - 42. The very first leg of the long, long journey is about sixty miles south and east to Succoth. This will carry the massive community away from the delta region and down to the northernmost tip of the Gulf of Suez, which is a finger of the Red Sea. The Bible estimates the number of travelers as _____ men on foot, not including women and children. *Think about that number*:

- Imagine that the number of women is roughly the same as the number of men. Then add in only one child for every man. That gives us a population projection of

    _____.

- If there were two children for every man, a number which is more likely in a world without contraception, we arrive at a population of _____ Israelites traveling through the desert.

What are all these people going to eat? The desert environment is much too harsh and arid for agriculture. Besides, the Jews are about to become nomads who never settle down long enough to cultivate and plant a garden. Imagine the prospects of naturally finding enough food for one million plus people traveling together through the desert! *You do the math*:

- Take the conservative estimate of 1.8 million travelers. If each person consumes only 2 pounds of food per day, how many pounds are required? _____
- Convert that number to tons of food (1 ton = 2,000 pounds:) _____ tons of food.

Week Five   The Truth Will Set You Free

- A 50' railroad car can generally transport ten tons in volume. Use that estimate to calculate how many railroad cars of food would be required by the Israelites every day: _____ railroad cars.
- *Note: This figure does not even include food for all the flocks and herds traveling with the Hebrews. (See 12:38)*

Don't forget that Moses has already spent forty years as a shepherd in the Desert of Midian. Nobody understands the severe limitations of desert life better than he does. *Where does Moses expect to find nearly 200 railroad cars of food every day?* Do you think he has sat down to calculate what will be required and where it can be obtained?

How would you summarize what Moses must be thinking about the food requirements for such a population traveling through the desert? Record your impressions here:

_____

_____

_____

Pause here and ask God how this applies to your life of faith today? When God calls you to a bold step of faith in a new direction, is it important that you can explain where you will find everything that you will require?
- [ ] Yes, it's important to have a logical plan to acquire everything I will need.
- [ ] No, it's not important to know where everything is coming from if God has called me in a new direction.
- [ ] I am torn because _____

_____

_____

12:40-42. How many years did Israel spend living in Egypt? _____ years. Take a moment to put that in perspective.
- How long has the United States been a nation? _____ years
- How long did the Babylonian Captivity last? *See Jeremiah 25:11.*

   _____ years

- *See 12:50.* During all these centuries in a foreign culture, do the Hebrews lose their tribal identity?
   [ ] YES   [ ] NO

109

v42. For generations to come, the families of Israel will keep a vigil on the night of Passover. According to the text, what will the vigil signify?_____

_____

Details of Passover: v43-50. When we're giving directions to others, we tend to repeat the details that are most important. Certain aspects of the Passover have already been reiterated in Exodus. Now Moses reaffirms some aspects yet again. *How highly should we regard these particular notes?*
- How does the Passover celebration reinforce the high priority of healthy, intact family?

_____

_____

_____

- How does the prohibition against breaking the bones of the Passover Lamb anticipate the cross of Christ? *(See John 19: 31 – 37)*

_____

_____

_____

Personal Application: What is the biggest step of faith God has called you to make in the past? Summarize it below:

_____

_____

_____

_____

Did you have any questions about what things might be required, where you'd get them, or how you might pay for them?

_____

_____

Week Five The Truth Will Set You Free

Did God provide everything you needed? [ ] YES [ ] NO

What is the most radical direction God has given you for the future?

_____

_____

Why are you waiting? *Check only the single best answer:*
  [ ] The Spirit has directed me to wait.
  [ ] I'm still waiting for all the details to come together.
  [ ] I'm anxious.
  [ ] People I respect have advised me against it.
  [ ] Other _____

_____

What should be your next step in this bold adventure?

_____

_____

Take a few moments and relive *Matthew 26: 36 – 46* with Jesus. Read the text several times, reflecting on the emotions that must be battling for control within the mind of our Lord.
- Is Christ in agony because of fear, knowledge about the pain of crucifixion, regret concerning all this rejection, or some other factor?

  _____

- If Jesus had stopped to make a list of possible advantages and possible disadvantages, which list do you think would have been longer?
  [ ] The list of advantages [ ] The list of disadvantages

- *v42.* How does he finally resolve his personal conflict?

  _____

Pause here for a few minutes to talk with the Father about his calling in your life. Confess any fears or anxieties you have. Commit yourself to the task at hand.

Day 4: Memories for the Next Generation
Read Exodus 13: 1 - 16
Read this brief text two or three times because it is less familiar than other passages we've read lately. Circle or highlight words or phrases that refer to offspring, descendants or future generations.

Exodus 13: 1 – 3. In God's command to Moses, the word translated "commemorate" is the Hebrew word *qadas*. It is the verb form of the word that gives us our adjective "holy." The term means to be holy, to make holy, or to treat as holy. The basic root means to set apart or set aside for a special, sacred purpose.

In our own postmodern age, it sometimes seems as though nothing is sacred, nothing is holy. If God is indeed timeless and changeless as we believe, however, there is still much that bears that designation. Read each of the following related texts, and summarize at right each of the things that God regards as holy.

- Exodus 20:8. _____ is holy.
- 1 Samuel 21:5. _____ were holy.
- Ezekiel 36:23 _____ is holy.

Select the single definition among the following which most adequately expresses the word "holy." *You may cross out a word/phrase or add one to improve the definition.*
  [ ] Holy: set on a distinctive path not taken by the majority
  [ ] Holy: not engaged in mundane functions, but reserved for higher, more noble pursuits
  [ ] Holy: unrelentingly religious
  [ ] Holy: having been transformed by involvement in sacred functions

v2. God decrees that the firstborn male born to anyone among the Israelites- either human beings or animals- _____ to God. As a result, every firstborn male must be bought back from him.

"I never knew that!" This may strike you as a strange idea- buying back the firstborn male from the Lord. It may sound so unfamiliar that you think you've never heard of it before! Think again. Take a moment to read *Luke 2:21 – 32. Then fill in the blanks below:*
- *v22.* After forty days, Joseph and Mary took infant Jesus to the Temple to _____ him _____.
- *v23.* In keeping with the Law, they offered _____ or two young _____.
- It was at this moment that a wise old man named _____ encountered Jesus and his parents. He had been promised by God that he would not die until he could see the Messiah.
- Simeon's vision extended beyond the Jews. He actually spoke of Jesus as "a light for revelation for the _____."

- This is significant because it was not until quite some time after Christ's resurrection and ascension that the Church actually realized the Gospel was for the whole world and not exclusively for the Jews.[30]

The fact that Mary and Joseph offered pigeons (or doves) is instructive. To get the rest of the story, consult *Leviticus 12: 1 – 8*. *Then answer these brief questions*:
  - Which animals were appropriate for this particular sacrifice?

  - What factor do you think determined whether the larger animal or the smaller one was offered to God?

  - What does this reveal about the financial status of Christ's stepfather and mother at the time of his birth?

Now let's return to Exodus and think further about the act of consecrating the firstborn males. Review *Exodus 11 and 12* if necessary. *Then answer these brief questions*:

  - All firstborn sons and male animals in Egypt had died except for one exempted community? What symbol set the homes of these males apart from others in Egypt?

  - Where was that specific symbol obtained in order to be placed on the gateways and doorposts?

  - Is it fair to say that the animals in question were sacrificed in order to save all the first born sons of Israel from death?
    [ ] YES   [ ] NO

- Hundreds of years later when the survivors of Egypt were long gone, what would this ritual of redeeming the firstborn communicate to the people of Israel? *Among the following check only those that apply:*
  ___ Our God is harsh and demanding.
  ___ We are profoundly indebted to God.
  ___ Redemption is expensive.
  ___ The Earth belongs to the Lord and everything in it.
  ___ Boys are more precious to God than girls.
  ___ A great price was paid for your freedom.
  ___ The future of our children and grandchildren is in God's hands.
  ___ Our tribe is unique because we are holy to the Lord.
  ___ Worship is difficult and time consuming.
  ___ Worship is a privilege.

Think about it. What unique traditions, beloved stories, and shared experiences must have been used by God to hold the Jews together as a nation through hundreds of devastating years in slavery? Think about heroes like Noah, Abraham, Jacob, Joseph, and their legacy, and record your impressions below:

_____
_____
_____
_____
_____
_____
_____

How would a sense of belonging to a special tribe have been an asset to this nation of slaves?

_____
_____
_____
_____
_____

Do you have any sense of "tribe" beyond your immediate family? Write about any larger sense of identity that you enjoy.

_____
_____
_____
_____
_____
_____

Read *Romans 11:17 – 24*. What does it mean that "wild branches" have been grafted into God's family tree, while some of the "natural branches" have been broken off?

_____
_____
_____
_____

If you have been grafted into God's family tree, do you belong to His Tribe?
    [ ] YES   [ ] NO

What is the name of your tribe?

_____

What rituals, ideas, stories and common experiences bind you to your tribe?

_____
_____
_____
_____
_____
_____

What factor or symbol is most important in reminding you personally of who you are in Christ and what he has done for you?

_____

_____

What habits can you cultivate to strengthen your sense of tribe/community and to remind you of your heritage in Christ?

_____

_____

_____

Take a few minutes to talk to God right now. Confer with him about your role within his Tribe.
- Confess the selfishness and blatant individualism which you and I naturally absorb from our pervasive US culture.
- Thank him for the larger identity you enjoy in his Body.
- Read *Ephesians 4: 1-6* aloud before the Lord.
- Commit yourself to embody these ideas
    - ✓ Living in a way that's worthy of your call to the Church
    - ✓ Humility, gentleness, patience
    - ✓ Making allowances for the weaknesses of other saints
    - ✓ Making every effort to live in unity
    - ✓ Embodying God's Oneness in His Church

WEEK SIX

WHO'S WATCHNG MY BACK?

He said, 'When God wishes to take pity on a soul and it rebels, not suffering anything and doing its own will, He permits it to suffer things it does not want, in order that it may seek Him again.' Abba Isaiah

The electrifying news goes buzzing through Goshen, from hut to hut, on a dark and mournful Egyptian night. A decree has come forth from the palace. The Pharaoh has issued a proclamation allowing the Israelite slaves to leave their masters and depart from Egypt. Now Moses has sent word that everyone must finish loading up their belongings and begin to assemble for the exodus- *in a hurry!*

In every other region of the Land of Pyramids, candles are burning and mothers are wailing in shock and grief. But in Goshen, there is laughter, and dancing and eager anticipation of life as free men and women. And perhaps in the strangest irony of all, the afflicted people of Egypt are opening up their treasures to the Jews- precious gems and family heirlooms, gold and silver. Suddenly an entire population living in bondage and poverty just an hour ago finds themselves on the very edge of freedom and riches!

Finally Moses appears in the distance, at the head of this massive tsunami of people with camels, sheep, goats, and creaking carts. A signal passes through the ranks and the nomadic nation begins to move- at first slow and halting, but finally with a comfortable degree of haste. Within hours the towering columns of the city and the glimmering lamps of Egypt begin to fade in the shadows behind them. But what lies ahead in the distance, obscured by the veil of darkness?

Darkness is the ideal time for traveling through the desert. There is no blistering, blinding heat from the sun- no superheated sand wedging into one's sandals and scorching the toes. Instead, there is an occasional breeze, and stars to point the way, and the rhythmic sounds of feet scuffling through the sand and carts groaning and creaking under their burdens.

After a few hours of chatter, a veil of silence and uncertainty descends. The darkness leaves each nomad cloistered in his own thoughts. Jubilation is now tempered by the dawning realization that this is a risky venture, laden with unanswered questions.
- The silver and gold from Egypt are precious gifts, but what will they purchase in a barren desert? *What will this hungry nation eat?*
- Everyone knows the most common feature of a desert is *waterlessness*. Where will this vast population find water when they need it?

- What destination awaits them? Surely their former homeland in Canaan has become prosperous and green once again, only to be overtaken by another nation. How will the *new inhabitants* feel about former owners returning to claim their lands?
- Who will survive? The people of Israel have been weakened by brutal conditions in slavery. How well will they fare in the unforgiving environment of the Sinai Desert?

For most of these travelers, the after taste of roasted lamb and bitter herbs is still in their throats and on their tongues. When will they enjoy a meal and a celebration like this again? They comfort themselves with the memory of God's most recent acts of deliverance: blood, frogs, boils, lightning mixed with hail. The shrieks and cries of mothers and siblings wailing over their first born children still resound in their minds. God could deliver death at precisely the appointed moment. Surely, he can deliver life in just as timely a manner!

Somewhere near the front of this mind boggling wagon train, a cart transports the bones of Joseph, who had asked not to be left behind in a grave in Egypt. Who could remember his amazing story and not be awed by the provision of the Almighty God? Many of the Jews must be thinking thoughts like these, and taking comfort in God's historic performances in the past. After all of that, what kind of fool could doubt him now?

And so time passes. Daylight comes and the caravan enjoys a respite. Then night returns followed by day followed by night. The desert miles run together. Then a vast, dark body of water appears in the foreground. The Red Sea looms just ahead. People begin to wonder what kind of detour is in store. Before long, they will discover that a detour is not necessary. And the Red Sea is not the problem.

During this week's journey, you will be able to answer questions like these:
- Day 1: Realizing that God has come through for you in the past, why is it so difficult to trust him for the next crisis?
- Day 2: Does God still get angry or has he become more tolerant?
- Day 3: What does it mean to "wait upon the Lord?"
- Day 4: How should you respond when the ideas of your church leadership don't conform to the way you believe things should be done?

Day 1: Trapped!
Read Exodus 13:17 – 14:30
Read this section of Exodus carefully. Use a pen or marker to highlight or underscore each instance in which God (or an agent of God) acts or intervenes in human history.

13:17-22. The caravan could proceed to the east and north upon leaving Egypt. This direct route would carry them around one corner of Sinai, near a line of Egyptian fortresses, through the land of the Philistines, and directly to Canaan. Instead, God leads them south and east toward the northern edge of the Red Sea. *See v17.* What is the divine rationale here?

Week Six   Who's Watching my Back?

_____

_____

_____

As comfortable as Joseph must have become in the palaces of Egypt, he never lost his first love for Canaan. How do we know this?

_____

_____

God appears before Israel as a pillar of cloud to guide them on their appointed path by day. (The Hebrew word translated "pillar" is *ammud*. This is the word used to describe the columns in the Philistine Temple which Samson topples to bring the building down in *Judges 16:26*.) Of course, night time provides the ideal conditions for traveling through the blistering heat and sand of the Sinai Desert. How does God adapt to allow Israel to travel at night as well?

_____

_____

14: 1 – 9. God literally leads Israel into a trap here, but it's not for them. Rather, he prompts the caravan to make a U-turn and move back toward the north *before again turning south*. When this is reported back to Pharaoh by his spies, it will appear that the Children of Israel are lost and wandering aimlessly. Why does God select this particular detour? *Select the single most likely answer below*:

- [ ] Baal Zephon may have some theological significance in God's mind that is not apparent to us today.
- [ ] This out of the way loop north will allow Pharaoh and his charioteers ample time to intercept the Jews alongside the Red Sea.
- [ ] God has apparently changed his mind about which strategy to use.
- [ ] Other _____

Once again, the Lord God hardens the Pharaoh's heart and prompts the king to change his mind. He regrets allowing the Hebrew slaves to go free, and calls for military intervention to recapture the Jews and return them to bondage in Egypt. In fact, Pharaoh mounts his chariot and leads the expedition.

14:10 – 20. The Israelites turn to see clouds of dust in the distance as the Egyptian Army bears down on them. *Fill in the blanks to describe what happens next.*
- The Israelites are so afraid they_____;
- They taunt Moses, "Were there no _____ in Egypt? Is that why you brought us here to die?"

- "We told you to leave us alone and let us _____ the _____!
  That would have been better than dying in the desert."

What's going on here? It's easy for you and me to dismiss the people of Israel as wimps and cry babies. Living in freedom ourselves, we cannot imagine how they can so easily change their minds and prefer Egyptian bondage to this chance at freedom. As it happens, we are not taking human nature into consideration. In fact, the Jews had become accustomed to their miserable lot as slaves. It was terrible and extremely limiting, but it had become familiar. Now, by contrast, following God and facing all this uncertainty has drawn them completely out of their comfort zone! Just like many abused wives who bounce back to violent husbands rather than adapt to the changes required for healthy lives, these broken people would prefer to retreat to the predictability of cruel slavery rather than sail boldly on the winds of change and risk everything in the desert.

v13-14. Moses delivers a fine motivational speech here. He insists the people should stand firm and see a great deliverance. He assures them God will fight for them. *But in fact, courageous Moses has no idea what's about to happen!*
- How do we know he is clueless at this moment? Pause here and look back to these verses in the Bible. Reread *v13-15* now, and explain aloud how we know Moses is momentarily clueless......
- *Answer*: Because *[v13]* Moses just told the people to stand still and watch. The Hebrew word *yasab* means "to take a position."
- Immediately God says *[v15]*, "What are you waiting for? Tell these people to *get moving!*"

Review the text and then label each of the following statements T/True or F/False. Use the passage to check your answers.

_____ God directs Moses to lift his rod, but Moses apparently has no idea
what will ensue when he does that.
_____ God will not only harden Pharaoh's heart here, but will stiffen the
resolve of the entire Egyptian Army as they charge into the sea.
_____ God will prove his might to the Egyptians by defeating their divine
Pharaoh on the battlefield as well.
_____ To protect his people while he parts the sea, God creates a giant
dust storm between the Hebrews and the Pharaoh's Army.
_____ When Moses lifts the rod of God toward the sea, it whips up a
strong wind that blows against the face of the sea all night.

What body of water is described here? In fact, the original Hebrew text does not specify the Red Sea. Rather, Moses uses the term *yam suph* which literally means the Reed Sea, or a sea of reeds. Does this denote a narrow inlet along the northern extremity of the Red Sea? There is quite a bit of debate about whether this term is a mistake by the King James translators and if it refers to some other body of water. However, in *Acts 7:36*, Stephen literally identifies the location as the Red Sea. For people who believe the Bible is God's inspired Word that seems to resolve the debate.

Week Six   Who's Watching my Back?

SECRETS OF THE DESERT
The Red Sea is the world's northernmost tropical sea, enjoying a comfy 61 - 65 degrees Fahrenheit through most of the year. Many of its underlying shelves are laden with beautiful coral formations. Geography suggests that the Israelites must have crossed at a northern extremity of the sea. That's because its widest region spans 186 miles, and could not have been covered on foot during in a few hours.

14: 21- 31. Under the unrelenting force of a powerful east wind, the sea divides. Moses shares two revealing details with us:
- *v21.* The floor of the sea that is exposed quickly becomes _____ so that the Hebrews can cross unimpeded.
- *v22.* As the people pass through, there is a _____ of water on their right, and another on their left.

The Hebrew verb for what happens when the Red Sea divides is most commonly translated "to break." The waters of the Red Sea literally break forth or break open! Some rabbis see references here to the way a pregnant woman's water breaks when she is about to give birth.
- They note that God is literally birthing a new nation at this point in the story. West of the Red Sea, the Jews had been reduced to a broken band of dispirited slaves. Emerging on the eastern shore of the sea stands the infant that will grow into a nation.
- Many Christians quite naturally perceive this as an allusion to baptism and the new life that follows when we walk in faith.

This is a monumental moment in the story of redemption. Pause here and think about the implications of God's work on behalf of his people. *Record your thoughts and impressions below.*

_____

_____

_____

_____

_____

v23-25. There are fascinating details included here which we commonly ignore or forget when dealing with the Exodus. *Fill in the blanks that follow.*
- When the Egyptian chariots reach the shores of the Red Sea and charge into the gap, God looks out from the pillar of fire and

  _____ _____.
- _____ fall off, leaving charioteers grounded and unable to move forward.

- The Egyptian soldiers conclude they need to retreat because _____ is fighting for the Israelites!

v27. It becomes apparent that all the Israelites have made their way through the sea during the night. *How can we conclude this?*

_____

_____

_____

Moses stretches forth the rod of God once again and the walls of water collapse, allowing the Red Sea to rush back into place and drowning the Egyptians. Take a moment to visualize the very natural reaction that is captured in words here.
- *v27.* There is a backwash that surges beyond the banks, sweeping in units that had been rushing toward the body of water as well.
- *v28.* Then, like a tide, the water pulls back, engulfing all the men and equipment that had already made their way into the gap.
- *v30.* Soon the situation looks normal again, except for all the dead Egyptians lying along the shore!

Verse *31* captures a defining moment for this emerging nation. Read this statement again and then summarize it in your own words.

_____

_____

Did you notice how God used natural forces to bring about a supernatural work of judgment? Of course, every natural disaster cannot be construed as a sign of judgment from God, but some crises and disasters clearly can. The things that set them apart would be:
- *Timing*: it happens at a moment directly related to a promise or principle of God;
- *Intensity*: it is more unusual that previous disasters that were similar in nature, and results in a more dramatic impact;
- *Limitations*: it ceases at the most opportune moment and is limited to individuals somehow related to a promise or principle of God.

Can you recall a crisis or painful event in your life in which you were sure God was demanding your attention? *Describe it briefly below:*

_____

_____

Week Six   Who's Watching my Back?

Is there an obstacle or barrier in your life that is threatening you or preventing you from serving God fully? *If so, what is it?*

_____

_____

Is it likely that the God who saved Israel from Egypt is adequate to take care of your problem as well?
    [ ] YES
    [ ] NO

Moses honestly has no idea what kind of rescue will result when he lifts his staff toward the Red Sea. He simply obeys and sees God fight the battle for him. *In your particular problem, what change or action would equate to the moment when Moses lifted his staff in obedience to God's command?*

_____

_____

_____

Has the moment arrived in your life when you must lift your staff and trust the Lord to take care of the obstacle?
    [ ] YES
    [ ] NO

Take a few moments and talk with your Heavenly Father about his calling, his destiny for you, and your willingness to follow whole heartedly.

Day 2: The Theology of Praise
Read Exodus 15: 1 - 21
Go back and review these twenty-one verses once again. Use a pencil or marker to highlight each adjective or phrase that describes the Almighty God.

Have you ever found yourself standing in worship, singing one of those very contemporary songs, and being slightly distracted by the bouncy, Top Forty-style melody? Suddenly, you think again about the lyrics and you realize you'd never, ever actually say something like that to God on you own?

There's none of that "Jesus is my boyfriend" pop music in the desert when Moses and the people of Israel get busy with the work of praise. As we shall see, their praise not only describes what God has just done for them, but it is true to his character as well; *who he is.*

15: 1 – 5. Moses explains that he and the people of Israel are singing the praises of their God because he _____.

- The English word "highly exalted" is a translation of the Hebrew word *ga'ah*, which means "to lift or raise up high." Think about how natural this is.

- When an athletic team wins a completely unexpected victory, how do they recognize the leadership of their coach?

  _____

  _____

- When an NFL team wins the Super Bowl and receives the trophy, what is the first thing someone does with that coveted award?

  _____

  _____

- The difference here is that God has elevated himself. Apart from the praise of his people, he has already distinguished himself as the God above all gods.

    ✓ v1. How has God lifted himself up in this particular case?

    _____

    _____

    ✓ The specific expression for what God has done to the horses and riders is used three times in this passage: verses 1,4,21. The Hebrew verb denotes shooting an arrow or throwing an object.

    ✓ But the previous chapter explains that the charioteers voluntarily followed Israel across the floor of the Red Sea. Why does Moses sing repeatedly that God *has hurled* the horses and riders into the sea? *Use an X to indicate the one explanation that best fits this situation*:
    [ ] Moses has become senile and confused.
    [ ] The Egyptians pursuing Israel were safe and dry until the walls of the sea collapsed, hurling them into the depths.
    [ ] Moses is speaking metaphorically to explain that the Egyptians unwittingly submitted to the divine power of the Almighty.
    [ ] Based on the accounts of God hardening Pharaoh's heart, it is safe to say that God made the charioteers more stubborn as well.

v2. Explain in your own words what Moses means when he uses the following expressions:

- The Lord is my strength.

  _____

  _____

- The Lord is my song.

  _____

  _____

- He has become my salvation.

  _____

v3. When Moses says "The Lord is his name," he uses the covenant name of God, YHWH. This is the name which was never pronounced. (I wonder if Moses simply sang out the letters.) It denotes the relational God of the Covenant.

Exodus 15: 6 – 12. As you review the next seven verses, recall the spectacle that has just played out across the Red Sea as Moses and the people of Israel begin to sing and chant! There had been gasps of terror when Pharaoh and his troops arrived with a mighty show of force. As the Egyptians had wandered around in a cloud of smoke and darkness, an all night wind had parted the Red Sea, allowing the Israelites to cross on dry land. Then as soon the people of God reached the opposite shore, turning to see Egyptians pursuing from the other side, those mighty walls of the Sea that had stood firm all night suddenly toppled and crashed onto the soldiers!

- The most popular form of Hebrew poetry, parallelism, is incorporated into this song. The poet sings a statement of truth, and then repeats the idea, changing it slightly. Sometimes the second part complements the first clause. On other occasions it shows contrasts.
    - ✓ That's why verse six includes two very similar statements about God's right hand.
    - ✓ God's hand is _____ and it _____ the enemy.
    - ✓ *Verse 7* captures the wrath of God falling upon the Egyptians and expresses it twice, using slightly different expressions.
    - ✓ God acts out of the greatness of his _____ and unleashes his burning _____.
    - ✓ Take a moment and scan the entire chapter. Mark or otherwise indicate each place where this technique comes into play.

- Notice that in Hebrew thought, the right hand is the hand of power.

Don't rush past this important doctrinal idea! Moses describes God acting out of righteous indignation (i.e. holy anger.) So many postmoderns are offended by the frequent outbursts of divine anger in the Old Testament that it has become popular to suppose God is not angry any more. It's more fashionable to depict the God of the New Testament as gentle, tender and sensitive, but never angry. And yet, is that good theology or just pop psychology?

Read these passages and answer the questions that correspond to each.
- *Romans 2:5*
    - ✓ Some of these New Testament readers are storing up _____ from God against themselves.
    - ✓ This will happen when God's righteous _____ is revealed.
- *1 Corinthians 11:28, 29*
    - ✓ Anyone who disrespects the fellowship while taking the Lord's Supper eats and drinks _____ on himself.
    - ✓ For this reason many are sick and others have actually _____.
- *Hebrews 10:30,31*
    - ✓ God declares his right to _____ and to _____.
    - ✓ It is a _____ thing to fall into the hands of the living God.
- *2 Peter 3:10*
    - ✓ The _____ of the _____ will arrive unexpectedly.
    - ✓ The heavens, earth and elements will be _____ by fire.

The wrath of God is not comparable to the outburst of a sinful, selfish human being who loses his temper. Unlike us, God is completely righteous. Righteousness is so integral to the core of his eternal character that he doesn't have to work up a rage. Like a detective who must follow the trail of a murderer, even though it ultimately brings his brother to justice for the crime, God's character must respond to sin and iniquity even though it leads to one of his beloved creations.

v11. "Who among the gods is like you?" Moses wonders in awe. Pause here and ponder exactly what qualities of God Moses has in mind. *What does he mean by these expressions?*

- Majestic in holiness: _____

_____

- Awesome in glory: _____

_____

- Working wonders: It's pretty obvious what Moses has in mind here, isn't it?

_____

Week Six Who's Watching my Back?

Exodus 15: 13 – 18. In unfailing love God will lead the people he has redeemed.
- The love of God is described by the Hebrew word *hesed*, which means "loving kindness."
- The term "redeemed" literally describes slaves who have been set free.

REMEMBER THE WORD

Exodus 15:13. "In your unfailing love you will lead the people you have redeemed. In your strength you will guide them to your holy dwelling." Take time this week to commit this powerful Scripture verse to memory. It will come in handy the next time you're anxious.

---

v14. "The nations will hear and tremble..."
Don't forget the scene that plays out in the Book of Joshua when the Israelite spies sneak into Jericho and encounter a woman named Rahab.
- Read *Joshua 2:11*.
- Write Rahab's statement below:

_____

_____

_____

v17. Three different phrases are used here to describe the tribe's destination in the Land of Canaan. Write them in the blanks below:
- The Mountain of your _____;
- The place you made for your _____;
- The _____ your hands established.

v20. Don't miss this oft overlooked detail. We know that Miriam is the sister of Moses. We are not surprised when she picks up a tambourine and leads the other women in dancing and singing. But we frequently miss her role in the story.

Q: What role or gift area has Moses assigned to her? She is called a _____.

YOUR PATH TO PRAISE
How did you come to be a follower of Jesus?
   [ ] God allowed me to be born again in a Christian home.
   [ ] The Lord sent a messenger with the Good News.
   [ ] He brought me safely through a trial and demonstrated my need and his power.
   [ ] Other _____

Which of God's qualities had been most evident in your life recently?
[ ] His work behind the scenes
[ ] His sovereign plan
[ ] His mercy
[ ] His convicting power
[ ] His ability to rescue
[ ] Other _____

Recall the most recent occasion when God rescued you from yourself or some serious hazard. *Summarize it here*:

_____

_____

_____

Now with all that information on hand, take a few minutes and write a message of Praise to your Heavenly Father. Think about his grace, his revelation, his rescue in your life. Do it your way: Hebrew parallelism, free verse, rhyme, or just a straightforward couple of paragraphs. Write your praise to God, and then read it aloud to Him.

_____

_____

_____

_____

Day 3: Those Who Wait Upon the Lord
Read Exodus 15: 22-27
Read these six verses several times. Then be still. Take a few minutes and meditate on this passage. Run the sentences through your mind again and again, emphasizing different words and pausing to ask questions like "Why?"

This vast band of nomads now crosses into the Arabian Desert, one of the largest, hottest, and least inhabited desert regions of the world. Water is extremely limited because rainfall is so scarce. Vegetation is rare and widely scattered. One desert explorer has written that such arid wilderness instills a different mind set in those who live there. In the West, we tend to believe in progress: that working today creates benefits tomorrow. But people who live in the world's vast deserts have learned from experience that the shifting sands and unrelenting winds do terrible things to optimism and positive attitudes. The desert reminds you that you are always a visitor at the disposal of an unyielding higher power.[31]

Exodus 15: 22 – 27. After only three days of trekking through the sand, the recent victory at the Red Sea must seem like ancient history. Water is difficult to transport. A single gallon weighs eight pounds. And so whatever water the travelers have enjoyed has been gone for seventy two long hours. *Pause here and personalize this.* What are some of the essential activities of life that are suddenly impossible when you're living in a desert and have no water?

1. _____
2. _____
3. _____
4. _____
5. _____

We tend to mock the Jews for their short memory and their small faith. But try to envision what this ordeal would be like for real people. These families have spent three days in a blistering desert without water, and at this moment, they have no prospects of finding any. Have you ever doubted God or complained in a situation far less perilous than that? *Ponder that question and write one recent example here:*

_____
_____
_____
_____
_____
_____

When scouts see green plant life in the distance, everyone's heart is lifted. Vegetation is a reliable sign of water. But unfortunately, the nomads arrive at the spring only to discover the place is named *Marah*. That term denotes that the water is bitter.

- *v24.* How do the Israelites respond?

_____

- *v25.* What does Moses do?

_____

- What does the Lord do?

_____

- What is the result?

  _____

v25-b. Here at Marah God creates a law, issues a judgment, and tests the faith of Israel. This particular word, *nasah,* [for testing] is used frequently in the Old Testament. Consult these texts and summarize the test/trial in each.
- *Genesis 22: 1 – 6* _____

  _____

- *Deuteronomy 13: 1 - 5* _____

  _____

Scripture is clear that God knows everything, including our innermost thoughts and attitudes. Later in the Old Testament, God reminds Samuel, "Man looks at the outward appearance but the Lord looks at the heart."[32] So it's wise to understand divine testing in the larger context of a tribe, community, or church in which people are finding their roles of service. *If God already knows what's in my heart, who actually learns more about my heart when my faith is publicly tested?*

1. _____

2. _____

Does Israel pass or fail this initial trial of their faith?
    [ ] Pass   [ ] Fail

Why? _____

_____

v25-b. God enters into a contract or covenant with his people. Read it carefully and then summarize it in your own words.
Israel's obligation: _____

_____

_____

God's promise: _____

_____

The Most High God reveals another of his names here:
- *YHWH*: The relational God of the Covenant.
- *Rapa*: to make well, make whole, or renew.
- *We would verbalize this Jehovah Rapa.*

v27. Then they came to Elim, a magnificent oasis with twelve springs and seventy palm trees! No wonder it's named *Elim*, meaning "palm tree."

What is God's lesson for his people here? Select only one of the following statements that best represents the divine principle at work here.
[ ] There's always an oasis just around the corner.
[ ] When you wait upon the Lord God, you will always have what you need.
[ ] Always keep a positive attitude.
[ ] Be patient and your luck will eventually change.

Don't overlook the obvious. Sometimes, the answer to my prayers requires that God perform a miracle. On other occasions, the answer to my prayer is actually only a few steps away. Finding water at Elim requires no supernatural intervention on God's part. It simply demands that the people of God continue to walk one more mile in faith and obedience.

Read *Isaiah 40: 27 – 31*. Think about the passage for a few moments. Then write out verse *31* in your own words.

_____

_____

_____

_____

In the Hebrew text, the word translated "hope" denotes a particular kind of hope. It's not the sort of empty hope that says "I hope I win the lottery one day." Rather, it has the connotation of arranging your life in a certain way because of what you expect to happen.
- *Job 7:2* begins, "Like a slave longing for the evening shadows or a hired man waiting eagerly for his wages..."
- That same word, *qawah*, is translated "waiting" here. It means to expect something you are sure is coming.

In other words, to wait upon the Lord does not mean that you glumly endure one ordeal after another because you believe your luck may eventually change. Rather, like a worker looking forward to pay day, you order your life based on the promises of God which you know will be fulfilled.
- Recall *Genesis 39: 1 – 6* (Joseph's purchase by Potiphar.) How did Joseph order his life in order to wait upon God's promise to give him greatness?

- Consult *1 Samuel 24: 1 - 12*. How did David order his life in order to wait upon God's promise to make him the next king?

Sometimes we confuse faith with other approaches to life that are actually based on luck or wrong thinking. Even the Hindu concept of Karma has become fashionable in some circles in the church. Be clear about what it means to trust in the Lord and wait upon him. *Match each attitude on the left with its definition on the right. Consult a dictionary if necessary.*

A. Fatalism   ____ I look for something positive in every situation.
B. Optimism   ____ I fully believe God will keep his promises to me.
C. Karma   ____ I believe that everything is fixed in advance.
D. Luck   ____ What happens to me is based on a previous life.
E. Faith   ____ Life is random but sometimes you catch a break.

Case Study #1
Your church is growing rapidly, and desperately needs to purchase an adjacent piece of property in order to add parking spaces. Unfortunately, the owner is an atheist who adamantly refuses to sell the vacant lot to a church. A member of your church who serves on the city council believes that the city can exploit a particular Eminent Domain Law to force the man to relinquish the property. *What actions might be appropriate for your church as you wait upon the Lord?*

Case Study #2
A young woman in your church plans to marry a young man who lives in a distant city. Because their wedding date is still more than a year away, she is getting impatient. One friend has suggested she should take a new job in his area and move into an apartment until the

wedding, but her job search has been fruitless so far. Some else has suggested she should simply go ahead and move in with him now, since they're going to be married anyway. She asks you for advice about what to do. *How will you counsel her?*

Is there any place in your life in which you are running ahead of God or attempting to manipulate his will into place? *If so, how should you order your life in order to wait on the Lord?*

Day 4: Yes, He Can
Read Exodus 16
Review this chapter, imagining yourself in this situation. Use a pencil or marker to circle each instance of gracious behavior on God's part. Then underscore each example of bad attitudes on the part of Israel.

How long have the Israelites been "on the road" so far? Take a moment and do the calculation.
- 16:1. What is the date as they arrive at the Desert of Sin?

- 12: 1-4. What date did the Passover occur? That's when the Jews began their journey.

- This means the people of Israel have been traveling and camping for

16: 1 – 8. As they reach the Wilderness of Sin, the Jews teach us a valuable lesson about selective memory. Sometimes, the brain shapes our memories so that we recall events as we wish they had happened, rather than as they really occurred. This is why eye witness testimony is not the best form of evidence in a criminal trial.
- v2. What do they recall about life in Egypt?

- What have they conveniently forgotten about life in Egypt?
    1.
    2.
    3.

v4-5. God promises to rain down bread from heaven. Notice that the sixth day will be different than days one through five. *Why?*

_____

_____

_____

v6-7. God promises two distinct events in which he will deliver food. What are they?

1. _____

2. _____

v8. Moses explains, "When you grumble and complain against Aaron and me, you are actually grumbling against _____."

- How does this apply to the gossip and complaining that sometimes goes on in churches about leadership decisions? *Select only one of the following:*
  [ ] This Old Covenant incident doesn't relate to the New Testament.
  [ ] It means our church leaders should be more like Moses.
  [ ] When we moan and groan about routine matters of church leadership, we are actually moaning and groaning against God.

- When you realize that God is working intently to create bonds of community among his people, why is grumbling and dissension so sinful?

  _____

  _____

- How should you respond when the ideas of your church leaders don't agree with the way you think things should be done? *Mark each of the following statements as A/Acceptable or U/Unacceptable.*
  ___ Start a petition drive.
  ___ If it's just a difference of opinion, you should accept it.
  ___ Organize a meeting of people who share your viewpoint.
  ___ If there's an ethical question, speak privately to the person in charge.
  ___ Pray quietly about it.
  ___ Call a special business meeting and recruit all your supporters.
  ___ Threaten to leave the church.
  ___ If the final decision is unbiblical and you are in the minority, leave the church.

v10. The people look toward the east, and the glory of God appears before them. What does it look like?

_____

v13. Realizing the way God works, one assumes the quail here are migratory birds which can fly short distances but stop to rest frequently. One scenario for this event is that God causes a flock of exhausted birds en route from Africa to land precisely where Moses and his hungry multitudes are waiting. Would that meet the criteria required for a miracle?
    _____ YES   _____ NO

v14. On the next morning after the dew dries, there are thin flakes remaining on the ground. Moses explains that this is the bread God had promised the day before.
- Notice that the people collecting the manna should only gather as much as they need- roughly two quarts for each person in the family. This corresponds to the directions at Passover that the meat should be carefully apportioned and not wasted. *In your mind, what's the point?*

_____

_____

_____

- *v19.* Why does God require that only one day's provision may be collected (except before the Sabbath?) *Hint- Matthew 6:11.*

_____

_____

v23. The manna is pretty versatile. Notice that it can be baked or boiled. And on the sixth day (only), it can be preserved for another day.

Which comes first: the Sabbath or the fourth commandment about the Sabbath?

_____

v24. Why would one mandated day of rest each week be a particular blessing to desert travelers?

_____

_____

_____

v31. The Israelites name the "wonder" bread *manna*. Ordinarily, that Hebrew term *man* (pronounced like "mon") means "What is it?" *Why do you suppose they give the bread this name?*

_____

_____

SECRETS OF THE DESERT

Coriander seed has been a familiar herb for thousands of years. The Egyptians used it for medicinal purposes- primarily as a cough medicine, but also as a tonic for the sick or weak. It also has alleged powers as an aphrodisiac. These seeds look like small round pebbles.

v34. As directed by God, a sample of the manna is sealed in a jar and saved as a testimony. What is God's desired purpose here?

_____

_____

Note: This memorial of God's provision will someday be placed inside the Ark of the Covenant, one token of God's presence with his people.[33]

Read John 6: 25 – 40. The story of the manna surfaces in the New Testament during the ministry of Jesus Christ.

- What does the crowd have in mind when they mention the manna?

    _____

    _____

- What is Christ's response to their request?

    _____

    _____

- What is the biggest difference between the manna and the Bread of Life?

    _____

- According to the words of Christ in this passage, what is the Father's will for his ministry?

- What doctrine do we derive from this promise?

BE STILL & KNOW
Take some time now to quietly reflect on God's provision in your life. Think about areas like gifts and abilities, family, vocation, accomplishments. What has been the role of the Father in the most critical areas of your life?

1.

2.

3.

4.

Pause now for a time of thanksgiving before the Lord.

WEEK SEVEN

WHAT EVERY LEADER MUST LEARN

Do not be surprised that you fall every day; do not give up, but stand your ground courageously. And assuredly, the angel who guards you will honor your patience. John of the Ladder

My friend Dave was a personnel exec for a giant auto maker. With a background in administration and a track record for moving complex responsibilities smoothly through a massive chain of command, he felt competent to assume a leadership role in one branch of the children's ministry at our church. With a clear job description, he courageously began the process of recruiting, training and scheduling his leaders.

Months passed. There were days of trial and error. There was evidence of growing success. The ministry began to move forward. One day, Dave walked into my office and collapsed into a chair. "Pastor," he confessed, tossing his baseball cap on the floor, "I hate leading this volunteer army!"

Happily, Dave was a warrior who never gave up. And as a result, he led that ministry to a higher level of excellence. But it was never quite as simple as in the corporate world of salaries and raises.

By contrast, another friend of mine served as Senior Pastor of a suburban church. He was a willing worker who loved the Lord, but he was forever complaining of his frustration with the failures of the people around him. The poor guy was never able to devote sufficient time to prayer and sermon preparation because he was overwhelmed by a never-ending "to do" list.

- He repaired faucets and changed light bulbs.
- He ran all his own errands and finalized his own manuscripts for his file.
- He gassed up the bus and went on every youth trip and children's trip.
- He helped serve Wednesday night suppers and sometimes cooked them.

My friend had a boundless supply of energy and fresh ideas, yet he was often exhausted and unhappy with the results. Nevertheless, his explanation was always the same, "I'd rather do it right the first time than do it over after someone else messes it up." In fact, other people who might not have done it precisely the way he did it, might well have done it better with the benefit of more time and expertise! And, my friend would have had more time to devote to the essentials of his own calling.

It's pretty common for leaders in churches to assume their job is to develop followers. In fact, if a church desires to grow in power and influence, it will need more than additional followers; it will require additional leaders as well. Every leader should see his role as the essential task of developing other leaders who can perform his job and a variety of others as well.

In Egypt, Moses had grown up in the midst of a governmental hierarchy. The Pharaoh had counselors who had aides who had assistants. Even the priests in the pagan temples had attendants who had acolytes. But when he fled into the desert, Moses became accustomed to a much more simple way of doing things. You see, there was this herd of sheep and each one needed his attention. There were wounds to dress, eyes to treat, and horns to trim, and over the course of time, one shepherd could take care of them all. Sheep could be stubborn and wayward, but they were fairly manageable because they were easily frightened.

So when this eighty year old shepherd finds himself in the desert at the head of this massive column of Israelites, maybe two million strong, it's not surprising that he relies on his most recent leadership experience. With time and patience, perhaps he can eventually get around to every sheep! *But can he really?* And even if this feat is humanly possible, will this particular herd of Israelites be as easily managed as the sheep back in Midian? One could make the case that these nomads are more stubborn and less easily intimidated than any of the livestock in Moses' memory! In fact, before long, Moses himself will make that case: "These people are impossible!"

There's a great deal we can learn by observing the very public successes and failures of this amazing man of God. He will cultivate the virtue of determination. In addition, he will learn the art of delegation.

Use this week to observe Moses and reflect on your own leadership abilities. Are you called to lead thousands, hundreds, or smaller groups? Are you naturally gifted at influencing others, or is leadership a discipline you will need to cultivate? And what is your area of expertise?
- Are you a teacher or an instructor?
- Are you a counselor or an adviser?
- Are you gifted to bless others by working with your hands?
- Are you especially adept at evangelism or encouragement?
- Are you most effective with adults, students or children?

General George S. Patton used to say, "Don't tell people how to do things. Tell them *what to do* and let them surprise you with the results." It worked in World War II, and it still works today. Learn to entrust a worthy task to a capable person. Then let that person own it.

Watch patiently as Moses faces adversity, and ask yourself how you might have responded in his situation. Be patient when he fouls up and loses his temper, and think about the last time you lost your emotional balance in a tense moment. And look around for budding leaders who are waiting just within the prophet's circle of influence. What is it that will eventually make Joshua and Caleb such amazing members of the leadership team? And why will others fail although their circumstances are similar?

Week Seven   What Every Leader Must Learn

This week Moses takes part in some on the job training for team building. He learns a couple of lessons in the School of Hard Knocks, and then his father-in-law arrives with the wisdom of an older man. You and I can learn a thing or two about leadership as well, just by working through what Moses discovers in the desert. Ask yourself these questions as you journey this week:
- Day 1: How can I be more intentional about modeling faith for the people in my realm of influence?
- Day 2: How do I learn to trust others and help them find their places in the vision God has given me?
- Day 3: How could an unhealthy view of family cause someone to be an ineffective follower of Christ?
- Day 4: Name a younger Christian you could begin to disciple, encourage and mentor.

Day 1: Cultivating Follow-ship
Read Exodus 17: 1 - 7
Read this very brief section of Exodus two or three times. Use a pen or marker to highlight each complaint the people make directly against Moses. Then circle each complaint the people make against the Lord God.

17: 1 – 7. And so the journey continues in accordance with the command of the Lord. Pause here and refresh your memory. How do we know that Moses is leading these people in a God-ordained direction?

- 3:12 _____
  _____

- 13:21,22. _____
  _____

Geographical note: The Israelites are moving east and south through a part of the world that is today known as Saudi Arabia. In fact, they are headed toward a region which has been known for centuries as the *Rub'al Khali*, meaning "the empty quarter." It is so named because there's virtually nothing there except blistering sand and superheated rocks. The area receives no annual rainfall to speak of. (Significantly, the area is oil rich, but that's all below the surface.)

The text mentions two complaints directed at Moses by his people as representative of their general tone and attitude. Record their comments here:
- *v2.* _____
- *v3.* _____
  _____

v2-b. Moses rebukes his people, insisting these remarks against him are actually directed against the Lord. Why would this be accurate?

_____

_____

_____

_____

_____

Moses accuses the people of "testing" the Lord.
- This is the same Hebrew term used in *15:25*. At Mara, God had tested the faith of this people.
- God is allowed to test us because one of his divine roles is to grow us up and mature us. We are not allowed to test the Lord because we are not in charge, and are not fully informed.
- Read *Deuteronomy 6: 16 – 19*. Then label each of the following statements as T/True or F/False.
  _____ Testing or tempting God is specifically forbidden.
  _____ One way to ensure that you don't test the Lord is by walking in conformity to his commands and principles.
  _____ Whether God chooses to bless you is never dependent on how you choose to live.
  _____ Success or failure in the Promised Land will depend not on the skill of the military, but on the day to day choices made by the people.

The Old Testament turns up in the New. Did you realize that when Jesus Christ was tempted by Satan in the wilderness, he answered all of Satan's challenges by quoting one book of the Old Testament- Deuteronomy?
- Read *Matthew 4: 5 – 7*.
- What is the behavior that Satan calls for but Jesus rejects as "testing God?"

_____

_____

- What is Satan's rationale that suggests his request is "biblical?"

_____

_____

It's important to stop for a moment and mentally process what God is teaching us here. *Think about it*:
- When the Israelites cross the Jordan River to conquer Jericho, God will command that the priests to carry the Ark of the Covenant into the river before the water actually parts to allow them to cross.[34]
- The Great Commission commands the Church to go into every part of the world, even the deadly, dangerous areas, on the basis of his promise that "I will be with you everyday."[35]
- *Think about it:* Why are those behaviors acceptable while jumping off a cliff and expecting God to keep a promise from *Psalm 91:11-12* is not acceptable? *Write your answer below.*

Which of the following amounts to testing/tempting God? *Check as many as apply:*
- [ ] Demanding that God do something now
- [ ] Risking my life to help a neighbor in danger
- [ ] Complaining about the spiritual leaders God has assigned me
- [ ] Grumbling about my misfortunes in life
- [ ] Hiking alone and unarmed into an area with lions because God protected Daniel
- [ ] Risking my life to encourage an underground church in a Muslim nation
- [ ] Giving a tithe to God because he has promised to more than compensate me for the amount I give back[36]
- [ ] Sharing my food with children during a famine because I believe God will keep his promises to me
- [ ] Smuggling Bibles into a country where the church is persecuted and Bibles are forbidden
- [ ] Asking cynically "Where is God now?"

v4. The mob is becoming so angry and disrespectful that Moses becomes concerned about his safety. It feels like he's just moments away from being stoned to death by the crowd!
- *v5.* God reminds Moses of others who share his responsibility. Who are they?

  _____

- As he did when Israel was trapped by the Red Sea, God reminds Moses of the symbol of his authority. What is that?

  _____

- *v6.* What must Moses do in order to produce water from the rock?

  _____

The Old Testament turns up in the New. This is one of those places where we can see the power and character of Christ in the shadows of the Old Testament. How does this incident of striking the rock relate to the ministry of the Messiah?
- *Matthew 26:31.* What does Christ say will happen to him?

  _____

- *John 4: 10 – 14.* What does Christ offer those who come to him?

  _____

- *Romans 9:32.* Who is the rock over which so many stumble?

  _____

- *1 Corinthians 10: 1 – 5.* Summarize Paul's idea in your own words.

  _____

  _____

  _____

v7. This campsite is forever remembered as *Massah* and *Meribah* (temptation and strife.) Although the people had challenged Moses, their behavior had posed a terrible question about God. What is that question?

_____

_____

LEAVING MASSAH & MERIBAH IN THE DUST

This painful incident in the life of Israel offers insight and guidance to our own generation, despite the fact that most of us live far from the desert, surrounded by water fountains and bottled water. Cool clean water is available, but resolute, unwavering faith in God is sometimes hard to find.

Take this lesson to heart by evaluating recent behavior and attitudes. Think through the following questions and comparisons. How can you become more intentional about living a life that demonstrates faith, and refuses to test the Almighty?

In your church and your circle of friends, are complaints and critiques an accepted part of normal conversation?
[ ] YES   [ ] NO

What is the difference between a healthy, constructive conversation among members of a faith community, and a gripe session among people who don't trust God?

_____

_____

_____

_____

Which of the following have you complained about most recently?
[ ] Your health   [ ] Your church
[ ] Your finances   [ ] A leader or ministry at your church
[ ] Your circumstances   [ ] Christians in general
[ ] Your family or friends [ ] The weather
[ ] Your appearance   [ ] Other _____

What might an unbelieving bystander have concluded from your conversation?
[ ] God is in control   [ ] Faith makes a real difference   [ ] Where is your God?

How should the Israelites have demonstrated their faith in God when they were waiting for water? *What would walking by faith have looked like?*

_____

_____

_____

How should you have demonstrated faith in God when you were undergoing your most recent time of struggling or waiting?

_____

_____

_____

How can you cultivate faith and constructive conversation among your friends and relatives who are more inclined to dwell on complaints and criticisms?

_____

_____

Day 2: The Chain of Command
Read Exodus 17: 8 - 16
Read these eight verses from Exodus 2-3 times. Imagine yourself as Moses and ask why you would say a certain thing or feel a certain way. Highlight or underline each instance in which Moses relies on someone (divine or human) other than himself.

As this chapter of the journey begins, don't lose sight of the Israelites' physical condition after years of slavery designed to break their spirits. You'll recall from *Exodus 13:17* how God has explained that too much warfare too soon might completely overwhelm them, sending them in full retreat to Egypt and bondage. So it's especially unfortunate when the army of Amalek attacks. But there's even more to this tragic story.

For the rest of this story, read *Deuteronomy 25: 17 – 19*. This account shares one significant detail that is omitted in the Exodus account.

- When the Amalekites launch a raid on the Israelites, they attack from the _____.

- Rather than facing advance parties and armed warriors who are organized along the front, they violently assault the weak and weary who are lagging behind. What groups or types of people would be traveling more slowly and exposed at the rear?
    - ✓ _____
    - ✓ _____

In God's righteous judgment, what must happen to the Amalekites?

_____

_____

Now, take a moment to trace God's fingerprints throughout history.

- Read *1 Samuel 15: 1 – 11*.

    What is God's command concerning the Amalekites?

    _____

    v8. What is the name of the king of the Amalekites?

    _____

- Read *1 Samuel 30: 1 – 20*.

    Who attacks Ziklag and carries away the families of David and his men?

    _____

    How does David respond to this situation?

    _____

    _____

- Read *Esther 3: 1-2; 9: 1 – 9*.

    Haman, the enemy of the Jews, is a descendant of whom?

    _____

    What happens to the descendants of Haman?

    _____

Exodus 17: 8 – 16. When Moses realizes that his people have been ambushed, to whom does he entrust the responsibility for a military response?

_____

Why do you think Moses positions himself at the top of the hill first thing the next morning? *Choose the single best answer.*
- [ ] So that he will have a better view of the battlefield
- [ ] So that his warriors can see the Staff of the Lord in his hand
- [ ] So that he will be out of the line of fire
- [ ] Other _____

Moses stands on the vista overlooking the battle and lifts the Staff of the Lord high in the sky. *What happens?*
- [ ] The Israelites are soundly defeated.
- [ ] The Israelites prevail until Moses gets weary and lowers his arms.
- [ ] The Israelites get all excited and the Amalekites are quickly routed.
- [ ] The Edomites join the attack.

In response to what happens on the field of battle, Moses takes a seat on a large rock and does something unique. *What is it?*
- [ ] He weeps.
- [ ] He enlists Aaron and a man named Hur to hold his arms up.
- [ ] He surrenders
- [ ] He calls down fire from Heaven.

Why do the Israelites succeed as long as the staff is lifted high? *If you're unsure, consult Exodus 4:5.*

_____

_____

v13. When the Bible explains that Israel overcomes the Amalekites with the sword, whose leadership is being credited with the victory?

_____

How do you explain that it's not about Joshua's sword but God's power?

_____

v14. The Lord God decrees that this command should be engraved in stone so that it can be permanent. Moses should be certain that Joshua understands what has happened here. For their merciless assault on the people of God, the Amalekites will forever be under a curse from God. He will pursue them until they are wiped off the face of the Earth. Moses builds an altar through which this moment of judgment will be affirmed and remembered forever and ever.

> ### SECRETS OF THE DESERT
>
> Who are the Amalekites and why do they take such delight in wreaking havoc on the people of Israel? The answer is found in *Genesis 36:9-12*. You will recall that Jacob unjustly takes the blessing and the birthright from his older brother Esau. When Esau is grown, he will have two sons, one named Eliphaz. That son will give birth to Amalek, whose descendants will long be a thorn in the side of Jacob's descendants.

v15. The name of the altar is "The Lord is my banner." The Hebrew word being translated here is *nes*. It denotes a banner, a standard, a symbol or a sign. Think about this for a moment.
- No banner has been displayed in this battle against the Amalekites.
- God has not authorized the men on the front to carry any sort of ensign or flag.
- What is the only symbol or sign which has played a prominent role in the victory over the Amalekites?

_____

- Hence, what is the likely meaning of the name *Jehovah Nissi*?

_____

- *Read Psalm 23:4.* What comforts David in the Valley of the Shadow?

_____

A leader must develop other leaders! Granted, the most important lesson in this story is that we must rely upon the Lord for the critical battles of life. His strength and majestic power will bring victories we could never reap on our own. Of course, this is true.

But don't miss a secondary lesson from the text. Because Moses is looking ahead to the next generation of leaders, he spreads his authority around and allows other capable leaders to share in this victory.
- What sort of responsibility is assigned to Joshua?
    [ ] Key Leadership
    [ ] Administrative Support
    [ ] Performing assigned tasks

- What sort of responsibility is assigned to Aaron and Hur?
  [ ] Key Leadership
  [ ] Administrative Support
  [ ] Performing assigned tasks

Think about your most important ministry role in the Kingdom of God at this moment. How would you describe your role?

_____

_____

- How would you classify this role you play?
  [ ] Key Leadership
  [ ] Administrative Support
  [ ] Performing assigned tasks

List the names of some people you are already mentoring or some that you need to enlist in order to expand your work and develop the next generation:

1. _____
2. _____
3. _____
4. _____

How can you be more intentional in involving these people in ministry and allowing them to share the responsibility and the victory?

_____

_____

_____

_____

Proverbs 27:17. "As iron sharpens iron, so one man sharpens another." This is equally true for men and women.

Day 3: The X-treme Blessing of Extended Family
Read Exodus 18: 1 - 12
Read this chapter a couple of times. Use a marker or pen to circle or identify words or phrases which highlight or suggest the value of one's larger family network.

Sometimes in our quest to afford and purchase more of life's luxuries, we inadvertently forfeit assets that are extremely precious, but free. One of those inexpensive treasures being lost in the dust of our mobile society is the blessing of extended family.

Americans have come to one of those periods in which we place a high premium on children. We work long hours and accept promotions to distant locations because we want to offer our kids all the advantages. But once again, in our quest for the pricey extras, we are quick to lose sight of an inexpensive necessity: grandparents, cousins, and the identity of a larger family.

While ministering in Kenya a few years ago, I had the privilege of spending a week with a godly young pastor and seeing many of his friends and relatives come to Christ. At the end of the week, he invited me to his village where he and his larger family prepared a feast of appreciation in my honor. It was the middle of a weekday, and a long table was set outdoors. The Pastor, his wife, their children, and several members of the extended family gathered to break bread with me. They were all able to attend on short notice because they lived in such proximity to one another. It was an absolutely beautiful day, and the food was simple but delicious. And as I enjoyed the privilege of getting to know members of the family, I thought we should do more of this back home in the States. Then it occurred to me: *we could never afford something this wonderful back home*! We are all too scattered, and our careers are too high a priority.

18: 1 – 6. Moses had originally carried his family with him into Egypt. Only now do we discover that, at some point in the ordeal, he had sent them home to Midian to stay with his father-in-law, Jethro. What are the names of Moses and Zipporah's sons, and what do they mean?

- _____ = _____

- _____ = _____

Why would you guess Moses sent them away?
  [ ] Polluted water, insects and disease, food shortages;
  [ ] Fear for their personal safety;
  [ ] Uncertainty about the future;
  [ ] Here's my guess: _____

Where are the Israelites camped when Moses learns he will soon be reunited with his family?

_____

It would seem that Moses did not accompany his wife and sons when he returned them home to Midian earlier. Reflect for a moment. Why would you suppose that Jethro, priest of Midian, personally accompanies them on their return to Moses?

_____

_____

_____

_____

18: 7 – 12. Make notations here of the customary acts of respect that Moses offers upon the arrival of his father-in-law:

1. _____
2. _____
3. _____

The older man listens eagerly as Moses recounts all that God has done to liberate his people from bondage and to protect them in the desert. No wonder. Think of the things we know Jethro has done to prepare Moses and support him in this leadership role.

1. _____
2. _____
3. _____

v11. What impact do the stories of Moses have on the faith of this older man who is a priest?

_____

_____

v12. What would be the significance of Moses inviting Aaron and the elders of Israel to share the evening meal with him and his father-in-law?

_____

_____

_____

_____

Read the following passages. Then list the role or contribution of family that is taught in each text:
- *Deuteronomy 6: 4 – 9*

  _____

- *Ruth 1: 1 – 19*

  _____

- *Psalm 127: 3 – 5*

  _____

- *1 Timothy 5: 1 – 8*

  _____

Read *1 Timothy 3:5*. What can you learn about someone's leadership skills by observing his family?

_____

_____

Why would extended family have been so important in a harsh world with few cities and no real social support network?

_____

_____

_____

What are some of the institutions and structures that we tend to substitute for our family network in our postmodern world?

1. _____
2. _____
3. _____
4. _____
5. _____

What are some of the real blessings extended family can provide in a world that has sometimes been called "high tech/low touch?"

1. _____
2. _____
3. _____
4. _____

In *1 Corinthians 7:33*, Paul explains how marriage can be a detriment to leadership and service. That is, a spouse can require time and energy that could otherwise be devoted to the Kingdom of God. However, there are also ways in which a spouse and family can enrich one's ability to lead and to serve. *What are some of the ways in which family can make you a more effective leader?*

1. _____
2. _____
3. _____
4. _____
5. _____

How could an unhealthy view of extended family cause a follower of Jesus Christ to become an inadequate member of the Body of Christ?

_____

_____

_____

Look over the following list of responsibilities. On the left, use an X to indicate responsibilities you owe members of your extended family. On the right use an X to indicate the selected areas in which you need to improve.

I OWE THIS	RESPONSIBILITY	MUST IMPROVE
____	Maintain healthy personal relationships	____
____	Show true concern for personal needs	____
____	Be a positive spiritual influence	____
____	Turn conflicts into seasons of growth	____
____	Offer occasional assistance	____
____	Be there in times of crisis	____
____	Pay personal visits	____
____	Care about special events in their family	____
____	Pray for God's blessings and guidance	____
____	Other _____	____

Personal Inventory: Who are the extended relatives you most commonly neglect? Write their names below, along with the reason you neglect them, and what their greatest need might be:

Name _____
- Why you neglect him/her:
- Greatest current need:

Name _____
- Why you neglect him/her:
- Greatest current need:

Name _____
- Why you neglect him/her:
- Greatest current need:

Set aside some time now to pray for your role in your extended family. Ask God to teach you about tribal faith by giving you insights through your own family. Pray for your relationships that are strained at the moment. Pray for relatives who may have been neglected. Thank God for the power of family in your life.

Day 4: The Discipline of Delegation
Read Exodus 18: 13 - 27
Read this section of the chapter carefully. Circle sentences or phrases that reflect faulty thinking. Underline sentences or phrases that reflect a healthier view of mission and responsibility.

18: 13 – 23. When Jethro observes Moses serving as judge on an ordinary day, how long does Moses have people waiting in line for his assistance?

_____

v16. What is Moses' purpose in serving as judge?

_____

_____

v17,18. It's apparent why assuming this sort of task will soon become exhausting and overwhelming for Moses. But why is it also exhausting and frustrating for the people who need assistance and counsel?

_____

Why is it so wasteful when one leader attempts to take responsibility for so many?

Jethro offers his son-in-law some powerful advice. He explains that at this level of leadership, Moses must act out his compassion and concern in a totally different way. Jethro advises he should take three steps:

- v19-b. _____
- v20. _____
- v21. _____

Will each appointed leader be given the same degree of responsibility?

v22. As Jethro explains it, why will this make the load so much lighter for Moses?
Indicate the one right answer with an X.
    [ ] Because this job is not worth the effort it requires
    [ ] Because Moses can now forget about all this minutia
    [ ] Because other qualified leaders are sharing his load
    [ ] Because other people are smarter and more effective than Moses

v23. *Notice one particular phrase in this statement.* How do we know that Jethro is a truly humble man, and that he does not want to interfere in the unique relationship between Moses and the Lord God?

Week Seven   What Every Leader Must Learn

Read *Deuteronomy 1: 9 – 18*. In this passage, Moses explains the directions given to the judges he has appointed. Write those directives below:

1. _____
2. _____
3. _____
4. _____

As you can observe in this passage, delegation is not the same thing as shirking responsibility. The irresponsible person neglects an assigned task because he values his own needs and desires more than the needs or desires of others. By contrast, a responsible leader delegates because the assigned task is so important that it must be done well. Although we tend to think of delegation as the act of moving responsibility to someone else, there are actually several acts involved in effective delegation. *Complete the statements below, finding each in Exodus 18 or Deuteronomy 1.*

1. Select _____ individuals who can share your responsibility.
2. Either train the new leaders or give them _____ directions.
3. Explain accountability and the chain of _____.

One of the most commonplace problems in churches and other Christian organizations is ineffective delegation. That manifests itself in a variety of ways. Read each of the following practices and then summarize why it so commonly leads to mediocrity or failure.

- Offer too few worthwhile tasks for talented people. Only seek out volunteers to serve in the nursery or the choir.

  _____
  _____

- Don't allow space for initiative and resourcefulness. Micromanage the project through an excessive number of rules or administrative meetings.

  _____
  _____

- Delegate jobs that are so big and/or so vague that volunteers can never feel successful or even get a handle of the scope of the task.

  _____
  _____

- Divide oversight or final authority for a task between several different individuals or committees.

  _____

- Recruit people who will quickly agree to serve, without respect to their qualifications for this particular task.

  _____

It's ironic that we in the church are not better known for our excellence in delegation. On one hand, the mission assigned to us is enormous. On the other hand, Scripture is full of texts which deal in one way or another with effective delegation. Read these texts and answer the questions below.

- *Matthew 10: 1 – 20*

    ✓ To whom is this task delegated? _____

    ✓ What are the directions? _____

    _____

- *Matthew 28: 16 – 20*

    ✓ To whom is this task assigned? _____

    ✓ What is the assignment? _____

    _____

- *Acts 6: 1 – 7*
    ✓ To whom is this task delegated? _____

    ✓ What are the qualifications? _____

    _____

- *2 Timothy 2: 1 – 7*
    ✓ To whom is this task assigned? _____

    ✓ What are the directions? _____

Week Seven   What Every Leader Must Learn

_____

_____

Now let's shift gears and allow you to process this truth in your own life. How are you doing in the work of mentoring people in your influence and raising up spiritual leaders for the next generation? *Use the following questions to begin the thinking process for yourself.*

Are you allowing yourself to be trained and mentored by anyone?

[ ] NO [ ] YES   Who? _____

Are you making the effort to mentor or guide a less experienced person in knowing Christ and serving him?

[ ] NO [ ] YES

If you just answered Yes, name that person here. If you just answered No, write the name of someone you could begin to disciple and encourage:

_____

Name one area where you are currently serving the Lord in which you could enlarge your impact and broaden your reach by enlisting leaders to share your responsibility:

_____

Read over the following prayer and determine if it expresses a need in your life. Change any words or phrases that don't sound like you. *Then take a few minutes to offer this prayer to the Lord.*

Heavenly Father,

I am grateful for the privilege of serving in your Kingdom and loving my world as a part of your team. Thank your for calling me and giving me a place where I can be a blessing.

Give me the power in this coming week to reach beyond myself and share my ministry with others. It's been good to be a follower in your Army, but I realize you are calling me to become a leader. Please show me how to reproduce my heart and my ability in the lives of other people I trust.

This week, I want to grow your Church by bringing new leaders on board. Please show me how to be an effective recruiter, a dynamic team builder, and a more productive servant. It's all your work and I just want to be a productive servant.

What an amazing thing that you have entrusted me with something this important. Even more, thank your for sharing your Son with me, and sending him to buy me back from slavery and death.

Help me to line up with Christ even as I offer this prayer in his name.

WEEK EIGHT

LOVING GOD

How can I have the face to look upon Thee, my God? I do not know what words to use in the attempt to justify myself in Thy presence, Lord. What excuse have I before Thee, seeing that all my hidden secrets are laid open before Thee? -Nonnus

There's an odd statement we often hear in churches today that actually has no logical place in our Judeo-Christian tradition. It happens whenever a believer asserts the authority of God to set limits, establish deadlines, or deliver judgment. Whenever concepts like these arise, someone often responds, "*My* God would never do that."

You could have made a claim like that in ancient Egypt where the state religion afforded a vast menu of contrasting gods and goddesses. You were required to worship them all, of course, but you were free to choose your favorite. Even later in Greece and Rome, a serious pagan could differentiate between "my God," and other gods and goddesses within the realms of a polytheistic system. It was necessary to pay homage to all, but every city had its patron deities, and individuals could pick and choose to determine their favorites. Hence, one might logically assert, "My god would never behave that way," although other gods might. Or so the mythology insisted.

But when Abram responded in faith to the call of God and began to worship the one true God, he introduced a brand new concept to an overwhelmingly pagan world- *monotheism*. Today we take the idea for granted because the success of Judaism and later Christianity has drastically altered the way our world perceives the heavens. It is the presupposition of most human beings today that there is one God. *But for most of the history of our world, almost everybody assumed there were many competing deities to be patronized and appeased.* This brings us back to the strange statement we often hear in churches about "my God" versus "your God."

There is only one Lord; the God of Abraham, Isaac and Jacob. He sent his Son who would raise the bar on holiness, and then would willingly offer up his life on a cross in order to ransom us from slavery to sin. This is the God who inspired the Bible and established the Church. He has many attributes, but only one personality. And he never changes.

So we cannot compare our gods- *only our theology*. In other words, "What do you know about God?" One might argue, "I can't imagine God doing that," but that idea is subject to the teachings of Scripture. If the Word of God insists God can indeed do that very thing, then that particular debate is settled. The only doubt that remains is whether or not you believe the Bible.

When the people of Israel bade goodbye to Egypt and followed Moses into the desert, they had no inspired documents to consult or study. They had stories of faith which had been passed along verbatim from generation to generation. Their very survival as a nation was a testimony to the faithfulness of the Almighty in keeping his promises. Occasionally they might pass ancient altars and landmarks which reminded them of God's activity in the past. But mostly, they had Moses standing before them to decree "Thus saith the Lord...!"

This was how they constructed their theology, their knowledge of God. They learned he was holy and all powerful. They discovered he was fully committed to promise keeping. They recognized that he was eternal and beyond their ability to comprehend or fully explain. Any time you think about the things you know about God, you are acting as a theologian. Theology is not about some esoteric philosophical argument that doesn't matter anyway. Theology is the study of what we know about the God we love. This is anything but insignificant.

In our own age when terms like "doctrine" and "obedience" sound like four-letter words to many people in churches, the Ten Commandments must seem like a massive burden God placed upon the backs of the poor Jews. Their pagan neighbors were free to behave as they wanted, but those poor Jews have to carry the weight of those ten impossible orders carved in granite or something like it!

This week we shall watch as God delivers those well-known commandments to Moses. And we shall discover they are neither a curse nor an obstacle. The Ten Commandments are a gift from the Eternal Father. They are not about legalism and limitations. They are about life, health, community and a powerful witness. They will make the people of God utterly unique, and that completely distinctive quality will serve a compelling purpose.

At Mount Sinai the earth will tremble and the mountain top will glow like molten lava. It will be an hour the Jews will never, ever forget. But it will draw them closer still to the Eternal Lord who will never, ever forget about them. Prepare yourself to travel through time and space to behold the wonder of the God of the Ages as he reveals his love and his purpose to the people he has chosen.

This week, we will answer questions like these:
- Day 1: Why did God elevate Israel to such a special status in his eyes, and does this automatically apply to the New Testament Church?
- Day 2: Why was the final approach to Mount Sinai such a terrifying experience, and what can we learn from it?
- Day 3: What's wrong with having other gods as long as God is #1?
- Day 4: What is the significance of the Sabbath, and why don't we keep it today?

Week Eight   Loving God

Day 1: Why Us?
Read Exodus 19: 1 - 9
Read this brief passage slowly 2-3 times. Now go back to look at the various expressions used to address or describe the people of God. Underscore or highlight those descriptive words and phrases.

Exodus 19: 1 – 8. Israel left Egypt on the fifteenth day of the first month. Based on the chronology in this passage, how long have they been traveling through the desert?

_____

v2. At this moment, where in the desert have they set up camp?

_____

Remember, it was for this moment that the Jews left Egypt in the first place. Moses originally asked the Pharaoh to let God's people go so that they could worship him on this mountain. Now that they have arrived, the time has come for the Almighty God to explain what comes next. So God calls out to Moses and gives him directions about what the people must be told.

v4. Fill in these blanks: "You yourselves have _____ what I did to Egypt; how I carried you on _____ _____, and brought you to _____."

Q: Why do you think the Israelites must be verbally and visually reminded so often of what God has done for them? *Indicate the single best answer below:*
    [ ] Because the blistering desert plays tricks on the mind;
    [ ] Slavery has damaged their ability to reason and remember.
    [ ] Because the miracles God has done can be easily explained away;
    [ ] We all have this human tendency to credit our own savvy and resourcefulness
       (rather than divine intervention) for surviving hard times in our lives.

Q: What quality does God have in mind when he says he has carried them on eagles' wings? *Indicate the single best answer.*
    [ ] The power of God, which has enabled them to travel like an eagle who
       rarely flaps his wings
    [ ] The speed with which they have made the journey to Sinai
    [ ] The ease and convenience of the desert trek to Sinai
    [ ] The extreme distance they have been able to accomplish

Q: From God's perspective, what is the significance of their arrival at Mount Sinai? *Select the single best answer.*
    [ ] They are so far from Egypt that they can no longer be pursued.
    [ ] This mountain represents the presence and dwelling of the Lord.
    [ ] This is the place God has promised as a homeland.
    [ ] This area is not as hot and barren as Egypt.

v3. The first part of this conditional sentence is given different shades of meaning by different interpreters.
- It is translated "Now if you obey me fully," by the NIV,
- It is rendered "If you obey my voice," by the KJV
- The connotation of obedience is clearly there, but the Hebrew literally reads, "If you will hear my voice." The term in question is *sama*.

The second part of the promise builds on the fact that the Jews will indeed stop and hear God's voice.
- "If you will hear my voice *and keep my covenant...*"
- The word translated "to keep" is *samar*, a variation of *sama* in the previous phrase. Its uses are insightful.
    - ✓ *Genesis 2:15*. This word is used when God directs Adam and Eve to keep or watch over the Garden of Eden.
    - ✓ *1 Samuel 26:15*. David uses this word when he tells his men to protect Absalom and keep him safe.
- With the core definitions of *sama* and *samar* firmly in mind, take a moment to write out the two conditions of this promise in your own words. Then use your own words to express the conditions clause.

    1. Now if _____

    _____

    2. If _____

    _____

This brings us to one of my favorite concepts. God promises that if Israel will hear his voice and remain faithful to his covenant, he will make them a "treasured possession." This particular Hebrew word is only used six times in the Old Testament. It affirms that Israel will be able to occupy a position like no other nation on Earth. Look up these verses and examine the result of this treasured status:
- *Deuteronomy 26:18,19*. What will occur because Israel enjoys this favored status?

    _____

    _____

- *Malachi 3:17,18*. What will become apparent when Israel is restored to "treasured possession" status?

    _____

    _____

Week Eight   Loving God

"If you hear my voice and remain faithful to my covenant, then out of all the nations, you will be my treasured possession...."

v5-b. Although the whole earth is mine, you will be for me
- a _____ of _____; and
- a _____ _____.

It's not as though Israel alone belongs to the Creator. He made the whole world, which explains why all the nations belong to him. And yet Israel will enjoy a more privileged, more intimate level of relationship. Being God's unique treasure is a privilege that carries a responsibility. And this is the part that Israel often forgot throughout their history: *they are people chosen for a divine purpose!*

What is a kingdom? It is a group of people organized around a _____.

What is a priest? This is an individual who facilitates the relationship between worshipers and _____.

With that in mind, use your own words to describe "a kingdom of priests."

_____

_____

_____

If you hear my voice and remain faithful to my covenant, then out of all the nations, you will be my treasured possession. And although all the nations are mine, you shall be a kingdom of priests..."

v6-b. "You shall be a kingdom of priests and a holy nation."
- The word translated "holy" is *qadosh*. It can be defined as sacred, or set apart. But perhaps the easiest way to catch its meaning is to consider what it doesn't mean.
- *It is the opposite of most things which are common, ordinary, or easily wasted.*
- Israel will be a nation reserved for the purposes of God.

Other nations will go about the usual business of government and politics: self-defense, self-interest, accumulating wealth, exploiting other nations. However, Israel will be a nation on reserve for God's special purpose: facilitating and encouraging the relationship between other people and the living God.

Q: Can we simply lift this specific idea from the Old Covenant and interject it automatically into the New Testament?
A: The Apostle Peter does exactly that!

Read *1 Peter 2: 9-12*.
Notice that Simon Peter has lifted *Exodus 19:6* from the Old Covenant and transferred it completely to the New Covenant.
- The Church is a chosen people, a royal priesthood, a holy nation, a people belonging to God.
- For what purpose?

    ✓ That [we] may _____
    _____

    ✓ Once [we] were not a people, but now [we] are _____
    _____

Read *Romans 2:28,29*.
Paul asserts that belonging to the true Israel is not a matter of genes or physical circumcision, but is instead a matter of _____
_____

Exodus 19: 7-8. Moses explains all that God has spoken. And the people of Israel respond as one, "We will do everything the Lord has said." As we shall see in the next lesson, they have no idea what they are promising. But God is a capable instructor.

Think about what it means today that the church is the true Israel, the treasured possession of God, a nation of priests. Then read the following statements and indicate whether it is T/True or F/False.

___ The role of the church is to lobby the government for specific legislation.
___ One of the highest priorities of the church must be building up a financial nest egg.
___ Christians should be actively involved in cultivating relationships between other people, even outsiders, and Jesus Christ, our King.
___ The life of the church should be positively distinctive from the life of the world.
___ Christians are healthier and more victorious because we spend more time focused on ourselves and our happiness.
___ It is God's design that people in the church should enjoy healthier, more productive lives than people in the world.
___ Being chosen is not only a privilege, but a sacred responsibility.

Week Eight   Loving God

Day 2: The Awesome Presence of the Lord
Read Exodus 19: 10 - 25
Read this passage slowly and carefully. Underscore or highlight every phrase, circumstance or prescribed activity that emphasizes the difference between God and the human beings who seek Him.

Exodus 19: 10 – 14. The ancient and timeless covenant between God and Abram is about to advance to a new level. God calls the descendants of Abram into a very special convocation. In this pivotal event, God will offer his people a matchless treasure that will make them unique among the nations, and will serve as evidence that they are his treasured possession.

v10. Two days are set aside to make the necessary preparations for bringing the Israelites into the personal presence of the Lord. Two processes must be initiated. First, Moses must lead the people in consecrating themselves. Once again, we come upon the Hebrew word *qadosh*, to make holy. The Israelites are required to do certain things to set themselves apart for God's purposes. *Specifically, they must:*

1. *v10-b* _____

2. *v14* _____

Don't ever forget that this is taking place in an arid desert environment. Washing oneself and ones clothing is useful and healthy, but it's not an everyday event because it requires extra water and, therefore, extra effort. The people don't have to do anything special to approach Moses or his lieutenants and ask for wisdom and counsel. But Moses is flesh and blood as they are. *God is different: elevated and set apart.* And he is completely uncorrupted and untainted by sin or imperfection. As a result, sinful humans find it dangerous, even deadly, to stand in his presence. So great care must be taken to be clean and dedicated, inside and outside.

Abstinence from the normal sexual activity that accompanies marriage is also required. Again, this reflects the fallen nature of man and the unique nature of this moment. This is not a casual, everyday event, and it cannot be approached as such.

v12. That brings us to the second step of preparation for the meeting: *barriers.* God directs Moses to establish certain boundaries to prevent the Israelites, their children and herds, from straying too close to the mountain of God.

- What happens to anyone who touches the mountain?

  _____

- *v13.* What methods are prescribed?

  _____

- *v13.* What is the significance of those particular methods?

  _____

v13-b. The people may climb the mountain only when they hear a long blast from a ram's horn. This ram's horn, called a *shofar*, will become a herald that will be used to summon the people of Israel to battle, to emergencies, and into the presence of the Lord.

v16-20. What a moment of awe, majesty and terror this must be! Work through this paragraph and try to visualize the scene at Sinai.
- The sky is rocked by _____ and _____.
- A thick _____ covers the mountain.
- When the long blast of the *shofar* pierces the air, everyone in the camp _____.
- *v17.* Moses leads the people to higher ground at the base of the mountain.
- *v18.* Mount Sinai is covered with _____ because the Lord has descended in _____.
- The smoke is so black and thick that it looks like it has been produced in a _____.
- The mountain begins to _____ violently.
- *v19.* The _____ blast grows louder and louder.
- Then Moses speaks and _____ answers.

Nothing you've ever seen in an *Indiana Jones* movie could compare to the spectacle that unfolds here as God incorporates a nightmarish firestorm and a molten, quaking mountain shrouded in clouds as an object lesson on divine holiness! *Who could miss the point here?* On your best day, your human morality can never approach the righteousness of the Eternal One! Even your most elevated moments of insight are not sufficient to comprehend the wonder and the mystery of the Almighty Creator of Heaven and Earth! These poor Jews must feel trapped between a rock and a hard place. Do they respond to the trumpet call and move toward a mountain that threatens to pummel them, or do they turn on their heels and run as fast as they can from the only one who can save them?

SECRETS OF THE DESERT

Where is Mount Sinai located? The fact is, we aren't sure and archaeologists are divided between several debatable sites. Some Roman Catholics believe the original site is marked by St. Catherine Monastery, which was built in the mountains of the southern Sinai Peninsula in 527 AD. This lofty campus boasts two claims to fame. The chapel overlooks an ancient, sprawling bush, related to the rose family, dating back many centuries and believed by some to be the original burning bush that was not consumed. In addition, one of our oldest Greek manuscripts of the Bible, *Codex Sinaiticus* (dating back to the 4th Century BC,) was discovered here in 1844. St. Catherine was reportedly constructed atop Mount Sinai, but this claim has never been authenticated.

v20-25. Amid all this chaos, there is clearly a great deal of panic and confusion. Twice the all-knowing Lord of Eternity warns Moses not to let the people rush the mountain. After the first

Week Eight Loving God

warning, Moses feels everything is under control, but God puts him on notice a second time. So Moses goes down the mountain to the masses yet again, and warns them to be calm and not rush past the barricades. Clearly something unprecedented is about to come to pass.

Read *Hebrews 12: 18 – 28*. The God of the Old Covenant is also the God of the New Covenant. His character never changes, but it's impossible to read Exodus 19 and this passage back to back and not sense a dramatic difference. Use the images of Hebrews 12 to contrast the Old Covenant and the New:

OLD COVENANT	NEW COVENANT
Untouchable, flaming mountain	v22 _____
Darkness, gloom, & storm	_____
Trumpet & terrifying voice	v23 _____
	_____
Moses trembling in fear	v24 _____
	_____

Q: How has the blood of Jesus Christ made such a difference between one's approach to God in the Old Covenant, and the very different perspective we have in the New Covenant?

_____

_____

_____

_____

In the Old Testament Temple that came later, the Ark of the Covenant remained in perpetual darkness in the Most Holy Place, shielded from light and prying eyes by a woven curtain seventy feet tall and twelve inches thick. Only the high priest could enter that sacred area. Even he was restricted to once a year on a particular day, and only after going to great lengths to be ceremonially clean. Any priest who entered without conformity to those rules would be instantly struck dead. But after the crucifixion of Christ, priests entered the temple in Jerusalem to encounter a shocking and unimaginable scene. The curtain that shrouded the Most Holy Place had been torn from top to bottom, leaving the Ark of the Covenant in plain sight![37] These men must have wondered why they weren't already dead!

Dr. John Phillips has commented that after centuries of warning, "Don't come in here or I'll kill you!" God had suddenly opened the door to smile and beckon, "Come in. Sit down and stay a while." The work of Jesus Christ changed everything!

Hebrews 12:25-29. The writer of Hebrews is writing to Jews who are apparently worshiping with Christians but refusing to confess Christ. Persecution has broken out and being identified with Christ could be costly. At worst, Jewish Christians can be arrested by the government or punished by angry neighbors. And even if they escape those kinds of consequences, they may still be disowned and disinherited by their Jewish families. It seems far easier to delay this decision to follow Christ until circumstances eventually improve.

v25. What will be the cost of postponing a decision to trust the Messiah?

_____

_____

_____

v27. What is the connotation of our inheriting a kingdom that cannot be shaken?
Indicate the single best answer.
 ___ God no longer uses natural forces like earthquakes.
 ___ Natural kingdoms are subject to catastrophes. A supernatural kingdom is not subject to such natural forces.
 ___ God is not as engaged in the New Testament as he was in the Old.
 ___ The writer is suggesting our faith is unshakeable.

v28. Hebrews calls upon people of faith to worship the Almighty with reverence and awe.
- The Greek word translated reverence, *aidos*, denotes a sense of modesty in approaching someone or something worthy of great respect or veneration.
- The word translated awe, *eulabia*, speaks of drawing back in response to the overwhelming greatness of someone or something before you.

Personal Inventory: How do you integrate reverence and awe into your times of worship with God?

_____

_____

_____

Week Eight Loving God

_____

_____

Read through this prayer and adjust the words or ideas until they reflect the ideas and attitudes you desire to express to God about living in his presence. Then read your prayer back to the Lord.

> Almighty Father,
> You are a consuming fire. You are a lamp to my feet and a light to my pathway.
> More than anything else, I desire to surrender my life fully to your leadership, your e ethic, and to keep my feet on the level path you have set before me.
>
> Forgive me for the occasions when I have approached you with a casual routine attitude. Forgive me for the times when I have treated my faith as a burden, or your presence as a chore. Melt away the dross in my life and give me a pure heart that can easily delight in you; that can gladly follow the call of your purpose.
>
> Thank you, Father, for the privilege of living in the light of the New Testament. I live my faith in the shadow of Old Testament heroes who paid the price to hand the faith down to my generation. My faith is a treasure that has been defended and protected for me by New Testament heroes who gave their very lives. Let me always live my life within sight of the cross, and the Savior who took the blows and died the death I deserve.   I lift this prayer in the name of your son, Jesus.

Day 3: One Lord
Read Exodus 20: 1 - 12
Read these verses until you can think beyond familiar rhythms and concepts. Then take a pen or pencil and number the first five commandments. Circle the most important verb in each command.

ALLEGIANCE
The first of the Ten Commandments is just one more reminder that the Christian Faith has never been about blind faith. Our faith is always a response to something evident God has done or something he has revealed to us.
- Abram responded in faith when God took the initiative and reached out to him with an amazing promise.
- Moses summoned the faith to follow only after God revealed his power through a burning bush and an array of miraculous signs.
- So it's not surprising that the Ten Commandments will be an expression of faith in a God who has loved first and liberated a nation of slaves.

The gift of faith is always a response to revelation and personal experience. So when God escalates his relationship with Israel to a high level of intimacy, the entire experience begins with God acting as the Lover, making the first move, revealing something of himself.

The Jews have spent sixty days waiting on the Lord, who has rescued them time after time with one miracle after another. The people of Israel are learning that God is reliable. What have you learned about God during the last eight weeks? Take a moment to review the previous chapters in the study. Then summarize three images or incidents from the first nineteen chapters of Exodus. *What has each image or incident taught you about the Father?*

1. The Event: _____

   The Lesson: _____

   _____

2. The Event: _____

   The Lesson: _____

   _____

3. The Event: _____

   The Lesson: _____

   _____

In Egypt, the names of all the competing gods and goddesses were well-known. Their painted images, carved statues, and tokens of authority were everywhere. There was Ra the sun god, Heqet the frog goddess, Hathor, Nut and a catalog of other figures as well. But now the Jews find themselves standing before a flaming mountain in a blistering wilderness, and there's only one amazing God in sight! By these standards, the first commandment should be a piece of cake, right?

In fact, the most insidious false god- the most popular alternative to the One True God- was not forsaken when Israel departed Egypt. This wannabe god could not be left behind in Egypt because it wasn't born there in the first place. No, this false god was born in a place called Eden when a woman named Eve concluded that the Creator God could not anticipate her needs nearly as well as she could. So Adam and Eve rejected the counsel of the One who made them, and attempted to make themselves gods.

That was the first appearance of Self in the Bible, but not nearly the last. Throughout the Bible- page after page, chapter after chapter- Self wages a full-scale war to steal the glory, the allegiance, that belongs to the Lord.

Read *Matthew 19:16 – 30*.

When this young man approaches Christ with such a reasonable question about receiving eternal life, why do you suppose Jesus replies with such an extreme demand? "Sell all your possessions and give to the poor." If this is a universal requirement for salvation, why did you and I get to keep our possessions? *Explore this true story and find some answers.*

- Christ's directive for the young man to sell everything and give to the poor is not the first extreme, jarring statement in this passage. What is the <u>first</u> statement that is unrealistic or out of kilter? *Clue: see verse 20.*

  _____

  _____

- Why does the young man's reaction in *verse 22* prove he was wrong in *verse 20*, and that he has broken the first commandment at the very least?

  _____

  _____

- Why is money such a key indicator of whether I worship God or Self?

  _____

  _____

  _____

  _____

NO IDOLATRY
Exodus 20:4. The second commandment fleshes out the first and adds more specificity. Beyond Self, there is also a vast array of idols created and exalted by people in our culture. There's a great deal of pressure for you and me to join in the worship. *Break the second commandment down into its various elements:*
- Don't make an idol for yourself;
- Don't _____;
- For I am a _____ God
  - ✓ punishing children for the sins of their fathers to the ___ and ___ generations;
  - ✓ but showing love to _____ generations of those who love me and keep my commandments.

Skeptics are offended by the idea of a "jealous" God. "If he's so big and awesome and incomparable, why is he so insecure and petty?" they ask. "Doesn't *1 Corinthians 13* teach that love is not jealous?" There are at least two compelling answers.
- Just as God's ways are not like ours, neither is his jealousy. There is no sin, no lust, no envy involved. For this reason, the Hebrew word translated "jealous" is only used six times in the Old Testament, and only in relationship to God.

173

- Secondly, faith is an intimate relationship- *not a shopping trip*. A shopper may come home with several kinds of bread, cookies, or soft drinks. But a husband comes home with one wife. A wife is loyal to one husband.

Once again, skeptics accuse God of cruelty for someone imposing a penalty on the children and grandchildren of people obsessed with sin. But this empty accusation overlooks the reality that sinful behavior has both short term and long term consequences.

- Can you think of three forms of sinful behavior that damage not only the sinner, but his/her children and grandchildren?
    1.
    2.
    3.

- If a man becomes so addicted to alcohol that he ultimately wrecks his marriage, his health, and his career, how does this damage his children and grandchildren?
    ✓ _____
    ✓ _____
    ✓ _____

- How can that cycle of sin be interrupted when a son, daughter or grandchild comes to faith in Christ?

_____

_____

_____

_____

- How will an individual's strong walk with Christ impact children, grandchildren and great grandchildren even before they become believers?
    1. _____
    2. _____
    3. _____

Read 1 Corinthians 10: 14 – 22.
Paul indicates that sharing in the Lord's Supper is a token of the fact that we belong to Christ. It's about allegiance, family, tribe. Then he explains that chasing after idols is disloyalty to Christ.
- Just because idols aren't alive doesn't mean idolatry is harmless.
- *v20.* Whoever worships an idol is actually worshiping _____!

Week Eight Loving God

An idol is any object that steals my attentions, affections, and energies from the one true God. It doesn't have to look like a god, any more than the various idols in Egypt, Greece and Rome looked like gods. They didn't. All those idols looked like animals, people or created things. Our twenty-first century idols are no different... *except that they're often powered by gasoline or electricity.*

Which of the following has "idol potential" in your life? Check as many as apply:
- [ ] Personal Computer
- [ ] Automobile, Truck, Tractor or Boat
- [ ] HD TV
- [ ] Refrigerator
- [ ] Golf Clubs
- [ ] Garden, home landscape
- [ ] Fashionable Clothing
- [ ] Money, credit cards
- [ ] Trophies and awards
- [ ] Video games
- [ ] Cell phone
- [ ] Other _____
- [ ] Other _____

Read Isaiah 62: 1 – 7.
Zion is a prophetic name for the homeland of the people of God. As you review this passage, note all the references to the relationship between God and Israel which is very much like marriage.
- *v2.* The Lord will give Israel something new. What is it?

    _____

- *v4.* Consult your Study Bible notes or work through the second part of this verse to define the two names given to Israel in the first section.
    - ✓ *Hepzibah* means _____
    - ✓ *Beulah* means _____

- *v5.* How does God describe himself in relationship to Israel?

    _____

The intimate nature of the relationship God desires with his people is the explanation for his basic requirement for fidelity. The first and second commandments affirm the desire of God to bless and enrich his family as a powerful king blesses and enriches his own family.

Day 4: Reverence, Rest & Respect
Read Exodus 20: 1 - 12

Take some time to memorize these first five commandments and commit them to memory. Ask someone else to hold your Bible and let you recite them without looking at the page. You will need to repeat them every day for a few days to make them a permanent memory.

THE NAME OF THE LORD

v7. The third commandment prohibits using the name of YHWH, the Lord of the Covenant, in a careless way that does not honor him. As you know, for the longest time this particular name of God was not even assigned vowels so that it could not be pronounced at all.

Jot down four or five ways people in this generation commonly misuse the name of the Lord.

- _____
- _____
- _____
- _____
- _____

Have you personally used any of those terms or even a variation of one in a way not related to bringing honor to the Lord?
   [ ] NO   [ ] YES

   If YES, explain _____
   _____

Q: Have you repented of abusing God's name? Have you confessed this as a sin and asked for grace? If not, pause now and consider that.

We have a very narrow concept of what it means to dishonor or profane the name of the Lord. However, the name and reputation of God is so high and holy, that God has a much broader view of this sin. Consult the following texts and explain the activities characterized as profaning God's name:

- *Leviticus 20:3* _____
  _____

- *Leviticus 22:2* _____
  _____

Week Eight Loving God

- *James 2: 5 – 7* _____
  _____

Stop and take this idea to heart. It's obviously a sin to exclaim "Jesus Christ!" when something suddenly goes wrong. It's probably also disrespectful to use variations of the term like "Jeez," or "Good Lord!" But when you and I seriously take pains to set the name of the Lord apart as high and holy[38], it's more than just a matter of semantics.

Read Psalm 118:24-26.
What does it mean when a diplomat travels somewhere in the name of the United States?

_____
_____

When a diplomat represents the USA, how important is his conduct when he leaves the Embassy or the meeting room in another country?

_____
_____

Should you appoint someone to go somewhere in your name, what expectations would you have for your personal representative's behavior?

_____
_____
_____

What does it mean then "to ask for something in the name of Christ?"[39]

_____
_____
_____

As followers of Jesus, people who belong to the body of Christ, we constantly live and travel in the name of Christ.[40] How do our habits and choices demonstrate reverence for the name of God we bear?

_____

_____

_____

THE SABBATH

Exodus 20:8-11. The fourth commandment designates the Sabbath as a day reserved as holy unto the Lord. It is different from the other days.

- *v8.* We know what a holy person is. What is a holy day?

   _____

- *v9.* What action sets this day apart from others?

   _____

- *v10.* Notice the detail that is invested in this commandment. A Jew must refrain from all labor on this day. But in addition, neither his _____ or _____; nor male or female _____; nor his _____; nor any _____ living with his household may be allowed to labor on the Sabbath!

- Read *Leviticus 25: 1-7.* In what other way are Jews required to observe the concept of Sabbath?

   _____

   _____

- *Exodus 20:11.* Upon what historical fact is this fourth commandment based?

   _____

The word Sabbath is a variant of the Hebrew word for seven. Obviously, it refers to the seventh day of the week, Saturday, rather than Sunday, the first day. On the Sabbath, Jews were to be intentional about refraining from labor and paying attention to the needs of their souls.

- At various places throughout the Old Testament, the Jews are taught that they should not travel far home, build a fire for the house, gather wood, or carry burdens on the Sabbath. The point is: "Not even a little work."
- Read *Nehemiah 13:16-17.* By simply allowing pagans to perform a particular act, the Jews profane the Sabbath. What is the offensive activity?

   _____

Week Eight Loving God

- *Psalm 92* is labeled "a song for the Sabbath." It speaks of making music in the name of the Lord, proclaiming his love and faithfulness all day, making melodies with harps and lyres. It is a time for reflection on the works of the Almighty.

Think about it. In our own age, we commonly point to the benefits of rest and leisure that could be afforded by the Sabbath. We elaborate on the dangers of stress, exhaustion and burn-out, and we prescribe taking off one day each week as a prescription for relief. Of course, this is all very practical, but God is emphatic about the true purpose of the Sabbath. And the primary purpose is not stress relief, is it?

What does *20:11* actually teach about the purpose of the Sabbath? Read the verse again and choose the one answer that best expresses the text:
[ ] The Sabbath is a divine way to prevent exhaustion and depression.
[ ] The Sabbath reflects the natural cycle of the universe.
[ ] The Sabbath is a testimony that God created the universe in 6 days.
[ ] The Sabbath was ordained because these nomads were exhausted.

Think about just some of the customs and habits prescribed for the Israelites by God:
- The refusal to erect idols and images of their God, although idols are commonplace among their neighbors;
- The annual celebration of a very unique Passover Feast to recall their deliverance by the Almighty God;
- Their unwillingness to intermarry with their neighbors, despite the fact that marriage with other nations forged useful political alliances;
- The refusal to do even minor labor one particular day each week, although the neighboring nations work every day to provide for themselves.

Q: Does it seem that God is more concerned with helping his people blend in with their pagan neighbors, or enabling them to stand out?

_____

Personal Application: Participating in worship on Sundays while your neighbors play golf, read the Sunday newspaper, or go to races is obviously a habit that makes you stand out. *What are some other habits that make your life visibly distinct from your neighbors?*

- _____
- _____
- _____

How intentional are you? When you assess your lifestyle and habits, do you spend more time working to "fit in" or to make your life visibly distinctive from unbelievers?

_____

If you are more intentional about 'fitting in' than standing out, what excuse(s) have you used to rationalize this tendency?

_____

_____

_____

Think of the most holy men and women you have ever known or read about. What habits or qualities vividly set their lives apart from the people around them?

- _____
- _____
- _____
- _____

There's a difference between tokenism and integrity. Tokens are things you do that aren't really sincere, but that lead other people to believe you are more than you are. (Displaying religious art that you don't really care for would amount to hypocrisy.) Integrity requires that anything you do to set your life apart should be authentic and personally meaningful. That could include anything from giving thanks over your meals every time you eat, to religiously visiting a rescue mission once a week, to setting apart a regular holy day in your own life. *How can you add more of a visible testimony to your routine life?*

_____

_____

_____

_____

WEEK NINE

LOVING YOUR NEIGHBOR

God is a fire that warms and kindles the heart and inward parts. Hence, if we feel in our hearts the cold which comes from the devil - for the devil is cold - let us call on the Lord. He will come to warm our hearts with perfect love, not only for Him but also for our neighbor -Seraphim of Sarov

My wife and I lived in Montgomery, Alabama for a few years. It was during those years that we became familiar with a place called the Montgomery Baptist Center. The Center itself was an ordinary, unimpressive building located in a rough inner city area. The heart of the ministry was a gray haired woman with deep creases in her face. Mrs. Gladys Farmer continued to direct the ministry of MBC despite the fact that she was more than eighty years old.

Early every morning this octogenarian drove her late model automobile into the roughest part of town. After dark every evening, she locked up the Center and drove home alone. But during those long days, her committed, well organized team of volunteers read to children, fed the hungry, coordinated literacy education, and coached boys and girls playing basketball and soccer.

One day Mrs. Farmer learned about an aging, black woman living alone in despair. She visited her home to discover an abandoned, hungry soul living in the most sordid conditions in a shack layered with dirt and grime, animal waste, cobwebs and other fecal matter. Although she was older than the woman she'd come to rescue, Mrs. Farmer spent a whole day cleaning, sanitizing, and organizing the house. She bathed the sick woman, prepared her a nourishing meal, and later sent volunteers to check on her.

Shortly before our family moved away, one federal organization or another recognized the city of Montgomery for making drastic reductions in crime over a five year period. When the Mayor received the award at a press conference, he explained that most of the decrease had come primarily as a result of one plucky, eighty-year old woman named Gladys Farmer and a place called the Montgomery Baptist Center.

Mrs. Farmer was not a glamorous woman. Her face was solemn and lined with wrinkles. Her horn-rimmed glasses were too thick, her gray hair was always wound tightly in a bun atop her head, and her swollen ankles were accented with clunky black shoes before clunky was fashionable. But for boys and girls at risk and for people in need of food, medication or education, her face must have always looked like a radiant welcome sign.

And her feet must have called to mind an exultation from Isaiah : "How beautiful on the mountains are the feet of those who bring good news, who proclaim peace, who bring good tidings, who proclaim salvation, who say to Zion, 'Your God reigns!'"[41]

The Ten Commandments were an amazing revelation to Moses and his generation. Their's was a world in which the overwhelming majority of human beings assumed the heavens were populated with gods and goddesses guilty of the same vices and bad attitudes that plagued the visible world below. Mount Olympus, where the legendary Greek gods lived, was a petty place marked by greed, lust, jealousy and constant rivalry.

But Mount Sinai was vastly different- a holy place where God reached down from the heavens to offer wisdom and guidance from his very throne room. This God could not have been more unlike the gods of Egypt, Assyria or Babylon. He towered far above the petty greed and lust so typical of his people. And from his eternal kingdom of justice and righteousness, he offered his chosen nation the kind of laws that would guarantee prosperity and make them unique among all the nations of the world.

Many centuries after the introduction of the Ten Commandments, Jesus Christ was asked to pick the greatest or most important commandment. He replied that those ten amazing commands could not be ranked or rated, but they could be summarized. "Love the Lord your God with all your heart, soul and mind; and love your neighbor as yourself," he replied. "In doing so you will keep all the commandments."[42]

This is one of those very direct teachings of Christ that somehow gets overlooked by religious people in our rush to select our favorite rules and commandments. Some of us elect not to drink, smoke, do drugs or gamble. Others of us prefer not to gossip, neglect the poor, overlook injustice, or fail to feed the hungry. Nevertheless, our lists are always incomplete and our righteousness is always selective. But if I love God with all my heart and my neighbor as myself, I will never dishonor God by worshiping an idol- *at least, not for long*; or offend my neighbor by stealing his money or his wife.

Before we crunch the ten down to two for simplicity, let's spend a few days examining the last six laws of Mount Sinai. They are more than just amazing guidelines for successful living. For in the specific ways God teaches us to love our neighbors, he reveals a great deal about our design and our Designer.

As you study this week, I'll once again be encouraging you to memorize the commandments. In addition, we'll be answering questions like these:
- Day 1: What does it mean to "honor" parents, and what does that virtue teach us about the character of God?
- Day 2: What does the eighth commandment teach me about maintaining healthy relationships with other people?

Week Nine Loving Your Neighbor

- Day 3: How does the constant barrage of commercial advertising and in-movie product placement feed the evil God calls covetousness?
- Day 4: As New Testament followers of Christ, what is our relationship to the Ten Commandments? Do we use them for making decisions, or do we simply treat them with reverence?

Day 1: Parents and Other Problem People
Read Exodus 20: 12 - 21

Read this passage three times. Set aside some time now to meditate on the fourth commandment. Allow it to cycle gently through you mind over and over again. Emphasize a different word as you repeat the command again and again. Ask the Holy Spirit to give you insights into the character of God.

HONOR YOUR PARENTS

Exodus 20:12. When God orders us to honor our parents, he uses a verb, *kabed*, that means to weigh heavily or cause to be weighty. It is related to the Hebrew word *kabod*, which denotes the glory of God. When God orders us to respect our mothers and fathers, he is directing us to add weight to their words and their counsel because of their position; to be intentional about giving them significance in our lives.

Jesus reminded us that this is the only commandment with a promise attached. The Jews are assured that in being careful to honor parents and the authority they represent, their nation will enjoy a long, long life in the land they've been given.

Q: Why would a nation that teaches respect for authority be more likely to thrive and endure for many generations than one that doesn't emphasize that ethic?

_____

_____

_____

_____

Q: This commandment has been likened to a bridge, connecting the first four commands relating to God with the last five which influence our behavior towards other people. How does respect for our parents relate both to the way we worship God and the way we treat other human beings?

_____

_____

_____

Treasure in the Sand

_____

_____

_____

Read Ruth 1: 1 – 22. The heroine of this story is not one of God's chosen people. Born among the people of Moab, she actually marries into the nation of Israel. And yet she clearly wins the favor of God; so much so that she will be included in the bloodline of the Messiah. *Reflect on her life and choose the correct answer to each of the following questions.*

- Ruth quickly wins our admiration, primarily through details of her relationship with:
  ___ God
  ___ Her husband Killion
  ___ Her mother
  ___ Her mother-in-law Naomi

- How would you describe Naomi's personality, at least during this moment in time?
  ___ Courageous and full of faith
  ___ Defeated and depressed
  ___ Self-centered and egotistical
  ___ Determined and optimistic

- Naomi seems to think God has forsaken her. In fact...
  ___ She is correct.
  ___ God has not abandoned her but is punishing her.
  ___ God has offered her an incredible blessing in the person of Ruth.
  ___ It's impossible to know what God is doing.

- How would you describe Ruth's character?
  ___ Typically pagan
  ___ Cautious and uncertain
  ___ Self-serving
  ___ Loyal and respectful

Why do you think Ruth remained with Naomi and treated her like her own mother?

_____

_____

If your parents are still alive, how would you describe your relationship with them? *Choose one.*
  [ ] I'm much too self-absorbed at the moment.
  [ ] My folks are much too self-absorbed at the moment.
  [ ] We're courteous but don't enjoy a meaningful relationship.
  [ ] We are fond of each other and see each other on occasion.
  [ ] Our relationship is full of love, respect and healthy times together.

Which of these things must be true if you honor and revere your parents as commanded? *Select as many as apply.*

[ ] The relationship is always happy and never stressful.
[ ] I am intentional about spending time with my parents.
[ ] I am concerned when they are having a problem.
[ ] I have my life, they have theirs and never the two shall meet.
[ ] We work through problems in our relationship even if it's difficult.
[ ] I share their hobbies and interests.
[ ] We eat lunch together every Sunday.
[ ] We belong to the same denomination.
[ ] I insist that my parents respect my spouse.
[ ] I pray for my parents, and pray with them if possible.
[ ] I must always follow my parents' advice.
[ ] I listen courteously even if I don't plan to heed their advice.
[ ] _____

Think about your relationship with your parents. Are you fulfilling your obligation to honor your parents and model this ethic for your own children, or is something missing? *Write your thoughts below.*

_____
_____
_____
_____

MURDER
Exodus 20:13. Human life is so sacred in the eyes of God that anyone who unjustly takes another human life is subject to the ultimate penalty- the loss of his own life. God explained to Noah, "And for your lifeblood I will surely demand an accounting. I will demand an accounting from every animal. And from each man, too, I will demand an accounting for the life of his fellow man. Whoever sheds the blood of man, by man shall his blood be shed; for in the image of God has God made man."[43]

Fifteen hundred years before the birth of Christ, there is no professional army or police force to protect ordinary citizens- particularly those who are nomads wandering through desolate places. When an invading army must be defeated or a marauding criminal requires apprehension, God has authorized members of the community to act. Ordinary men must rise to take care of unpleasant tasks like these. *As a result, there are a variety of Hebrew words that denote killing.*

- The word *mut* is employed whenever the law requires that someone must be put to death either by a soldier or someone acting in an official capacity. For example, when God later directs King Saul to kill all the Amalekites because of their earlier attack on Israel, he uses this word. Saul is authorized to act justly on behalf of God and the community.[44]
- The fifth commandment uses the term *rasah*, which means to murder or kill someone in an unjust manner. It does not apply to the brother of an Old Testament murder victim who is authorized by God to avenge the manslayer. It does, however, apply to someone who commits manslaughter, killing someone unintentionally.

Read Genesis 4: 1 – 16. This is a particularly notable incident, involving not only the first siblings in the history of mankind, but the first murder as well. Reflect on the passage and ask yourselves questions about Cain's attitudes and resulting actions. *Then complete the questions that follow*:

- In one word, what is Cain's motive for slaying his brother?

  _____

- *v8.* How do we know Cain's act is premeditated rather than the result of sudden rage?

  _____

  _____

- *v11.* What does this rebuke from God reveal about the spiritual impact of murder within the governance and heart of the Almighty?

  _____

  _____

  _____

- *v13.* At this moment at the dawn of civilization, long before laws or governments have come to mind, Cain automatically assumes that people who encounter him will take his life. What does this reveal about his instinctive guilt?

  _____

  _____

  _____

- *v15-16.* Within a few generations, God will ordain the penalty of death for the crime of murder. And yet here, he puts a mark on Cain to ensure that he will not be punished,

Week Nine Loving Your Neighbor

but will be allowed to wander the earth outside of God's presence. *What's your best guess about God's motivation in this?*

_____

_____

_____

_____

Read Matthew 5:21-24. In the New Testament, Christ raises the bar. Not only is murder forbidden, but so is the offense of hatred or resentment. In terms of the tribe God desires to build, what makes enmity so destructive and unacceptable?

_____

_____

_____

_____

v23. Thinking in terms of tribe and community, why is reconciliation so important that it should precede our worship of God?

_____

_____

_____

Is there any trace of hatred or resentment in your heart today? Is there anyone who hurt you years ago whom you have simply tried to forget- to block out of your memory? Are there people you'd banish from your presence if you had the authority? Search your heart in prayer for a few minutes. If God reveals offensive individuals or areas that need your attention, jot them here.
    1.
    2.
    3.

Take a few minutes to commit yourself to act in faith as the Father has directed you. "Blessed are the peace makers, for they shall be called the children of God."[45]

Day 2: Adultery and the Failure of Faith
Read Exodus 20: 14-15; 2 Samuel 11: 1 – 12:14

Work on your memorization of the Ten Commandments. Then read the 2 Samuel passage prayerfully, using a pen or marker to highlight each key turning point in which the King allows his lustful desires to escalate to a more serious condition.

ADULTERY

Exodus 20:14. This commandment is about as simple and straightforward as you can get. God says "You must not commit adultery." There are no complex words here with shades of meaning. The Hebrew term translated "adultery" means just that.

For years, I assumed that our English words "adultery" and "adult" were somehow related to the same Latin root word. That seemed strange. Why would such obviously self-centered and irresponsible conduct be considered "adult" in any way? Then I did a bit of research and came across a surprise.

The English term 'adult' does indeed come from a Latin term: *adolescere*, meaning to grow up or become mature. We speak of adolescence as that distinct time when children begin moving more rapidly toward adulthood. But the English word 'adultery' is not rooted in the Latin. Rather the term comes from an old French word, *avoutrie*. It means "to corrupt." Adultery is a behavior that corrupts your character, your marriage, and your relationship with the Father. The action is a sexual one, but the word denotes not pleasure, but destruction. It's quite common that the individual caught up in the adulterous affair seems completely unable to grasp a fact that is crystal clear to mere bystanders: one's life is unraveling!

2 Samuel 11: 1 - 2. As this tragic episode begins to unravel, beloved King David overlooks symptoms of sin sickness in his own life that you and I can easily diagnose.

- *v1.* When David was just a lad with no professional obligations, he ran to the battle with Goliath. Explain why the behavior of this verse is so out of character for David. What does it reveal about his interior life?

_____

_____

_____

_____

_____

- *v2.* The Hebrew term *hereb*, means a specific time of day: early evening at sundown. If David is sleeping all afternoon and then rising at sunset to pace the roof of the palace like a caged tiger, what can we surmise about his attitudes and his thought life?

Week Nine Loving Your Neighbor

_____

_____

_____

_____

Unlike some other sins, adultery is not an impulsive, spur of the moment moral failure. Rather, this kind of behavior requires a defiant spirit that refuses to heed warnings or pause for spiritual evaluation. Explain how each of the following verses reveals a moment when David might have stopped the downward spiral and saved the life of a loyal friend.

- v3. _____
- v11. _____
- v13. _____

2 Samuel 12; 1 – 31. The king refuses to repent or even pause to consider how far he has fallen, so God dispatches a prophet. Briefly summarize the story Nathan narrates in order to get David's attention.

_____

_____

_____

_____

_____

Why do you think David immediately gauges the injustice in Nathan's story when he was utterly blind to his own evil behavior that has been much more offensive and destructive? Select the one most likely explanation from the following:

- [ ] The story is told by a man of God whom David respects.
- [ ] The story allows David to perceive the basic events uncomplicated by his own passion and personality.
- [ ] Because David was a shepherd during his childhood, he still cares a great deal about sheep and their treatment.
- [ ] David has been haunted by guilt and has been looking for an opportunity to come clean.

Why is it so much easier to spot sin in the life of another person, than to recognize it in your own life?

_____

_____

_____

Adultery is the betrayal and rejection of an entire range of people: a) your own spouse; b) the husband or wife of your partner in sin; c) your own children and those of your conspirator. It is also an affront to many other people who depend on your character for their jobs, or their own spiritual well being.

And yet when David writes about the guilt he has experienced as a result of his sin with Bathsheba, he makes a thought provoking confession. Speaking to God in *Psalm 51:4*, he confesses, "Against you, *you only*, have I sinned and done what is evil in your sight." How can you justify his statement that he has sinned against God alone?

_____

_____

_____

_____

In *Matthew 5: 27-28*, Christ teaches, "You have heard that it was said, 'Do not commit adultery." But I tell you that anyone who has looked at a woman lustfully has already committed adultery with her in his heart."

Christ does not elaborate on the definition of looking "with lust in the heart." How do you define that phrase? *Choose the answer that best fits your conviction:*
    ____ Enjoying an admiring glance
    ____ Looking a second time and thinking about sex
    ____ Staring in hopes the person will return your glance
    ____ Watching intently and planning a liaison

What are some intentional steps you can take in order to confront the sin while it's still in your mind? How does one avoid especially tempting situations?

   1. _____
   2. _____
   3. _____

How could an accountability partner who regularly asks hard questions about your interior life be an asset to you?

_____

_____

_____

THEFT
Exodus 20:15. Many of us think this simple command doesn't relate to us. Stealing sounds just so much like shop lifting, something most of us have never done or even wanted to do. When we're challenged to broaden our definition a bit, we commonly think about bringing pens and office supplies home from the place where we work. "Yes," we confess half-heartedly, "I am guilty of stealing from the office." In fact, while that may or may not be considered pilfering at the place where you work, God has more profound issues in mind than that.

I recently heard someone explain that the best way to gauge your driving skills is not by counting the number of wrecks you've had. Instead, the author explained, you should count the number of close calls you've had. If you're constantly escaping near misses, you're probably an unsafe driver even if you haven't sustained a crash recently.

Likewise, when you think about the temptation to steal, don't measure your vulnerability by actual thefts. Rather, examine the core attitudes in your life which bring you into close calls and near misses. Which of the following attitudes have surfaced in your life in recent years? (Check all that apply.)
   [ ] These rules apply to other people, but I'm special.
   [ ] It's not fair that other people have ____ and I don't.
   [ ] God helps those who help themselves.[46]
   [ ] It's easier to get forgiveness than permission.
   [ ] One way or the other, I will have one of those for myself.
   [ ] It may be wrong, but who cares?
   [ ] Yes, but everybody sins once in a while anyway.

Before theft becomes an action it begins with two corrupt attitudes that seep into my head and combine to create spontaneous combustion.

- I cannot trust God to provide what I need.
- If I need something, I have a right to take it.

In sharp contradiction are the two attitudes of faith. Read the following verses and briefly express the faith attitudes you and I must cultivate in our lives.

Matthew 6:31 – 34

_____

_____

- *Luke 6:38*

_____

_____

Personal Reflection: Why do you think American believers are so prone to confuse the things we "need" with the things we "want?"

_____

_____

_____

Do you agree that we in America have a sense of entitlement- an attitude that we are justified in demanding bigger houses, newer cars, more expensive clothes? If this is true, how do we square these expectations with the call of Christ to pick up a cross and follow Him?

_____

_____

_____

Is it possible to steal from God? If so, how does this happen?

_____

_____

Spiritual Growth Exercise: Try this once a week for the next four weeks. Identify one useful, practical item you can give away each week. This can range from a Bible or book to an envelope with money inside to a computer or a used car.

- What will you give away?
    1. _____
    2. _____

3. _____
4. _____

- Pray about the exercise, asking God to reveal the people to whom you should give these items, or the method by which you pass them along to those who need them. *Who are the some of the people, or how will you make the gifts?*

    1. _____
    2. _____
    3. _____
    4. _____

- Keep this in confidence between you, the recipients, and the Lord.

- Track the results in your own life. Do you miss the items/cash you gave away, or do you have a growing desire to do more?

A Closing Prayer
Read the following prayer over quietly. Make any changes or edits necessary in order to make it your own. Then kneel in a quiet, out of the way place and read this back to God.

Father, I praise you for your Grace, and for the generous way you deal with me. Paul promised us, "My God will meet all your needs according to His glorious riches in Christ." This has always been my experience with you.

I thank you for calling me into your family, and for making a way through Christ. I thank you for placing me here with a purpose, and for equipping me to be your hands. The richest moments in my life have been those occasions when I have found myself in service to you.

May I never steal your glory by pampering myself with life's riches. Help me to never contradict the promises you make by the way I live. Help me to be lavish toward you and your Kingdom, rather than my own desires and creature comforts. Convict me anytime this week I behave in a selfish way. And help me to live as a river that sends the wealth downstream to others. Forgive me for the times I have lived like a reservoir, storing up your riches merely for myself and my benefit.

Day 3: Hurtful Tongues and Hungry Eyes
Read Exodus 20: 16-17; Numbers 16: 1 – 15
Read both passages carefully, allowing the message to sink in. Take a few minutes to firm up your memorization of the Ten Commandments. Ask someone to check them off as you recite them. Then work through the questions that follow.

SLANDER & GOSSIP
Exodus 20: 16. You shall not give false _____ against your neighbor.

I find that people often miss the point when they think of the ninth commandment. It's a very direct statement and yet it seems that most people interpret this as a warning against lies and dishonesty. In fact, this commandment deals with an affront even more serious and damaging than merely lying.

Think about it: Abram lied about Sarai[47] when he told the king of Egypt she was his sister, rather than risking his life and admitting she was his wife.[48] God rescued Sarai, enriched Abram, and no one seemed the worse for it. Before the Israelites crossed the Jordan, Rahab lied about the whereabouts of the Hebrew spies in order to save their lives.[49] The spies escaped to inform their countrymen who successfully invaded Jericho and spared Rahab and her family. During the reign of King Saul, David pretended to be insane while living in Gath to escape Saul's dragnet.[50] David's comments to King Achish while feigning madness were certainly a form of dishonesty, but God spared David's life and the lie was never mentioned again.

Don't misunderstand. Lying when lives are not at risk is unethical, and Scripture is clear that God hates a lying tongue,[51] but the ninth commandment does not forbid all forms of lying. In fact, even the "lying tongue" in the proverb just cited has one particular kind of lie in mind. God commands that you must never give false, destructive testimony about your neighbor.

Numbers 16: 1 – 15. Do you remember Aaron's rod- the one that budded and was ultimately saved as Testimony to the Lord? One historic event produced the blossoms and almonds on that rod overnight. Here's the rest of the story.

Exodus closes with the Israelites departing Mount Sinai with the Ten Commandments in hand, and with the Tabernacle providing God a place to rest among them. Numbers picks up the story and explains why God ultimately adds another forty years to their estimated time of arrival. However, in this incident, some of the priests are attempting to foment an uprising by slandering Moses.
- *v3.* The leaders give their rationale for opposing Moses. Why is this charge against Moses invalid?

- *v13.* Why is this characterization of riches in Egypt so dishonest?

- *v14.* Why is this accusation disingenuous?

The human heart can deceive us, can't it? Korah and his followers know in their heads that all these accusations are bogus. What drives them to such slander and exaggeration?

God gives Israel only six commands for living in healthy community and building a united nation. We generally understand why murder, theft and adultery must be forbidden by healthy nations. Why is slander so significant that it is also included among those six?

In what ways is slander similar to murder?

Can you remember the most recent occasion when you allowed yourself to be drawn into a gossip-based conversation?

- Did you know from the first moment that you were stepping into sin, or did a healthy conversation suddenly go south?

- What motive led you to remain in the discussion after you realized it was slanderous?
  [ ] I was angry at the person who was being criticized.
  [ ] I was having a bad day and it felt good to hash over another person's problems.
  [ ] I was deflecting possible criticism of my own mistakes.
  [ ] I was trying to earn chips and make a good impression on someone else in the conversation.
  [ ] I did not want to look like some Holy Joe by walking away.
  [ ] I was too insecure to defend the victim or suggest there might be more to the story.
  [ ] The conversation was juicy and it seemed like fun at the time.
  [ ] Other _____

- Looking back, how could you have handled the situation in a more Christ-like manner?

  _____

  _____

  _____

COVETOUSNESS

Exodus 20:17. You shall not covet your neighbor's house, or his wife, or his servants, or his livestock, or _____
_____

A number of Hebrew verbs can be translated "to desire" or "to want" something.
- *Bahar* means to prefer something. In other words, I can have what's behind Door #1 or what's behind the curtain.
- *Hepes* means to delight or take pleasure in. Proverbs 3:15 comments, "Nothing you can desire compares to her (wisdom.)"

The tenth commandment incorporates the term *hamad*, which means "to lust," "to take great pleasure in," "to passionately long for." In other words, this is far more intense than walking into a palace and casually thinking, "I wish I had a house like this!" To covet something that does not belong to you is to burn inwardly for that person or object, to devote a great deal of thought to it.

This is perhaps the commandment that is most easily violated, for this sin can begin with something as innocent as working online when a well-timed advertisement pops onto your screen. It can take root in a mundane situation as innocuous as shopping with a neighbor or taking a stroll through a car dealership or a marina. That's right, the merchants who own all those consumer goods and expensive machines you fantasize about are also numbered among your "neighbors."

Week Nine Loving Your Neighbor

A secular person might argue that coveting is a victimless crime because it's all in your head. Who is the victim of this sin, and why is it ranked with such destructive acts as murder, theft and adultery?

_____

_____

_____

_____

Read *Romans 7: 4 – 8*. Paul explains that we have died to the Law so that we can live in the Spirit.

- *v5.* How could the law actually arouse sinful passions? In other words, when I command you not to think about an elephant, why does your mind immediately produce a pachyderm?

_____

_____

_____

- *v6.* Practically speaking, how does one "die" to the things that once bound him?

_____

_____

_____

Q: Would you agree that covetousness/materialism is one of the most insidious and prevalent sins that afflicts believers in the USA? What unique conditions contribute to this problem?

_____

_____

_____

_____

Why are materialism and surrender to Christ mutually exclusive?

_____

_____

_____

Practically speaking, what must you do in order to die to the temptation to covet material things? From the following areas of discipline, select one that seems most essential for you at this moment in your walk:

    [ ] I must cultivate a life and a set of priorities that are simple and less self-indulgent.
    [ ] I must dramatically cut back on my use of credit to purchase consumer goods and non-essentials.
    [ ] I must cultivate the disciplines of fasting and sacrificial giving.
    [ ] I must sell my unusually expensive house or automobiles, and acquire something more practical and less wasteful.
    [ ] Other _____

_____

Spiritual Exercise: Believe it or not, I'm going to ask you to watch an hour of television. You can do this in one session or two, and can build this time around your favorite shows or just watch something randomly.

- Count the number of commercials that are broadcast in that hour.
- Concisely evaluate each commercial along these lines:
  - ✓ Product: _____
  - ✓ What image is associated with the item? (i.e. sexuality, success, popularity, etc.) _____
  - ✓ What is the implied reason I should make this purchase? (i.e. become more beautiful, more successful, happier, etc.)

_____

_____

- How many of the commercials promise things they truly cannot deliver?

_____

- Do most advertisers seem to believe consumers are complex and rational, or merely superficial and emotional?

    _____

How does God's vision for your life differ from the lifestyle encouraged by most television advertisers? Prayerfully list some of the differences.
1. God desires _____
   while TV encourages_____
2. God desires _____
   while TV encourages_____
3. God desires _____
   while TV encourages_____
4. God desires _____
   while TV encourages_____

Day 4: Precautions Against Sin
Read Exodus 20: 18 - 26
Read this passage several times. Use a pen or marker to indicate words or phrases that indicate either a fear or God or a reverence for the Almighty. Work on your memorization of the Ten Commandments for a few minutes. Then proceed through this session.

I wish I could remember the name of my seminary professor who first made this simple but insightful comment to my class. He explained, "It's very common today for church people to treat sin like a deep, deadly chasm we can see just ahead. We know it's deadly, but we're curious. So we make it a practice to discover how closely we can approach the edge of the chasm without falling in. But in fact, because the chasm is so deadly and precipitous, it is the goal of our Heavenly Father that we should strive to see how far removed from sin we can keep ourselves- *without even being tempted to draw near!*"

Exodus 20: 18 – 21. That idea about staying far from the chasm is one explanation for all the drama and fireworks associated with Mount Sinai, isn't it?

v19. What emotion or sensation leads to the people's preference that Moses should instruct them rather than God?

_____

_____

_____

_____

v20. In just a few words, Moses explains God's motives. What is God's purpose here?

_____

_____

_____

v21. Why does the Lord employ the possibility of violent death to keep the Israelites observing all this from a respectful distance?

_____

_____

_____

20: 22 - 26. This section of the chapter at first seems obscure and almost insignificant. In fact, God establishes a critical principle here. He clearly prefers that the Jews offer their sacrifices on rudimentary altars of earth or stacked stones. He insists that they must not use blades or other instruments to shape the altar or the stones they use to erect it. Why would God be so wary of attempts at craftsmanship in building altars of worship?

_____

_____

_____

_____

While you and I no longer build altars for sacrifices to God, there is an underlying principle here. Summarize that spiritual precaution below:

_____

_____

_____

Read *1 Timothy 1: 3 – 11.*
Why does Paul insist that some extremely interesting religious conversations are harmful and confusing rather than helpful and edifying?

_____

Week Nine   Loving Your Neighbor

_____
_____

1 Timothy 1: 8-9. Paul admits that the Law is not for people who have obtained righteousness! Rather, it is for a different group of people. Who are the people for whom the Law is intended?

_____
_____

Why should a follower of Jesus Christ teach the Ten Commandments to his/her small children?

_____
_____
_____

Read Galatians 3: 19 – 24.
Amazing! The Ten Commandments did not make the wandering Israelites more righteous as individuals. Fact is, these ten little commandments were extremely hard to keep. What the commandments did accomplish was to teach the people about God and establish a higher standard of living for the people of God. They would not always be morally perfect, but they would recognize a higher, more eternal calling to which they had been summoned- one that would require divine assistance to fulfill.

Summarize the key ideas of Galatians 3 by filling in these blanks.
- v19. The Law was put in effect by angels in order to _____.
- v23. The whole world was filled with _____ locked up until _____ could be revealed.
- v24. The Law was put in charge to _____ us to Christ.
- v25. Now that faith has come, we are no longer under the _____ of the Law.

Read Galatians 5: 16 – 18.
What does Paul mean when he insists that if we live in the Spirit, we will not gratify the sins of the flesh?

_____
_____
_____

Practically speaking, how does a believer become more proficient at walking in the Spirit? In my own life, I have found these elements to be critical:
- Consistent prayer, often several times a day;
- Periods of being still, listening for God's small still voice;
- Waiting on the Lord to take the first step or offer guidance when much is at stake;
- Acting quickly when I receive an impulse from the Spirit.

Years ago, I served as pastor of a rapidly growing church that found it necessary to relocate to larger facilities four miles away. The process of leading the church in this direction was long and sometimes controversial. And along the way, one extremely inflexible church member came to truly resent me. Over the course of a couple of years, she made her low appraisal of me clear to anyone who cared to listen.

One morning as I was praying in my office, the Holy Spirit brought this lady to my mind and prompted me to call on her. As you can imagine, the very idea was so unpleasant that I postponed it for a bit. But before the morning was over, I finally relented and accepted the Spirit's guidance. I drove over to the frustrated woman's house and nervously knocked on her door.

When she finally appeared, there were tears in her eyes. She looked at me in surprise and finally asked, "How did you know?"

It turned out that she'd received a telephone call about two hours earlier notifying her that her elderly mother who lived in another state had passed away suddenly. Not expecting such news, the lady from our church had been too emotionally devastated to call any of her friends. She had sat there, grieving bitterly in solitude, until the Holy Spirit summoned her "insensitive" pastor to drop in and pray for her.

The Holy Spirit can also sound some extraordinarily loud warning buzzers in your life when sin is crouching at your door. No wonder Paul encourages us to walk continually in step with the Spirit.

Q: How can you be more intentional about listening for the Spirit, and walking in sync with him?

_____

_____

_____

_____

WEEK TEN

A FOUNDATION THAT ENDURES

Do not be surprised that you fall every day; do not give up, but stand your ground courageously. And assuredly, the angel who guards you will honor your patience. -John of the Ladder

One of the most striking features of the House Chamber in the US Capitol is the collection of marble relief portraits of history's most celebrated lawgivers. Located just above the gallery doors, they include the faces of Justinian, Hammurabi, George Mason and a host of other well known historical figures. Of the twenty-three faces, twenty-two are shown in profile.

Only one is depicted face forward, and his countenance is prominently positioned at the center of the room, gazing down onto the desk occupied by the Speaker of the House. This is the face of Moses, honored here in the House Chamber as history's Greatest Lawgiver.

People who have grown up in an orderly nation of laws can easily take the Law of Moses for granted. We don't always agree with the verdicts returned in celebrated cases of our day, and judges sometimes seem completely out of touch with the real world. But with all its warts and blemishes, our system of justice generally keeps us safe and holds offenders accountable. It could be better, but it still works!

The world in which Moses followed God could not have been more different. There were no legislative bodies to hammer out laws, just as there were no police departments to enforce them. Civil rights emanated from affluence and influence, so wealthy, privileged men had more rights than almost anybody else. If you wanted something and had the means to take it from someone else, that was generally expected. And if a stranger murdered your brother, it was the responsibility of your family to track him down and impose justice on him.

Communities were ruled by tribal chieftains who could render life changing decisions based on an impulse. You could be whipped if you were caught stealing something. Or you could have your hand chopped off. But if you were foolish enough to steal from someone with connections to the chief, you might be eligible for the death penalty!

God's principle of "an eye for an eye, and a tooth for a tooth" may sound harsh or even brutal in our era, but in the lifetime of Moses, it was an amazing breakthrough! For the first time, a nation established that the penalty imposed by justice should be proportional to the crime. If someone accidentally killed your ox, you could demand his prize ox or have that animal killed as well. But you could not slaughter his entire herd and burn down his house in a fit of rage! If a neighbor's carelessness caused you to lose an arm, justice could demand that his arm be cut off. But you could not torture and murder his entire family before executing him on the spot.

The Law of Moses raised the bar to require that justice must be measured. In keeping things proportional, God not only established that offenders had certain rights as well, but deliberately interrupted the cycle of violence which could lead to generational feuds as families responded to one injustice with another and another.

Of course, the tricky part of fashioning new laws for a society is in knowing when to stop. Over the centuries, virtually every law-making body has occasionally gone to extremes attempting to regulate the most minute and insignificant offenses. This very human tendency has resulted in tens of thousands of comical and outrageous laws like the following, many of which are still on record:

- In one American city, it is illegal for a barber to threaten to cut off a child's ears.
- In another city, it's against the law to make a monkey smoke a cigarette.
- One municipality forbids a driver from backing into a parking space as this prevents law enforcement from seeing the license plate.
- A town in Ohio prohibits women from wearing patent leather shoes lest men see the reflection of their underwear.
- Numerous cities and states make it illegal for four or five women to live in the same house.

All this is very human, isn't it? But what if you could read a set of laws decreed by the One True God of Eternity? In that case, you would probably expect those divinely inspired laws to be wise, clearly ahead of their time, and accompanied by reasonable penalties. And you would not expect to find one silly, quirky, irrelevant ordinance among them.

Guess what? You are about to spend some time studying a set of laws ordained by the Most High God. Not surprisingly, you will find them to be precisely what you would expect of divine legislation: wisdom, prescience, proportional penalties, and not one silly, outrageous ringer in the whole lot.

Nations that enjoy the order and stability of the rule of law owe a great debt to Moses and the Lord God who taught him. The Ten Commandments and the laws of Moses were a brilliant and unprecedented light shining into a world where the power of government was either completely unlimited in some regions, and non-existent in others.

You've probably never studied this particular set of laws of guiding principles before. You might have even assumed they were mere technicalities with nothing to say to us in the twenty-first century. In that case, you're in for a big surprise.

This week we'll be answering questions like these:

- Day 1: How have the ideas of Moses impacted our own view of justice and civil rights today?
- Day 2: What does it say about the kind of character God desires to cultivate in his people when he orders us not to boil a young goat in its mother's milk? Is there any relevance here for us today?
- Day 3: Why did God position Israel in their current location and what can we learn from them about living up to God's calling?
- Day 4: Do American believers sometimes miss the glory of God because we demand something instant and flashy, while God's priorities call for something eternal that develops more slowly?

Day 1: The Promise of Justice in an Unjust World
Read Exodus 21
Read this text carefully and thoughtfully. Use a pen or marker to indicate laws which strike you as demonstrating an advanced understanding of human nature. Look for offenses for which the penalty depends on the circumstances surrounding the crime. Indicate these with a check mark or asterisk in the margins.

21: 1 – 11. It is misleading to approach Old Testament slavery from our enlightened perspective two thousand years *after* Jesus Christ changed the world. We enjoy a highly developed sense of God-given liberties, leading most nations to expand the definition of civil rights every decade. Fifteen hundred years *before* Christ, however, the sinful world operated around the un-democratic idea that might makes right, and only the strongest survive.

The human race was far less numerous and much more scattered when the Hebrews departed Egypt. There was no mass communication to advise people in famine areas that conditions were better in distant places. And when news from afar finally reached a hungry population, there was no speedy mass transit to get them safely to the nearest pocket of prosperity. In a world with no social safety net for the most desperate souls, slavery was preferable to dying of starvation.

The Hebrews did not invent slavery. Their experience in Egypt reminds us that the bitterest forms of slavery had been around for centuries by the time Moses was born. However, the Law of Moses breaks dramatic new ground in this area of human relations.
- Slaves have always been regarded as "livestock" or possessions. For the first time, God establishes that slaves are human beings who have rights.
- The conditions of slavery had always been dependent on the desires and impulses of the slave owner. *For the first time anywhere,* God regulates slavery, setting up conditions and guidelines requiring reasonable treatment.

As you read this passage, recall that there are numerous forms of legal slavery here at the dawn of civilization. In the absence of our more recent idea of paid employment, **voluntary servitude** allowed a person to sell himself or members of his family for a limited period of time in order to take care of a financial obligation. (Fathers commonly sold themselves and sometimes sold their children.) **Involuntary servitude** involved people whose nations were defeated in battle by stronger neighbors. In the wake of military conquest, vanquished citizens generally lost their property rights, their liberty, and oftentimes their lives. Being taken captive was an agonizing life change, but it kept alive the possibility of a second chance and a new life.

Now, read the passage and answer questions like these:
- *v2.* A Hebrew can only sell himself for _____ years, and must be allowed to depart at the beginning of the next year.
- *v3,4.* Under what conditions was a freed slave not allowed to take his family with him, at least immediately?

_____

_____

- *v7.* As you interpret this text, remember that marriage is generally an economic arrangement in the world of Moses, and buying a slave is one legal way of acquiring a wife for oneself or one's heirs. (*Even a man who marries a free woman has to offer her family a dowry of cattle and livestock in exchange for her.*) Once again, God did not invent the system, but does begin to regulate it to guard the people most at risk.
- *v8.* In what way does God demonstrate his love for a Jewish woman in slavery when he forbids an unhappy owner from selling her to foreigners?

_____

_____

- *v10, 11* If a man fails to provide a slave/wife with food, clothing, and the rights that accompany marriage, what civil right does God grant her?

_____

_____

20:12 – 36. Moses outlines a very practical guide for personal liability and the assessment of damages caused by the actions of a neighbor. Look for ways in which God raises the bar for conduct among his people, but be careful not to expect twenty-first century civil rights some 3500 years previous.
- *v12.* What is the penalty for deliberately and unjustly taking another human life?

_____

- What does this penalty say about the value of human life in the eyes of society?

_____

Week Ten   A Foundation that Endures

- *v13.* What form of mercy is allowed for the one who accidentally or unintentionally causes the death of another human being?

- *v17.* This sounds harsh to us, of course. But at the dawn of a new society, why might God assign such a serious penalty to dishonoring ones parents?

- *v18.* Why is there a choice of penalties for someone who strikes another person with a stone or blunt object?

- *v20.* It offends us that nothing happens to a man who beats his slave if the victim recovers in a day or two. But what divine principle does God establish when he denies a man the right to kill a slave he has purchased with his own resources?

- *v22- 25.* Did you notice the subject under consideration when God issues his standard for justice- *an eye for an eye, a tooth for a tooth?* The victim is a pregnant woman who has been injured inadvertently by two men during a fight. If she gives birth prematurely and the child is injured, the penalty to the offenders is proportionate to what happens to the child- life for life, eye for eye, tooth for tooth. In a world where children are treated as possessions that can be abandoned or sacrificed to pagan deities, what does God establish about the life of an unborn child?

21:28-36. God reinforces the sanctity of human life by citing common occurrences involving valuable livestock and agricultural practices. Review these verses and answer the questions that follow. Check as many answers as apply.

- What is the point of killing the bull who merely acted instinctively?
    - [ ] It allows the victim's family to act out their rage without killing an innocent person.
    - [ ] The principle of justice demands that a sacred human life must be avenged to balance the scales.
    - [ ] Savagery demands savagery.
    - [ ] It underscores the fact that a human life is more valuable than an animal's life.

- What is the connotation of leaving the dead carcass uneaten?
    - [ ] It underscores that the loss of a human life should not be treated casually or routinely.
    - [ ] Consuming the meat would transfer guilt to anyone who ate the animal.
    - [ ] The bull's death should have no other value than simple justice.
    - [ ] The meat will be given to the victim's survivors.

- If the owner should have kept the bull penned, he must be stoned as well. But if the bull has never been violent before, the owner merely pays a fine to the family. *What message does this send to the Israelites?*
    - [ ] If you knowingly allow another human being to die unjustly, you also share in the guilt.
    - [ ] Overpopulation has always been a concern in the mind of God.
    - [ ] Animals are inexpensive and easy to replace.
    - [ ] Even if you could not have anticipated the tragedy, justice demands that you compensate the family for the damage done by your bull.

- Why should a man be penalized if he innocently digs a ditch and a careless ox falls into it and must be put down?
    - [ ] Animal rights are more important than property rights.
    - [ ] The animal's owner has suffered a loss and the farmer should have covered the ditch as a precaution.
    - [ ] By addressing the owner's loss, the law precludes further violence that might ensue if the wronged man nurses a grudge against the farmer.
    - [ ] Digging ditches is criminal behavior.

- If one man's bull kills the livestock of another man, the offending bull must be put to death. What principle is at stake here?
    - [ ] The importance of animal sacrifice
    - [ ] The right to own private property
    - [ ] The right to life
    - [ ] The right to equal justice if the choices of another person somehow result in the loss of your rights

Q: How have the principles God revealed to Moses dramatically affected the way we understand justice and civil rights today? How is our view of justice different from the world before Moses?

___

Day 2: Human Relations Department
Read Exodus 22 – 23: 19
Read these chapters a couple of times, looking for the principles that underlie each of the laws and required penalties. When there are contrasting penalties for the same offense, ask why. Use a pen or marker to indicate offenses related to money or monetary value.

Exodus 22: 1 – 5. Be on the look-out for ideas which are very familiar to us but would have shocked or surprised the Israelites to whom Moses was speaking.

v2. Breaking into someone's house for the purpose of robbery is penalized much more serious after dark than it is during the day. (The owner is not accountable for murdering a thief who breaks in at night.) Why is breaking into a home by night treated more seriously?

___

v3b-4. A thief who has no funds to repay his victim must be sold as a slave in order to satisfy the demands of justice. Why aren't offenders like these simply placed in jail?

___

If you are stumped, consult Exodus 40:36-38.

v7- 13. What sorts of cases require the intervention of the judges appointed earlier by Moses?

___

v15. How does this law protect a less wealthy Israelite from an unscrupulous neighbor?

_____

_____

_____

Exodus 22: 16 – 31. These ordinances deal with a variety of unrelated offenses involving sex, sorcery and shekels.

v16 - 17. If a man seduces a young woman to whom he is not pledged to be married, why must he pay a dowry to her family even if she is not allowed to marry him?

_____

_____

_____

v18. At this formative moment in the development of Israel, why would God deal so harshly with a sorceress?

_____

_____

_____

_____

v19 -20. We now understand why a nomadic people living in tents could not lock offenders up in jail. But why not banish such offenders and force them to leave camp, rather than executing them?

_____

_____

_____

_____

If you need help, consult Genesis 21: 14 – 16.

Week Ten A Foundation that Endures

v21. How would you explain God's sympathy for immigrants who are abused in a strange land?

_____

v22 - 23. Why is God so sensitive to the plight of widows and orphans, as he was to Rahab and Ishmael when they were banished unmercifully to the desert?

_____

_____

If you aren't sure, see Psalm 68:5.

v25 – 27. God encourages his people to be merciful to others, especially when another Israelite is in need. Two things are forbidden here. List them:

v25. _____

v26. _____

_____

v28. Why is cursing the leader of your country equated with the act of dishonoring God?

_____

_____

_____

If you are uncertain, consult Romans 13: 1.

v29. This warning is actually a reminder that Israel is in store for a homeland and a productive future. It doesn't even apply to this moment in the life of Israel. *Why?*

_____

_____

If you don't know the answer, consult Exodus 40:36-38 again.

v31. What is the most likely reason for the ban against eating the meat of an animal torn by wild beasts? *See Leviticus 17:15.*

_____

_____

Exodus 23: 1 – 19. Here Moses calls the people of God to distinguish themselves from their pagan neighbors by not only seeking justice, but by being people of integrity and mercy.

v1 – 3. The people of God are to be intentional in their honesty, even when it seems more profitable to shade the truth.
- They should not assist a wicked man by sharing a false testimony.
- They should be truthful even when it means going against peer pressure.
- They should not stretch the truth in order to assist a poor man who happens to be the underdog in a conflict.

v4 – 9. If a Jew discovers an enemy's ox has strayed, he should return it to his enemy. If he comes upon someone whose donkey has fallen under its load, he should assist the neighbor in getting the donkey back to its feet, even if this particular neighbor despises him. This sets the precedent for the words of Christ which will come much later: "You have heard that it was said, 'Love your neighbor and hate your enemy.' But I say to you, 'Love your enemies, and pray for those who persecute you that you may be sons of your Father in Heaven.'"[52] The Jews had most certainly heard that it was acceptable to hate their enemies, but they hadn't heard it from Moses!

v10-11. What does God reveal about the kind of character he aspires to develop in his people when he commands them to allow even their most fertile soil to rest every seventh year?

_____

_____

_____

_____

v12. In this directive, God expands on the fourth commandment. In addition to allowing a devout Jew to rest and reflect, what other benefits does the Sabbath rest bestow?

_____

_____

_____

_____

v14 – 19. It is easy to overlook the radical form of faith God requires in a command that sounds quite harmless to us.
- Imagine an ancient world in which enemies are constantly spying on their neighbors looking for moments of weakness: the death of a king, a disaster, any sort of event distracting from self-defense.
- If all the males convene in one central place on a designated occasion three times annually, what sort of opening will that provide predatory neighboring nations along the borders?

Week Ten A Foundation that Endures

- How will obedience in this command demonstrate faith in the Lord God?

v19-b. I must confess this particular tenet of the Law seemed for a while like it might be the first example of pettiness or over-reach in the Laws of God. At first, I couldn't explain it, but I maintain this deep, abiding conviction that every word of God is flawless, and that it is a shield to those who take refuge in him.[53] Over the years, I have come to realize that whenever a passage in God's Word seems really tricky or difficult to explain; if I search, and pray, and sometimes just relax to give God time to teach me, I eventually discover that the difficult text is rich with insight and meaning.

So I thought about this whole concept of not boiling a young goat in its mother's milk. I prayed about it, wondering what sort of mercy or reverence for the Lord this odd prohibition might demonstrate. Providentially, I came across a rabbinic website called Kolel.org. The scholars there drew an interesting comparison that was new to me.

There are other "odd" commands through the Pentateuch that are similar to the ban on cooking a baby goat in its mother's milk. One text commands that an Israelite must not slaughter an adult cow and its offspring on the same day.[54] Yet another scripture directs that if a Jew discovers a bird's nest with fresh eggs inside, he may take the eggs, but must not harm the mother.[55]

Together, these passages reveal a Creator God who allows us to take full advantage of the bounty of the world he has given us, but who expects us to show reverence for life. Only human life is sacred, because only man is made in God's image. But even as we are permitted to take the lives of animals for meat, leather, and other necessities, God expects us to do it with reverence for the one who gave us life. God's people should be the last people in all the earth to treat lesser life in a callous or cavalier manner.

Q: It's easy to mock fringe radicals like PETA[56] who equate the life of a frog or a spider with the life of a human being. That is clearly an ignorant and unbiblical position. But how should a follower of Jesus Christ demonstrate an appreciation for the divine origins of all life *without drifting into the error of Pantheism?*

_____

_____

_____

_____

_____

_____

Day 3: The Angel and the Inheritance
Read Exodus 23:19 - 32
Read this short passage and then review it. Use a pen or marker to indicate phrases in which God promises to take care of one problem or another through his sovereign power. Ask yourself what is the single most important thing God desires to communicate in this particular text.

Exodus 23: 20 – 26. God begins to lay out his strategy for planting his chosen people in the sacred land he has chosen for them. No longer will there be a pillar of clouds by day and a column of fire at night. Instead God will speak to Israel through an angel, presumably with Moses as the intermediary. If the Israelites pay attention to the directions offered by the angel, God will cause them to prosper and will bring them to the Land of Canaan, a place he had in mind for them before the world began.

23:20. As God speaks to the Israelites at Mount Sinai, the Land of Canaan awaits them hundreds of miles north and slightly east. The terminology God uses here is quite revealing. He doesn't say "I will send my angel before you who will take you to the place I have prepared." Rather, God says the angel will *bring* you to the land I have prepared for you." *What does this reveal about the Almighty?*

_____

_____

_____

_____

Week Ten A Foundation that Endures

If the Canaanite tribes are still embedded in their homeland, what must God mean by the phrase "the land I have prepared for you?"

_____

_____

_____

v22-23. God assures the people of Israel that if they will observe the principles and precepts offered by his angel, the Almighty will go before them as the enemy of their enemies.
- Notice that these people waiting ahead are all tribes related to a larger family called the Canaanites.
- Read *Genesis 10:15.* Who is their common ancestor? _____
- Read *Genesis 9:22-25.* Who is his father? _____
- Read *Joshua 15:8.* When we speak the name "Jerusalem," which tribe do we inadvertently remember? _____

v24-26. There is a fascinating comparison here. The angel of the Lord will go before the Israelites to break up and destroy the people who live in Canaan. But once the Israelites arrive safely, what are they commanded to break up and destroy?

_____

v27-28. Notice the extremely visual language employed by the Lord as he describes how He will divinely clear the path for Israel's arrival in Canaan. He promises to send "the hornet" ahead of them.

The hornets of Palestine are larger than ours in North America, and they are intensely aggressive. Much like the African Killer bees that infested the American Southwest a generation ago, desert hornets travel in noisy swarms and don't hesitate to attack. They have been credited with driving livestock insane through their furious assaults, and have sometimes killed large animals.

I can vividly recall a Saturday afternoon when my son and I were mowing the lawn and trimming our front yard when I drove the mower over a yellow jacket nest in the ground. Yellow jackets are not nearly as large or terrifying as hornets, but within seconds, I was off the mower racing across the yard with my son close behind! That's a mild version of the image being conveyed in *verse 27* when God speaks of the terror he will send ahead of his people. The bottom line is not that they will have to fight, but that they will simply have to go forward in faith.

v29-30. God promises the process of driving the Canaanites out of the land will be gradual rather than instant. *Why?*

_____

_____

v31. The Sea of the Philistines is another name for the Mediterranean Sea. What are the borders of the land God will deliver over to Israel?
- From the Sea of Reeds to the Mediterranean;
- From the desert to the Jordan River.

This is a very small corner of land, and Israel will never actually occupy even all of this. Locate a world map and you can't miss the fact that Israel is a tiny nation, surrounded by much larger nations like Egypt, Saudi Arabia, Iran and Iraq. These aren't nearly the largest nations on Earth, but Israel is a tiny sliver of land even compared to them.

Now pause here and catch a big thought you might have never entertained before. Think about all the great civilizations throughout history that have risen to power, using their riches and weapons to expand their borders by conquering all their neighbors. Egypt did it. Assyria and Babylon each captured a large share of the world during their glory days. Alexander the Great spread the Greek Empire until he came to the sea and wept that he had no more lands to conquer. The Romans dominated the world with their sprawling Empire. And this doesn't even take into account the ambitions of men who would come later- Napoleon, Hitler, and Stalin.

How many world class powers of history can you name who never attempted to conquer their neighbors and grow their borders as far as possible? There's really only one: *Israel*.
- Granted, God will drive out the inhabitants of Canaan to give His people this one small slice of land.
- But once the homeland is established, the borders will change little over all the centuries, and Israel will never threaten peaceful neighbors.

It might be useful to pause here and take a bird's eye view of God's original purpose for His chosen people.
- *Review Exodus 19: 3-6.* The term "treasured possession" clearly denotes a role for Israel that involves privilege and blessings. But what kind of role do phrases like "kingdom of priests" and "holy nation" require?

_____

_____

_____

_____

Week Ten A Foundation that Endures

- *Read Isaiah 58: 5-9.* While the wayward people of Israel might prefer to offer up some symbolic outward piety as tokens of their faith, what sort of religious fervor does God desire?

   _____
   _____
   _____

- When the people of Israel become involved in the work of rescuing the oppressed, feeding the hungry, and showing mercy to those in need, what kind of impact does the Lord God promise?

   _____
   _____
   _____
   _____

- *Read 1 Kings 10: 1 – 13.* Why does the Queen of Sheba visit King Solomon's court?

   _____
   _____

- According to *1 Kings 10: 23-24*, what impact does the glory of Israel have on the neighboring nations?

   _____
   _____
   _____

Q: Historically, church people have commonly been tempted to settle for religious behaviors and a certain level of morality, rather than genuinely sacrificing to rescue the hopeless and the hurting, as well as being moral people. *Why do you believe this is so often the case?*

   _____
   _____
   _____
   _____

Personal Assessment: Which of the following are generally true in your life?
- ___ Whenever people share a personal prayer request I follow through and pray for them every time.
- ___ I have practically assisted someone in need during the last 7 days.
- ___ I financially support at least one ministry or relief organization in addition to giving my tithes and offerings to my local church.
- ___ I sometimes have a twinge of anxiety about whether I am saving enough or if I'm too generous with needy people around me.
- ___ I contribute small amounts of cash on the spot with no expectation of a tax deduction.
- ___ I have asked God to bless me with even greater resources so that I can be more helpful to other people in need.
- ___ I find that God has increased my resources, so that I have become more generous in meeting spiritual and human needs around me.
- ___ I make it a habit of leaving generous tips at restaurants so that I can leave my server a gospel tract as well.
- ___ I have occasionally noticed I've collected too many Bibles at home, so I have given some away.
- ___ I have on occasion visited a food distribution center or homeless shelter to help out and get a better sense of human need in my area.

What do you imagine it will look like when your light finally breaks through like the dawn, and when your righteousness will shine like the noonday sun?

_____

_____

_____

_____

_____

_____

Week Ten A Foundation that Endures

Day 4: Into the Clouds
Read Exodus 24
Read this chapter with care, trying to imagine the scene. Highlight or underscore each use of numbers in the passage. Pause and ask what God might have in mind with these numerical values.

Less than ninety days ago, before these dramatic events at Mount Sinai, Moses stood before the mightiest king on the face of the Earth. The walls of the palace in Memphis were lined with gold, precious stones, and elaborate artwork. Armed soldiers stood at the Pharaoh's right and left hands, poised to defend him. And the ruler himself, regarded as divine, was decked out in gold and jewels, resting on a massive throne of hammered gold. Moses could stand in the presence of the great king with no preparation more elaborate than having a herald announce his arrival.

How different things are on this day as the weary prophet prepares to climb Mount Sinai for a personal audience with the Most High God. There have already been fireworks and earthquakes, smoke and clouds, and the thundering voice of the Almighty echoing from the mount. But even those awe inspiring and fearsome experiences cannot match what will happen next. Moses and the elders are just hours away from a mountaintop experience so unique that it occurs only once in the entire Bible. Isaiah, Ezekiel and Daniel will one day recount visions of the Eternal God, but Moses and his men will behold an eternal spectacle unfolding in real time and real space.

Before we climb Sinai with Moses, it will be helpful to give ourselves a quick refresher course in Hebrew numeric meanings. In the Hebrew mindset, many primary numbers are also intricately linked with a theological ideal. For instance:
- 3 denotes God, His presence, His authority
- 5 is associated with grace or God's divine generosity
- 6 speaks of the incomplete, ambitious nature of man
- 7 represents perfection or completeness
- 10 is associated with government or governing authority
- 12 denotes the tribe, the church, the community of God

Exodus 24: 1 – 7. It might be useful to begin this chapter by asking, "Who are all the people anyway, and why are they here?" Let's answer that question.
- v1. The elders are men of Israel who have risen to leadership roles because of their age, wisdom and influence. What is the significance of seventy?

_____

_____

- Who are Nadab and Abihu? For details, return to *Exodus 6:23*.

_____

What do we know so far about Joshua and Hur? *See Exodus 17:8-13.*

- *v2.* Why might God want all the elders present here, though only Moses will advance to the top for the divine summit?

v4. Moses constructs one altar at the base of the mountain. Then he erects twelve stone pillars around the altar. What is their significance?

v5. What image or images come to your mind when Moses sprinkles the blood on the altar of sacrifice?

v7. What is this Book of the Covenant? *(See v4.)*

v8. What image or images come to your mind when Moses speaks of "the blood of the covenant," and sprinkles it on the people?

Week Ten A Foundation that Endures

_____

_____

_____

v9 - 11. Let the power of this moment sink into your consciousness. This is an historic experience- not a vision. Virtually no one else in Scripture, other than Christ Jesus Himself, ever gets to physically see the Father and still survive.
- God's feet are resting on something like a pavement of sapphire. The Hebrew word can also be translated *lapis lazuli*, which was extremely popular back in Egypt for use in amulets and jewelry. Moses may have never seen a sapphire, but he would have seen many, many artifacts of lapis lazuli back at the royal palace. The surface beneath God's throne is the intense blue color of the unique, but it is transparent.
- See *Revelation 4:5*. How is the vision that John experienced similar to the reality that Moses and the elders behold?

_____

_____

- *v11.* There is no other scene like this in the Old Testament.
   - ✓ God doesn't _____ them.
   - ✓ They _____ and _____ in His presence.

v12. Moses has already written the words of God on some handy but fragile substance- vellum (sheepskin) or papyrus. Now God summons him to the top of the mountain to receive a copy carved into _____.
- We customarily imagine two tablets with five commandments on each.
- Because this is a covenant or contract, it's likely that the same information is carved on both tablets, denoting two parties to the contract.

v13-14. One man, _____, will accompany Moses at least part of the way to the summit. The word translated "his aide" by the NIV literally means "his minister."
- Two other trusted leaders, _____ and _____ will remain behind with the elders.
- How is this scene similar to the narrative from the Garden of Gethsemane in *Matthew 26:36 – 46*?

_____

_____

_____

v15 – 18. A cloud descends and completely conceals the summit. Moses and Joshua approach the cloud and wait to be summoned.
- The glory of God settles on the top of the mountain and creates strange atmospheric conditions for six days.
- *v17.* How does the glory of God appear to people watching from a distance?

  _____

- On the seventh day, God speaks from the cloud and invites Moses to come inside. What is the significance of the seventh day?

  _____

  _____

- How long will Moses remain alone with God on the mountain top?

  _____

The wheels of eternity apparently move slowly, don't they? So far, the Israelites have spent three days getting ready to hear the first message from God. An unspecified amount of time has passed while Moses has built an altar and pillars and made other preparations. After finally ascending the mount, Moses will delay another six days waiting on God's timing. And finally, he will spend forty days in the presence of God without sending any words of assurance back to the people below.

Q: Do you think all that time was required because the ancient world did not value time, or was so much time required because God is unhurried by nature?
   [ ] I think the world moved much more slowly a long time ago.
   [ ] I believe God is unhurried by nature or circumstances.
   [ ] Other _____

Q: Do you ever suspect that we American believers sometimes miss the glory of God because we demand instant results while God does his work at a slower pace?

_____

_____

_____

When was the last time you experienced an intense and life changing time of being in the presence of the Father?
- [ ] In the last six months
- [ ] In the last 2 years
- [ ] Three or more years ago
- [ ] A long, long time ago
- [ ] When I was a teenager

Personal Preparation: What is required in order for you to relax, slow down, and wait quietly for God's presence?
- Do you need quiet music or do you relax best in silence?
- Do you need to read a Psalm or do you more often hear from God through the Gospels?
- Do you need a list of prayer concerns or just a blank sheet of paper and a pen to write with?
- Do you have a particular space in your house, your office or your yard where you can be undisturbed with the Almighty?
- Are you more comfortable with your shoes on or off?

An Audience with God: Do whatever is required to create those conditions for personal surrender right now. Allot an hour just to wait on the Lord. Ask your family not to disturb you. Don't expect anything in particular except to be still as an act of adoration.

Now sit down, kneel or lie facedown on the floor or the ground. Ask God for permission to be still in his presence for a while. Now surrender............

WEEK ELEVEN

EVERY PICTURE TELLS A STORY

Do not seek the perfection of the law in human virtues, for it is not found perfect in them. Its perfection is hidden in the Cross of Christ. Mark the Ascetic

To be frank with you, I had never wanted to visit the Holy Land. I'm sure that's not what you'd expect of someone who studies history and has a passion for the Word of God. But during my days at seminary, a buddy of mine had gone on a field trip with the church history department. He had returned a few weeks later with disappointing stories about every important spot being totally obscured by a massive, ugly church building! So I had innocently concluded that this was not for me.

Imagine my surprise then when, while serving a church in Tennessee, friends offered my wife and me a trip to Israel as a gift! I was forced to conceal my lack of enthusiasm. I really wasn't interested but could not imagine a pastoral way to tell a godly family, "Sorry, I'm not interested in the country where most of the Bible took place." So that is how my wife and I reluctantly made our first trip to that place once known as the Land of Canaan.

As you might guess, I could not have been more mistaken about Israel. Yes, there are some old, blocky Greek Orthodox Church buildings located at key sites in Bethlehem and Jerusalem. And it's true that the food includes odd things like falafels (bean-filled pita sandwiches) and St. Peter's fish (dry and unattractive with the head and eyes still in place.) But for followers of Jesus, seeing Israel can be a deeply emotional experience.

Arriving at a place you've often read about in the Bible is always marked by a powerful sense of déjà vu. In Jerusalem, there's a stone path on the way to the site of the Governor's place, which historians believe dates back to the First Century. The location means it is almost certain that Christ's feet would have stepped on these very stones en route to his trial. The place is heavy with memories, even if you've never visited before!

The Jordan River is muddy and quite ordinary, but to eyes which have read the Bible, it shines with all the luster of a cherished haunt from your childhood. And Mount Carmel is not that much different from a hill you'd find in West Virginia- yet it's completely different. Standing at the spot where Elijah made his historic stand, and looking onto the plain of Megiddo down below and Mount Tabor across the way, all the stories and details come rushing through your mind. The world's final conflict will climax here. And Jesus spent his boyhood in Nazareth just over there. He would have gazed upon this valley many times as he ran errands with his family. Your eyes drink in unfamiliar sights, even as your heart cries out, "I *know* this place!"

I believe that "been here before" quality that sets Israel apart will be even more evident in the Kingdom of Heaven. Don't you think arriving there must surely feel like coming home? On one hand, your place there has been designed by someone who knows you better than anyone ever has or ever could. And on the other hand, you've studied the laws of Heaven and images of that kingdom for years every time you have opened your Bible. On the day you step inside those eagerly awaited gates for the very first time, your eyes will be dazzled by the one of a kind wonders, even as your heart exults, "*I know this place!*"

God designed it that way, of course. As far back as the second book of the Bible, he began to show us the road map to eternity. Bondage in Egypt was an object lesson in the power of sin to capture and detain us. The journey through the wilderness, ever awaiting the next watering hole, was designed to afford us an advance look at the walk of faith. And the Promised Land, that verdant destination overflowing with milk and honey, has always offered us a foretaste of Heaven.

Worship serves a similar function- *orienting us for home*. The Letter to the Hebrews explains that Jesus, our high priest in Heaven, has human counterparts playing that role on the Earth. "They serve at a sanctuary that is a copy and shadow of what is in Heaven. This is why Moses was warned when he was about to build the Tabernacle, 'See to it that you make everything according to the pattern shown you on the mountain.'"[57]

This week and next, we will take pains to examine some ancient earthly structures designed by our Father to show us pictures of Heaven. We won't move sequentially because the closing chapters of Exodus are sometimes redundant with detail, but we will cover every chapter. Our strategy will be to begin with the priests, their prescribed roles and their divinely ordained apparel. Then we will advance to the various elements of the Tabernacle: the Ark of the Covenant, the Table of Presence, the amazing, golden Lampstand that has inspired the Jews throughout the centuries. Then finally, we will spend a couple of days walking through a tent like no other portable shelter the world has ever seen. This tent endures for a full generation as the earthly house of the Most High God.

These will be our themes as we break off a slice of the Bread of Life this week:
- Day 1: What do the items of clothing prescribed for the priests teach us about God and his Kingdom?
- Day 2: What does the role of the priests reveal about the governance of Heaven?
- Day 3: Why did Aaron lead the people into pagan worship only forty short days after Moses disappeared on Mount Sinai?
- Day 4: Why was Moses forced to wear a veil, and why should we care?

Think about families and photo albums as you study this week. My earthly dad has been gone for years, but I still keep a photo of him on my dresser. Until the day he died, my father was a symbol of security and belonging for my siblings and me. Some Saturdays we'd take the family car over to visit relatives in another county. We'd stay all day and return home at night, arriving with little ones like me sleeping soundly in the back seat. And every time, in a process of which I was not even aware, my father would lift my small body into his strong arms to carry me inside and gently tuck me into bed. Having fallen asleep listening to the hum of the engine and the rhythmic sounds of the highway, I would awaken in my own bed in a room with familiar items that reminded me, "This is where you belong."

I am convinced that Heaven will be much the same. I will fall asleep distracted by the sounds and rhythms of life. And I will awaken in a place that is distinctly mine; a home that will dazzle my eyes, and comfort my heart. "I know this place. I have seen it many times before."

Study notes: The final fifteen chapters of Exodus offer one small challenge to us in this study. Several chapters reveal details of the forty day conversation with God about the Priesthood, the Tabernacle, and the various pieces of sacred furniture which will be placed in it. Later when the tent and all those objects are actually produced, all the details are repeated to demonstrate the care with which the craftsmen worked. To avoid redundant lessons, we will combine chapters with identical details. This means we will study the final chapters of Exodus out of order for these final two weeks. We will ultimately include every chapter, however.

This week our theme will be the priesthood and the essential character of service to God. We'll address these chapters and topics:
- Day 1: Chapters 28 and 39; special garments that must be worn by the Priests when serving in the Tabernacle
- Day 2: Chapters 29 and 30; consecrating the priests for their work
- Day 3: Chapter 32; The Golden Calf
- Day 4: Chapters 33 and 34; Moses and the Glory of the Lord

Day 1: Robed in Righteousness
Read Exodus 28, 39: 1 - 30
Read these texts thoughtfully. Mark or otherwise indicate every word or phrase that refers to the tribe, the family, the clan or the blood of Jacob that unites the people of Israel. Try to visualize in your mind how the various pieces of the uniforms would fit together, and how the final product would look to worshipers.

28: 1 – 5. The Lord selects Aaron, Nadab, Abihu, Eleazar, and Ithamar to serve as priests. At this moment, we know only one thing that all these men have in common. *What is it?*

_____

v2. The sacred garments will endow the priests with dignity and honor.
- "Dignity" comes from the Hebrew word *kabod*, which speaks of glory. Most commonly, this word- which is derived from the root word for "heavy-"is associated with the glory of God.
- "Honor" stems from the Hebrew term *tipharah*, meaning splendor.

- ✓ *Deuteronomy 25:19*. God promises to raise his people up in splendor as a holy nation.
- ✓ *Lamentations 2:1* recalls a time when in His anger, God cast the splendor of Israel down to the Earth.

Q: What sort of message will the priestly uniforms convey? *Check only one:*
- [ ] Aaron and his sons are noble, extremely wise individuals.
- [ ] The people of Israel are a noble and extremely virtuous tribe.
- [ ] God will invest His nation with his own glory and splendor.
- [ ] Priests and spiritual leaders are remarkable, elevated people.

v3. The most talented craftsmen will be asked to prepare this remarkable priestly apparel that Aaron will wear for his consecration ceremony.
- Consecration comes from the Hebrew root that gives us "holy" or "to make holy."
- In the ceremony, Aaron and his sons will be set on a different path from other men, with a different mission; much like the nation of Israel will be a holy nation with a different mission.

v4. The artisans are to craft six pieces for each uniform. What materials are required by God for the production of the clothing?

- _____ ;

- _____ yarn;

- _____ .

Where would nomads like these, traveling through the desert, be expected to acquire gold, expensive yarn, costly linen, and expensive stones?

_____

_____

_____

If you've forgotten, see Exodus 12: 35-36.

Frankly, what other value or practical purpose would luxury consumer goods like these have in a barren desert environment?

_____

_____

_____

Week Eleven   Every Picture Tells a Story

SECRETS OF THE DESERT

When you're reading about the linen and colorful yarns required for the priestly garments, it can be a surprise to study the Hebrew words. For example, the word *tola* that is translated "scarlet," also means a "worm or maggot!" What does a worm have to do with a brilliant and beautiful color? In fact, the dried bodies of a particular female worm, the *coccus ilicis*, are ground up to produce the scarlet dyes of the ancient world.

Aaron and each of his sons will require several pieces of clothing: an ephod, a breastplate, a woven tunic, a turban, and a sash. Let's examine them:

1. The Ephod: *v6 – 14*
    - Imagine the ephod very much like an apron that loops over the priest's shoulders to cover his chest, back, and midsection.
    - Two onyx stones are mounted on gold filigree as shoulder pieces. What is engraved on the precious stones?

      _____

      _____

    - What is the theological purpose for the stones?

      _____

    - Of what material are the two chains made? _____

2. The Breastplate: *v15 – 30*
    - This is attached to the front of the ephod.
    - What is its purpose? _____
    - There are four rows of precious stones aligned on the breastplate. What do the stones represent?

      _____

    - What is engraved on each of the stones?

      _____

    - Why do you think God calls for a different precious stone for each of the twelve tribes of Israel?

      _____

_____

_____

- The *Urim* and *Thummin* are believed by some to be sacred lots which can be cast by the priest whenever he must choose regarding the will of God. Others suggest the two stones were used to reflect light onto the stones of the breastplate for spelling out words. It seems they are contained in a pocket on the breastplate near the priest's heart.[58]

3. The Robe: *v31 – 35*
    - The robe is much longer, worn under the apron-like ephod.
    - It is made entirely of _____
    - Two special kinds of objects alternate around the entire length of the hem: _____ and _____
    - Pomegranates represent fruitfulness and abundance. They will frequently be incorporated into the design of the Temple.[59]
    - As long as the high priest is ministering inside the holy place, the bells ring as he moves. If they stop ringing, it is an indication that he is ceremonially unclean and has been struck dead.

4. The Turban: *v36 – 38*

    - On the front of the turban is a gold plate, or possibly a gold crown. What is inscribed on the gold?

      _____

    - What is the purpose of the gold plate or crown?

      _____

      _____

v39 – 43. The tunic is a long linen robe worn closest to the body, extending from neck to feet. The underwear is also made of linen.
- *v42.* Aaron and his sons will wear them in the Tent of Meeting to preclude personal guilt. What does this mean?
- Read *Ezekiel 44: 17-18*. Why was linen required for priests in the Tabernacle, rather than less costly fabrics?

_____

_____

Week Eleven Every Picture Tells a Story

What's the Point?
Something is clearly afoot here, but what? The Bible devotes only two short chapters to the wondrous and mind boggling process of God creating the cosmos! Now that same Bible spends an entire chapter talking about clothing for priests! What's so highly significant about the way priests dress for their work of sacrifice and intercession?

Think about it: *although Aaron and his sons are selected by God because of their bloodline, they are only capable of ministering in the Tabernacle if they are wearing the right clothes.* Without this apparel, neither their DNA nor their moral behavior qualifies them to serve in God's presence. Without the prescribed uniform, they will be rejected outright or even struck down. They dare not stand in the presence of the Almighty without some form of outside intervention.

Read Isaiah 61: 10 – 11. Isaiah delights in his garments of salvation.
- In which particular garment is he arrayed?

  _____

- Who has provided this particular garment?

  _____

Read Matthew 22: 1 – 14. Think about these details of an ancient wedding for a moment.
- Who are the guests who are invited after the original guests reject the host and his wedding feast?

  _____

- What do we learn from the fact that the guests must wear wedding garments to be accepted at this celebration?

  _____

  _____

  _____

Read Revelation 7: 9 – 17. The scene reveals a group of people who are serving before the throne of God. According to *7:14*, who are these ministers?

  _____

  _____

What qualifies YOU to minister grace before the throne of God? *Choose only one*:
    [ ] Your standards of morality
    [ ] Your particular church or denomination

[ ] The frequency of your Bible reading
[ ] Particular talents you've been granted
[ ] The robe of righteousness in which Christ has arrayed you

Day 2: Men in White
Read Exodus 29-30
Read these chapters carefully, using your imagination. Use a pen or pencil to circle or highlight every reference to an animal or substance offered on the altar of sacrifice. Ask yourself why some sacrifices are larger and why each is required for that particular setting.

In this sacred moment, which will actually continue for a week, the high priest and his sons are set apart for the high calling of God. During the course of the next seven days, sacrifices will be made first for the high priest and his sons, and then for the sanctity of the altar itself.

29: 1 – 9. Elaborate preparations are set in place. The elements of a feast are presented to the Lord: a bullock, two rams, unleavened bread, cakes and wafers.
- When hospitality became such a high priority to the Jews, what did it say about their relationships to God and one another?

_____

- What is suggested by the act of setting a feast before the Most High God?

_____

_____

Next, the candidates for priesthood are set before the Lord; first the high priest, and then his sons. Three things are done to prepare the high priest. They are:

1. _____ v4
2. _____ v5
3. _____ v7

Read Psalm 117. David compares the impact of living together in unity to the fragrance of precious anointing oil running down Aaron's head and beard.
- The special oil was not poured sparingly. It was poured liberally over his head, streaking the robes and pooling at his feet.
- The one of a kind fragrance would have drifted through the air, alerting people who were out of sight that a special event was underway at the Tabernacle.
- David compares unity among the family of faith to that unique fragrance that communicates something extraordinary is underway.

29: 10 – 14. There are different kinds of burnt offerings: sin, fellowship, meal, drink. What kind of offering is this first one made during the consecration of the high priest and son?

A bull is the largest animal offered as a burnt offering, and it's offered for the priests. (On the Day of Atonement, a goat is offered for the sins of the nation.[60]) Why would such a large sacrifice be made for the sins of a priest?

v13-14. Note that most of the bull's carcass is burned outside the camp. Only the liver, kidneys, and fat around those parts are burned on the altar for the priest. In the Hebrew world of this age, the kidneys are associated with the emotions, conscience and decision making.[61] What would be the significance of placing these parts on the altar as a priest is set apart for service?

29: 15 – 18. The first ram is cut into pieces, washed thoroughly, and then offered up in entirety. What is the significance of washing the ram throughout before committing it to the Lord on behalf of the priesthood?

29: 19 – 28. Before the second ram is offered up, Aaron and his sons lay their hands on the animal's head. What are they communicating here? *Choose one:*

[ ] We feel sorry for the poor ram and want to comfort it.
[ ] In God's eyes, this animal will now be identified with our sins.
[ ] We are happy to kill this ram.
[ ] This animal has rights too, and we are praying for it.

This ram's blood is placed on the high priest and his sons: on the lobe of the right ear; on the thumb of the right hand; on the toe of the right foot. What might that denote?

_____

_____

v22. Once again notice that the kidneys and liver are prominently identified. Old Testament sacrifices never specify the heart.

v25. The wave offering: imagine this wave offering in which portions of meat and bread are held above the head and waved forward and backward before the Lord. What do you think this might represent? *Choose only one*:
[ ] Taking credit for raising the animal and baking the bread
[ ] Gratitude for all that God has provided
[ ] Enthusiasm for worship
[ ] Other _____

v27-34. The fellowship/peace offering: This meal celebrates a healthy, cordial relationship between the worshipper and the Almighty, much like breaking bread together at the dinner table.
- *Read Romans 5: 1,2.*
- How does this peace offering remind you of Jesus Christ?

_____

v35. This seven day consecration ceremony obviously runs through the Sabbath. Why would this sort of work be acceptable on the day of rest?

_____

_____

v37. "Anything that touches the altar will be holy." What does this teach? Is holiness transferable from one person to another?

_____

_____

29: 38 – 45. Notice that as the offerings are made, God comes to meet with his people. His plan is to dwell with them. This sounds very similar to the concept of the peace offering, in which people of faith offer the Lord hospitality and invite him to come and break bread with them. And herein is one of the chief distinctions between the One True God and all the pagan gods and false deities of history. In religion, men and women attempt to appease a distant God in order to approach him. In the Bible, we are taught that if we consecrate ourselves in faith, the Holy One will approach us and dwell with us. This is a completely different concept from the rationale of paganism!

- *Read John 3:17. Do we go to God or does He come to us?*

_____

- *Read Revelation 3:20. How does Christ desire to relate to us?*

_____

_____

_____

30: 1 – 10. This golden altar is used to fill the air with fragrant incense, a gesture of reverence toward the Holy God. We can't be sure what the incense represents. Is it a visible expression of our prayers to God, or does it reflect the pleasing work of God underway in our world?
- *See Psalm 141:1,2*
- *See Ezekiel 20:41*
- What's your best guess about incense and its purpose in the Tabernacle?

_____

_____

Jump ahead momentarily to *30: 34 – 38* to see the ingredients of the incense.
- Gum resin would smell much like our pine resin or turpentine.
- Onycha is extracted from the shell of a certain snail soaked in wine.
- Galbanum is known for its bitter scent, perhaps denoting the nature of unrepentant sinners.
- Frankincense, "the incense of the gods," emits a mossy fragrance similar to pine but more distinctive.

30: 11 – 16. God establishes that whenever it is necessary to count the people, an offering must be made by each one being counted. This offering is the same for rich or poor, denoting the equal value of each life. This is an act of thanksgiving for being delivered and being providentially cared for.

- This little known law explains an otherwise baffling incident that occurs centuries later when David is King.
- If you're curious, consult *2 Samuel 24*.

30: 17 – 21. The Law is filled with commands similar to this one which involves washing the hands. Don't forget that Moses and his people are living in an age more than 3,000 years before the discovery of germs- *tiny organisms invisible to the human eye, which can make one sick unless they are removed by hand washing.* Not until the 1840's will a Jewish doctor named Ignaz Semmelweiss[62] teach his doctors and medical aides to wash their hands frequently to prevent the transmission of deadly germs from one patient to another! Even in the 1840's, the idea will still be controversial!

30: 22 – 33. The sacred anointing oil contains a unique formula which may not be mixed or used for any purpose other than anointing sacred people and objects. As you read the formula, take note of the ingredients and the large quantities of each.

- For example, 500 shekels is about 12 ½ pounds
- Myrrh has a clean, pungent fragrance a bit like pine resin or turpentine. Cassia has a fragrance similar to cinnamon, but is sharper, and not as delicate in scent as true cinnamon.
- List the ingredients and try to imagine the resulting fragrance:
    - ✓ 500 shekels: _____
    - ✓ 250 shekels: _____
    - ✓ 250 shekels: _____
    - ✓ 500 shekels: _____
    - ✓ A hin (4 quarts): _____

Now spend some time just reflecting and using your imagination. Envision yourself as an Israelite arriving at the Tabernacle for something you've never seen before: the consecration of the high priest. Recall the boredom and tedium, the unchanging desert scenery, the blinding glare of the sun and the livestock smells that are a routine part of your daily life. Now imagine seeing, hearing, and smelling all the utterly unique sensations associated with this ceremony. What messages are you receiving about the Holy God? Jot down some impressions as you mentally sift through the process.

1. _____
2. _____
3. _____
4. _____
5. _____

Week Eleven Every Picture Tells a Story

Day 3: Old Habits Die Hard
Read Exodus 32
Read this chapter twice. Look for any verse that might reveal the motive of the Israelites in this offensive action. Circle that verse. Then look for any verse or statement that might explain Aaron's reasoning in allowing the uprising. Underscore that verse or statement.

It was in *Exodus 24:15* that the Israelites last saw Moses as he ascended Mount Sinai and disappeared into a cloud to meet with the Almighty God. Meanwhile, Moses has been occupied with a major revelation from the Lord, but the Israelites have simply been waiting- *and wondering*. By the time Moses re-emerges later in this *32:15*, he will have been absent for eight chapters and forty days. To frame this with a bit of human perspective, remember that Israel had only been in the desert sixty days when they arrived at Sinai to receive the Ten Commandments in the first place.

Exodus 32: 1 – 8. After weeks of waiting with no word from God's man Moses, the Israelites are finally overcome by either anxiety or boredom. You can easily imagine some of the complaints and comments hurled at poor old Aaron. Take a moment and imagine some of the most likely feedback Aaron might have received:

1. "Have you thought about the fact that _____
   _____

2. "I hate to say this but _____
   _____

3. _____
   _____

v3 - 4. Scripture does not reveal what Aaron is actually thinking. One commentator suggests that Aaron is attempting to use psychology rather than simply rebuking the people for sinful attitudes. It is suggested that he hopes that when he asks for their gold ornaments, many of the vain, superficial people will draw the line at giving up their trinkets.[63] What Aaron is thinking isn't apparent, but what he does is obvious.

- Where does he get the gold used to produce the idol?

  _____

- What does he do with the gold once it was in his possession?

  _____

In the ancient world, a golden image of a bull might be expected to have the same impact that a photograph of a BMW convertible might have today. It symbolizes virility, and suggests a greater degree of wealth. In addition, bulls are powerful beasts of burden that can also be eaten as steaks! Glistening and gleaming in the desert sun, this 14 carat bull seems to shout, "It's party time!"

No wonder God has continually found it necessary to remind the Israelites that he brought them out of bondage in Egypt! The moment the idol is set before them, what is their conclusion?

_____

_____

v5. It seems here that Aaron is shocked and horrified by this spectacle, and that he attempts to restore some sanity to the situation. What suggests this?

_____

_____

_____

v6. Why is it clear that Aaron's so-called attempt at revival has completely failed to bring conviction or shame?

_____

_____

_____

32: 7 – 14. This particular moment in the saga recalls the words of the second commandment just forty days ago. "You shall not bow down to idols or worship them for I, the Lord your God, am a jealous God."
- This particular term for "jealous" is only used for God. His holy passion is not accompanied by insecurity or irrationality.
- However, God can spur spiritual growth in Moses by raising the question, "What's the point? Why not just destroy these failed creatures?"
- The all-knowing God of eternity has known all along things like this will happen, which explains his reminders about who actually brought the Israelites out of bondage. But Moses is left to wonder, unable to imagine all the tracks which are moving in God's endless mind simultaneously.

Week Eleven   Every Picture Tells a Story

Notice God's precise words: "You must go back down because..."
- *v7*. Your people have _____;
- *v8*. They have been _____ to turn away from what I commanded;
- They have bowed down to an idol, sacrificed to it, and said, "_____

  _____."

v9-10. God suggests two actions: 1) _____ the Israelites, and 2) Build a new nation through _____.

Moses responds by reminding the Lord of two priorities so important and so central to his character, that God could never have forgotten them in the first place. Use this space to elaborate on them.
- *v12*. God's reputation in the mind of the Egyptians

  _____

  _____

- *v13*. God's eternal promises to earlier generations

  _____

  _____

  _____

v14. God chooses to employ a different strategy. The KJV uses the phrase "repented of the evil." This particular verb and tense can be translated "And God felt sorry and was moved to compassion. The "evil" he turns from is not moral evil. Rather, this Hebrew word speaks of painful, catastrophic or tragic events; not immoral ones.

32: 15 – 35. What do we know for sure about the tablets containing the Ten Commandments?
- There are _____ of them.
- They are engraved on both _____.
- _____ did the engraving.

v19. These amazing clay tablets contain the Law in the actual handwriting of God! *Why in the world would Moses break them?* Choose the one answer that best fits the biblical evidence.
- [ ] *Guilt*: Moses feels so personally responsible for this sinful development that he simply drops the tablets in feelings of despair and helplessness.
- [ ] *Revulsion*: The sight of God's people celebrating around a pagan idol is so revolting to Moses that he shatters the tablets in disgust.

[ ] *Futility*: Moses angrily breaks the tablets on the ground as a token of what these compromised people have done with their retreat to paganism.

[ ] *Rage*: Moses is famous for his temper and he justifiably loses control on this occasion.

What message does Moses convey when he grinds up the idol into gold dust, mixes it with water, and forces the people to drink it? *Choose only one of the following.*

[ ] You have wasted your lives, just like you've wasted this gold!

[ ] You have whipped up this sinful brew; now you must drink the consequences!

[ ] I'm so angry I can't think straight!

[ ] Other _____

_____

v21 – 24. Moses finally utters the words all of us are asking: "Aaron, what in the world were you thinking, anyway?" What is so irresponsible and impossible about Aaron's explanation?

_____

_____

v25 - 26. In the words of the NIV, Moses realizes that the people are "running wild!" The Hebrew word in question has a broad range of possible meanings: to let loose; to unbind; to be uncovered; to be naked; to relinquish control.

- Like many words in Greek, Hebrew and even in English, it has more or less intensity depending on the context.
- The situation unfolding here is as serious as things can get: thousands being put to death. This lends support to the KJV interpretation that some of the people are naked and caught up in rank debauchery.

This chapter concludes with insight into two distinct qualities in the life of Moses: his high priority for justice, and his deep, compassionate desire for mercy.

- *v26 – 29.* How does Moses impose justice to bring this riotous hour of sin to a conclusion?

_____

_____

_____

Week Eleven   Every Picture Tells a Story

- *v30 – 35*. How does this passage demonstrate the compassion of Moses?

  _____

Moses refers to a "book" God has written. It apparently contains the names of people who walk by faith. God goes on to explain that unforgiven sin is the only reason for which people are blotted out of this book. It is interesting that while God's Book of Life is not described until Psalms, and then later in Revelation, Moses already knows about such a book at this early moment in scriptural history.

Review 32: 4, 8. Take note of the exact wording. Do you suppose the Israelites have completely renounced the One True God, or does it seem they are merely trying to worship God plus the golden calf?

_____

What happens after Aaron calls them to repent and devote a day to the worship of the God of Israel?

_____

Do you think that worshiping God + popular idols is a problem in the US Church today?
  [ ] Very much so
  [ ] Probably
  [ ] Maybe a little
  [ ] No

Have you recently found yourself worshiping God + a popular idol from our own day? If YES, explain.
  [ ] NO   [ ] YES _____

Have you ever noticed which kinds of circumstances create the greatest temptation for idolatry for you? Check the most prevalent one listed below:
  [ ] Anxiety
  [ ] Fear
  [ ] Self Doubt
  [ ] Sensuality
  [ ] Absence from God
  [ ] Peer Pressure
  [ ] Other _____

Take a few moments to be still and talk to God. Talk to him about wholehearted allegiance: what it means to you, and how you plan to grow in that area.

Day 4: The Power and the Glory
Read Exodus 33 - 34
Read these chapters slowly. Use a pen or marker to indicate each sentence or phrase that amounts to a promise from the Most High God.

What is the Glory of God? Scripture teaches that the heavens reveal it[64]. And yet it must be more than the majestic results of the power of God. Moses saw the might of God on display when the gods of Egypt were shattered and thrown to the ground by the power of the Most High God. But even after witnessing all those feats of wonder, Moses will still ask that he might see God's glory. Notice that God does not reply by saying, "But Moses, you already have."

Exodus 33: 1 – 11. This chapter begins on a surprising note with God telling his people he will not be traveling with them as they journey to Canaan. Instead he will send an angel ahead to lead them. What is God's rationale for not traveling with them?

v5. He directs them to take off their earrings and gold ornaments. Recall the events associated with the golden calf for a moment. Why might God command them to remove their jewelry?

v7 - 11. The tent mentioned here is not the Tabernacle, which will be constructed very shortly. Rather, this is simply an ordinary tent Moses sets aside for the sacred purpose of meeting with the Lord. What have we learned about this particular tent and its use?
- How do spectators know when God has arrived to meet with Moses?

- What happens in the area surrounding the tent when God and Moses are in session?

- How does the text characterize the quality of the relationship between God and Moses?

- Moses frequently leaves the tent to return to camp. Who stays inside and never vacates the tent?

v12 – 13. Moses makes a personal and very practical request of the Almighty. What does Moses request?

_____

_____

_____

v15 - 16. Moses implies that one fact distinguishes the Jews from all the other people of the world. It's the same quality that set Joseph apart when he first arrived in Egypt. What would that be?

_____

v17. Sometimes church people talk as though the Old Covenant is a contract based on works, while the New Covenant is a contract based on grace. The first assumption is utterly misguided, however. The phrase which the NIV renders "because I am pleased with you," is the same phrase translated "You have found favor with me" in *verse twelve*. It literally means, "You have found grace in my sight."
- "You have found _____ in my sight;
- "And I know you by _____."

Think about that sentence: "I know you by name." It's not the same thing as merely knowing someone's proper name. God knows everyone's name, not to mention their DNA! *But knowing a person by name is quite different.*
- Think of all the celebrities, business executives and sports figures whose names you know. Even though you may refer to them by first names, you have no relationship with them. *They don't know you at all.*
- To "know someone by name" is to be able to speak to them with familiarity, gain their attention by calling their name, and relate to them conversationally.
- That second way is how God knows Moses, and how he desires to know you and me.

v18. What Moses will request next is contingent upon the promise God has just made. The point is this: "If you do indeed know my name, and if I have found grace in your sight, then O Lord, please _____ _____ _____ _____.

What is Moses asking of God? What is he thinking? Some have suggested he wants some token of divine respect. Others believe Moses thinks he needs more insight to become a more effective leader of God's people. But I believe the scriptures are demonstrating that Moses has become so caught up in the amazing, unearthly love of God that he has become consumed with expectation. He has experienced more of the Holy One than any other human being since Adam and Eve, and yet he realizes he has scarcely touched the surface. The heavens radiate the glory of God and yet as vast and unsearchable as the evening sky seems, God is even more vast and unsearchable.

Read Psalm 63: 1 – 3. Like Moses, David is living a nomadic experience in the wilderness when he writes this song. And quite similar to Moses, he is surrounded by people who are not his relatives and yet who are dependant on him for their survival.
- To what physical sensation does David compare his deep, yearning to know God more intimately?

   _____

- Where does David say he has experienced God's glory?

   _____

Read Isaiah 6: 1 – 5. It's hard to say if Isaiah is describing a vision or a literal experience. One tends to assume this is a vision because had he literally seen the face of the King, he would have surely died. Nevertheless, the sensation seems intensely real to the prophet.
- Where can the Glory of God be found?

   _____

- What is Isaiah's response to this sense of intimacy with God?

   _____

Remember the promise of *Isaiah 55:6*? "Seek the Lord while he may be found. Call upon him while he is near."
- It reflects the promise of *Deuteronomy 4:29*. "But if from there you seek the Lord, you will find him if you look for him with all your heart, and with all your soul."
- It leads to the promise of Christ in *Matthew 7:7*. "Ask and it will be given to you; seek and you will find; knock and the door will be opened to you." And the emphasis is on asking, seeking and knocking tirelessly.

Is there always visible evidence that "God is near?"

_____
_____

What does God have in mind when he calls us to search for him with the whole heart and the entire soul?

_____
_____
_____

Week Eleven   Every Picture Tells a Story

Why do you believe God desires that people who love him should search for him so tirelessly?

_____

_____

33: 14,19. God grants both of Moses' requests. He will go before His people and reveal himself to Moses, the one who speaks with him like a friend. And although a human being cannot witness the face of God, Moses will be allowed to see the glory of God passing.

Now, take note of one more fact which is often overlooked in this incident!
- ✓ In *Exodus 32:15*, when Moses returned from the presence of God, with the original tablets of the Law in his arms, his appearance was unremarkable.
- ✓ In *Exodus 34:2*, when Moses once again comes down the mountainside with the second set of the Ten Commandments, something about him is very different. What has changed?

_____

v34. Moses is not aware that anything is different until people keep staring at him in shock and fear! What custom does the man of God develop as a result of this?

_____

Read *2 Corinthians 3: 12 – 18*. Paul's point here is that in the Old Testament, the images of Christ are "veiled" because they are conveyed in symbols. The Glory of God will be concealed behind a veil, a thick curtain, and reverenced in the Most Holy Place of the Tabernacle. But with the arrival of Christ in the New Covenant, we have experienced a profound unveiling!
- *v17.* What does it mean: "where the Spirit of the Lord is, there is freedom?"

_____

_____

- *v18.* How do you and I reflect the Glory of God?

_____

_____

There must be more! Think of some of the avenues in which you and I can seek the Lord with our whole heart to catch glimpses of His true glory?

1. _____
2. _____

3. _____
4. _____
5. _____

Now take a few moments to sit perfectly still in reverence before the Lord. Let the palms of your hands face upward, indicating a desire to relinquish some things and a willingness to receive others.

- To go after God, what are some things you must personally relinquish?

- What are the things you desire from God?

Now turn to *Psalm 27*. Read through it quietly to catch a sense of the message, the passion, the celebration.
- Now read it to God as a whisper.
- Finally, read it aloud to the Lord once again, and this time with feeling.

"Wait for the Lord; be strong and take heart and wait for the Lord!"

WEEK TWELVE

THE GLORY OF THE GOD WHO CAME NEAR

Be always, every moment, with God, especially when you pray to Him. If you are inconstant, you will fall away from life, and will cast yourself into sorrow and straitness. John of Kronstadt

"*Have I really beaten the grave robbers?*" That unlikely and amazing question must have electrified archeologist Howard Carter one notable Egyptian morning in November, 1922. Carter and his team had just begun their final excavation in Luxor's Valley of the Kings. His men had secured the ruins of some ancient huts when they uncovered a step which had been carved into an underlying rock. Within two days, workmen had unearthed twelve such steps leading downwards to a partially blocked entrance. After 31 years of sifting through history, Carter finally seemed to have stumbled on something big- perhaps the dream of his lifetime!

He secured the site and posted guards to allow some time to collect himself. He contacted the sponsor of his expedition, Lord Carnarvon, advising him to come at once. Then everything was placed on hold for nearly three weeks until the necessary arrangements could be made.

At last, the morning of the grand opening arrived. With a crowd looking on, Carter carefully proceeded. There were four additional steps to uncover. There were seals on the door, each containing the name of a king called Tutankhamen. A tiny crevice was broken in the upper left hand corner of the doorway. Candles were used to test for the presence of toxic gases. The crevice was widened slightly. Finally the scholar placed a candle inside and leaned forward to peer into the chamber beyond the sealed door. Carter would later write in his journal:

"At first I could see nothing, the hot air escaping from the chamber causing the candle flame to flicker, but presently, as my eyes grew accustomed to the light, details of the room within emerged slowly from the mist, strange animals, statues, and gold - everywhere the glint of gold."

Although King Tut had been a fairly minor figure on the grand stage of Egyptian history, his tomb became a sensation. Unlike so many other burial chambers of legendary pharaohs, this one had been virtually undisturbed for 3,000 years. The solid gold burial vaults, gold furnishings, and jewel encrusted artwork had survived to bear witness to the elaborate quality of ancient Egyptian religion. But unfortunately for King Tutankhamen, although his treasure was intact, the gods and goddesses he had relied upon were all gone. They had disappeared into the smoke and dust of legend many centuries before.

That episode from the history of Egypt stands in sharp contrast to the story of Israel. When the God of Abraham, Isaac and Jacob directed his people to honor him with objects of gold, he ordained a tent, not a tomb. This would be no resting place for a dead king. Rather, this would be the throne room of a living God, a personal God who would travel with his nomadic people.

The Lord God would ordain an elaborate tent called the Tabernacle. He would give details and dimensions for a gold altar, a golden table, a hammered gold lamp stand, and a treasure box called the Ark of the Covenant. The Ark would be sealed with a solid gold lid, known as the Mercy Seat. And there, cloistered in darkness, the Almighty One would reside with his people as they traveled the desert.

The Ark of the Covenant would meet the needs of God and Israel for nearly a thousand years. Of course, today it is gone, having mysteriously disappeared several centuries ago. In truth, all those amazing gold furnishings are lost to us. Some were stolen and no doubt melted down. Some were simply destroyed. Others were perhaps lost and ultimately buried.

But three thousand years later, the God to whom they were dedicated remains a force to be reckoned with in our postmodern world! He continues to grow his Church, his Kingdom. He continues to perform miracles, answer prayers, and keep promises. And while he once occupied a seat of gold in a chamber of darkness, the whole Earth is now filled with his glory.

The gilded artwork and wall hangings of the Egyptians spoke of mythical gods and goddesses who watched from afar. It was believed they did their work in the shadowy realms of the netherworld somewhere beyond that border between death and eternity.

By contrast, the furnishings of the Tabernacle celebrate a God who is close by. He is not only the God of the dead, but of the living as well. He intervenes in human history to achieve his most noble purposes. He breaks through the walls of time and space to inject his power into human lives, flesh and blood circumstances, and historic outcomes. He brings his power, love, wisdom, and righteousness to bear in a way that creates a divine combustion and reveals something more precious than gold- his Glory.

That's why on the night when Christ was born, the shepherds were awestruck by their experience with the angels. They had spent many, many long evenings scanning the heavens and marveling at the distant lights. But on this special occasion when the angels sang, the light was so close and so intense that the men were stupefied! The Kingdom of Heaven was very near.

The baby Christ would grow up to become an unprecedented healer, a revolutionary teacher, a holy martyr, and a resurrected savior. And just before departing the Earth, he would give his disciples a charge and a promise.

Week Twelve The Glory of the God Who Came Near

- *The charge*: Bring the whole world to me.
- *The promise*: I am with you everyday until the world ends!

As we wrap up our journey through Egypt and the Exodus, let's devote our final week to some treasure that still captivates the imagination of the world. The Ark of the Covenant is celebrated in popular movies and best-selling books. There is even a tradition that it survives today, resting in secrecy in a city called Aksum in Ethiopia. It is impossible to verify if the story is fact-based or complete fiction.

But even if the Ark still remains in some secret location on the planet Earth, it would today amount to nothing more than an extremely valuable relic. Granted, it would reflect on the veracity of the Old Testament. And it would be fascinating to see on display in a museum. But it would remain a relic, nothing more.

Jesus came to give life and fulfillment to everything the Ark of the Covenant represented. And in Christ, the veil was torn down that separated the Most Holy Place of God from the rest of life.
- In him we are called to join the Tribe of God and escape the bondage of sin.
- In him we have been summoned to the deserts of life, to grow as a community, and to worship and adore the Lord God Almighty.
- In him, we shall one day reach the Land of Promise, the splendid shores of Heaven, where the Glory of God keeps all darkness at bay.

This week, we will explore the Tabernacle and its furnishings. We'll be working through the final chapters and topics of Exodus in this order:
- Day 1: Chapters 25, 35, and 37; The Ark of the Covenant and the Table of Presence
- Day 2: Chapters 37 and 38; The Lampstand and the Bronze Altar
- Day 3: Chapters 26, 36, and 40; The Tabernacle and the Glory of God
- Day 4: Hebrews 9 and 10; How this all comes together in Christ

It should be an exciting and insightful week. Thanks for sharing this journey with me and the Family of God.

Day 1: The Amazing Gold Box
Read Exodus 25, 35, & 37
Read each chapter slowly. Use a pencil and paper to do a rough line drawing of each item, approximating its shape and jotting the dimensions along each line. Try to create a mental image of how each item might have looked.

25: 1 – 9. This chapter begins with a voluntary offering. What items are people invited to offer to the Lord? (The same inventory is repeated in Exodus 35.)
- _____, _____ & _____;
- _____, _____, & _____ yarn;
- Fine _____ and goat _____;
- Hides of sea cows and rams dyed _____;

- _____ wood, _____ oil, spices, fragrant _____;
- _____ stones and other _____.

v8. What is the purpose of this structure God has authorized?

_____

_____

v9. Notice the precision that God desires. Each sacred object must be built according to the

_____ he has provided.

The Ark of the Covenant
25: 10 – 22. Using familiar US measures, what would be the dimensions of the chest for the Ark of the Covenant? (Consult your Study Bible notes, or calculate 1 cubit = 1 ½ feet.)

- Length: _____
- Width: _____
- Height: _____

Note: What some translations identity as "shittim wood" is thought to be acacia, a hard and extremely durable wood often used for furniture in the Middle East. This particular wood was probably fragrant as well, which may have explained why it was averse to wood-eating insects. The acacia or thorn tree is one of the most familiar trees along the plains of Africa.

v11. What substance is prescribed by God to be hammered in order to completely cover the wooden chest? _____

v12 – 15. The Ark is designed with very specific structures for use whenever it must be transported. In order to take advantage of this particular structure, how should the Ark be transported?

_____

What would you think is the significance of the requirement that the poles must be inserted through the rings and never removed?

_____

_____

Week Twelve The Glory of the God Who Came Near

Note: This explains what happens much later in *2 Samuel 6* when David attempts to transport the Tabernacle back to the center of public life in Jerusalem. The young king's purpose is noble, but he carelessly permits his helpers to transport the Ark on an ox cart. When an ox stumbles and the Ark almost topples over, a servant name Uzzah extends his hand to steady the sacred box. He dies instantly!

v16. God explains that the golden box will contain "The Testimony" which he will define later. *Are you ready for a surprise?*

- Do you know what will ultimately be placed in the Ark? If so, write it in this space: _____

- If your list contains three items, it probably matches *Hebrews 9:4*. Read that passage and write its inventory below:

  _____

  Does your list match this one?

- Now read *2 Chronicles 5:10*. When King Solomon built the first Temple and the Ark was transferred to the Holy of Holies in that new building, what was contained in the box?

  _____

- I suspect that this discrepancy is one that surprises most Christians. But it cannot simply be a contradiction in Scripture. The writer of Hebrews is intimately familiar with the details and history of the Old Testament, of which he has entire books memorized. Hence, something this significant cannot be the result of an oversight. There are two possible solutions:

  ✓ In *1 Samuel 4-6*, the Ark is captured by the Philistines and taken back to their homeland where it creates havoc. It is ultimately returned to Israel where seventy careless men open the Ark, look inside and are struck dead. If the jar of Manna and Aaron's rod were in the Ark at this time, they might have been removed by some of these individuals who defiled the Ark.
  ✓ Exodus[65] mentions that some of the manna should be kept as a Testimony, but does not mention being kept inside the Ark. Numbers[66] mentions that Aaron's rod would be kept as Testimony, but does not require it be kept in the Ark. It may be that a High Priest felt led by God to add those things to the Ark after the time of King Solomon.

Exodus 25: 17 – 22. The mercy seat, the lid covering the Ark, is intended by God as a sort of throne. Here above the mercy seat and between images of two angels facing one another, God promises to meet with his people and converse with them.

- The Hebrew term translated "converse" or "commune" is *dabar*.
- The tense on this occasion serves to intensify the action, denoting an intimate conversation or the making of a promise.

What do these particular attributes of the mercy seat denote to you? *Choose the one best answer for what each of the following implies:*
- The solid gold lid
  - [ ] God is rich and powerful.
  - [ ] God is the King who is worthy of our very best.
  - [ ] The gold represents the weight and splendor of God's Glory.

- Seated between two angels facing each other
  - [ ] God has angelic servants watching to do his bidding (*Matthew 18:10*.)
  - [ ] God is worthy of reverence.
  - [ ] God requires honor guards.

The Table of Presence
25: 23 – 40. Using familiar US measures, what would be the dimensions of the chest for the table? (Consult your Study Bible notes, or calculate 1 cubit = 1 ½ feet.)

- Length: _____
- Width: _____
- Height: _____

The table is acacia wood covered in gold. The plates and utensils that accompany it are hammered from pure gold. What are the gold plates for the table intended to hold?

_____

Consult *Leviticus 24:5 – 9*. How many loaves are placed on this table? _____
What must that number represent? _____

Have you noticed how frequently God continues to emphasize the tribal quality of his relationship with Israel. In recent chapters, we've seen the twelve tribes emphasized repeatedly.
- When Moses confirmed the covenant with God[67], he sacrificed on an altar surrounded by twelve pillars.
- The number of tribes and the names of the tribes are emphasized in the design of the high priest's garments.[68]
- Now we find that when God ordains this reminder that he is always present with his people, he again incorporates the motif of twelve tribes.

What do you think God desires to communicate when he represents the twelve tribes on the sacred table that assures the Israelites He is present with them?

Week Twelve   The Glory of the God Who Came Near

_____

_____

_____

_____

What would loaves of bread have to do with the presence of God with his people?

_____

_____

Consult *1 Samuel 21: 1 – 6*. This narrative documents an unprecedented use of the Bread of Presence. Is the priest right or wrong in his actions? *Explain your answer.*

_____

_____

_____

How does the Bread of Presence foreshadow the life and ministry of Jesus?

_____

Hint: See John 6: 32-40.

Thinking About the God Who Came Near

There's something quite unique about this idea of "approaching God," having God "commune with us," or "go with us." It's something you and I take for granted, but it was virtually unheard of until God revealed Himself to the Jews. Even today, this relational quality of the One True God sets his Church apart from all the other religions of the world.

Allah, the god of Islam, does not seek a relationship with Muslims. The Koran commands Muslims to submit and, consequently, obey. Neither did the gods and goddesses of ancient Egypt speak in terms of relationship. They were distant, aloof, and constantly in need of appeasement. And although they might offer a few tokens of blessing in regard to this life, they were, for the most part, just waiting out there in the shadows in order to assist worshipers after death.

In sharp contrast, the God of Abraham, Isaac, Jacob and Jesus is jealous for relationship with the people who know Him. He teaches us to call him "Father." He constantly compares Israel to his bride. He explains in 1 John that he *is love*. He offers to adopt those who believe upon his Name.

In closing, what does the Ark of the Covenant teach you and me today about the priorities of God?

_____

_____

What does the Ark/mercy seat teach us about the practical impact of our sin?

_____

_____

Day 2: The Light of the World
Read Exodus 37, 38
Read each chapter, reflecting carefully. Once again use a pencil and paper to do a rough line drawing of each item, approximating its shape and jotting the dimensions along each line. Try to create a mental image of how each item might have looked.

Exodus 37: 17 - 24. The lampstand will be made of pure, hammered gold, just about 65 pounds. (God directs that a talent of gold, seventy-five pounds, should be used for the stand plus its accessories.)
- How many lights will burn on this menorah? _____
- The cups holding the lamps will be shaped like _____ blossoms.
- See *Jeremiah 1:11-12*. The particular tree is called "the watchful tree' because it is always the first to blossom.
- What would the use of these blossoms communicate about God's presence?

_____

_____

See *Exodus 27: 20-21*. How many hours each day does God require that this lampstand should be lighted? _____

What does that communicate about God's presence with us?

_____

1 Samuel 3: 1 – 10. The gold lampstand will figure prominently in this pivotal moment in the unfolding history of Israel.
- *v3.* Why was the hero of this story found inside the Tabernacle so late at night?

_____

Week Twelve   The Glory of the God Who Came Near

- Twice each day, a priest was charged with refilling the olive oil in the lamps and trimming the wicks so that the flames could be maintained continuously.[69]

Read *Revelation 1: 12 – 20*. In writing to seven churches during an age of hardship and violent persecution, John draws on the familiar image of the Old Testament menorah.
- How many lampstands does he describe? _____
- In light of the fact that John is addressing seven churches, what would be the significance of seven lamp stands rather than only one?

_____

_____

- Who is standing in the midst of the lamps? _____
- What message would persecuted saints receive from this image in John's Revelation? *Select the single best answer.*
  [ ] The answer to your problems is found in the Old Testament.
  [ ] Christ has not forgotten or abandoned you, but is standing in your midst.
  [ ] God deserves your very best.
  [ ] This is all good, for you are being refined as by fire.

Selah. It's useful to pause here and think about the power of beloved images. For example, in the United States the American flag is a powerful symbol for many, many people. The sight of Old Glory waving at historic moments can bring tears to the eyes of US citizens. Prisoners of war have been known to draw strength and comfort from small, crude replicas of the US flag constructed of tiny scraps of cloth and paper.

While the American flag is slightly more than 200 years old, the gold lampstand of the Holy Place had been a cherished symbol for more than 1500 years by the time of Christ. Throughout all those centuries, one tabernacle and three temples, the menorah had been a visual reminder of God's presence, his power, and his love for his people. With that in mind, imagine the rush of emotion and joy the first-century saints must have experienced when a messenger arrived with a letter from John the Apostle. Meeting in tunnels amid underground graves just to escape arrest and trial, they must have hurriedly clustered together to listen. And when the stranger began to read, the very first image he described was Christ standing by the sacred lampstand.

The Altar of Incense
Exodus 37: 25 – 28. This altar will rest just in front of the curtain which covers the doorway to the Holy of Holies. Acacia wood covered in gold, it will stand just about 1 ½' wide and 3' tall. It will constantly emit a specially ordained fragrance.

Q: How would incense suggest the reality and the power of prayers being offered faithfully to the Almighty?

_____

_____

The Bronze Altar of Sacrifice
38: 1 – 7. Take note that this is by far the largest piece of all the furnishings God has appointed for his Tabernacle. Using the calculation of 1 cubit = 1 ½ feet, estimate the dimensions of this altar.
- 3 cubits high = _____ ' tall
- 5 cubits long = _____ ' long
- 5 cubits wide = _____ ' wide

Why would it be necessary that the altar for burnt offerings be so large?

_____

_____

Hint: if you're stumped, consult Numbers 7: 1 – 10.

Read *Leviticus 4 :27 - 31.* Why must Israelites continually sacrifice animals on this bronze altar? In a word, the answer is "sin." Temptation is so seductive and sin is so pervasive that people not only violate the Law willfully, but sometimes do so unintentionally.

- *v29.* Why must he lay his own hand on the head of the sacrificial animal?

   _____

   _____

- *Leviticus 17:11* teaches, "For the life of the creature is in the blood, and I have given it to you to make atonement for yourselves on the altar: it is the blood that makes atonement for one's life."
   - ✓ What does the death of a choice animal teach us about the destructive power of our sin?
   - ✓ This principle is called "substitutionary atonement." What does that mean?

   _____

   _____

   _____

- ✓ Someone has said that the word "atonement" is self-defining. It simply must be broken up directly: at- one- ment. What does that suggest to you?

  _____

  _____

- ✓ The word translated "atonement" is the Hebrew term *kaphar*, meaning "to cover." What must be covered in order for us to experience atonement before God?

  _____

Why would the bronze altar necessarily be the first object a priest would encounter upon approaching the Tabernacle to stand in the presence of God?

_____

_____

How does the Old Testament altar of sacrifice relate to the New Testament ministry of Jesus Christ?

_____

_____

The Basin
Exodus 38:8. Standing between the altar and the entrance to the sacred tent, the basin was dedicated to ceremonial washing before entering the Holy Place. This basin may have been a forerunner of baptism by immersion, which was commonly practiced among the Jews by the time of John the Baptist.

1 John 1:9. "If we _____ our sins, he is faithful and just and will forgive our sins, and _____ us of all unrighteousness."

The Courtyard
Exodus 38: 9 – 19. The sacred tent will be surrounded by a fenced area or courtyard. Calculate the dimensions:
- 100 cubits long = _____' long
- 50 cubits wide = _____' wide

The sacred tent itself is not nearly so long or wide. What would all this empty space teach about God's holiness?

_____

_____

v18. While the curtains setting off the courtyard are made of fine linen, the entrance to the courtyard is made of finely twisted linen interwoven with blue, scarlet and purple yarn.
- What do you think is the significance of the purple, scarlet and blue yarn decorating the entrance?

_____

_____

_____

- Although the structure is quite large, there is only one entryway- one doorway to the presence of God. What truth does this detail foreshadow?

_____

See John 14:6.

Exodus 38: 21 – 31. The Israelites were quite generous in supplying the materials required for the Tent of God's Presence. Using familiar measures, the quantities would look more like this:
- Gold: 29 Talents, 730 Shekels = Slightly more than a ton
- Silver: 100 Talents, 1775 Shekels = 3 ¾ tons
- Bronze: 70 Talents, 2,400 Shekels = 2 ½ tons

Day 3: A Portrait of Atonement
Read Exodus 26, 36, & 40

These chapters are filled with dimensions, materials, and directions for building the tent where the Lord will dwell. Don't be overwhelmed by the numbers. Look carefully for theological truths embedded in this structure and its design.

Exodus 36: 1 – 7. Again we cannot help but notice the way God loves to speak and record the names of His people. After the people of Israel generously donate some of their treasures, God appoints two craftsmen to construct the Tabernacle and its furnishings. Their names are:

- _____

- _____

36: 8 – 38. Many of these details might be lost on you and me, but we can understand how some of them would have spoken to the Hebrews.

- *v8.* The blue, purple and scarlet yarn would have brought to mind the color of the heavens, the power of royalty, the atonement through blood.
- *v19.* The red covering over the tent would have indicated that our sins are covered (atoned for) by blood. Today you and I realize how that has been fulfilled in Jesus Christ.
- *v38.* The five posts at the front of the tent would have represented grace, a concept commonly associated with the number five. In God's grace, he would ultimately give them five books of the Law.

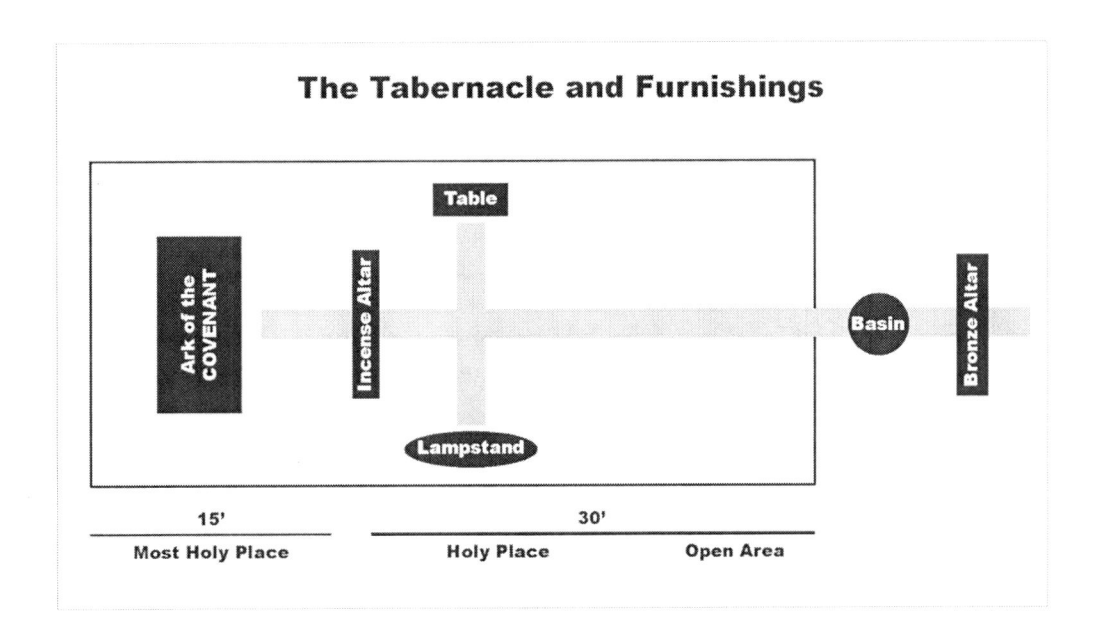

The Tabernacle and Furnishings

Ark of the COVENANT | Incense Altar | Table | Lampstand | Basin | Bronze Altar

15' Most Holy Place — 30' Holy Place — Open Area

Exodus 40: 1 – 33. Because God is so specific with even the most minute details of the design, we know the Tabernacle is a divine object lesson. Let's explore some of the details:

v3. As soon as the Tent is in place, the Ark of the Covenant is the first thing that is installed. It is placed in the Holy of Holies and shielded by an elaborate curtain. What is the theological significance of the Ark being in place first?

_____

_____

_____

v4. The Table of Presence is placed along the north wall of the tent, with the Gold Lampstand standing opposite on the south wall. Glance at the diagram and you'll recognize that these two pieces of sacred furniture form the arms of a cross. *It is no accident that the path from the solitary outside gate to the inner sanctuary of God follows the path of a cross.*

v6. The Bronze Altar is set in place just inside the gate, the first step on the path to the presence of God. How does this altar of sacrifice foreshadow the work of Christ on the cross?

_____

_____

_____

v7. The journey into God's presence begins with sacrifice. The next object on the path to peace is the basin. What does this water represent in the walk of faith that brings us to reconciliation with God?

_____

_____

v8. The sheets of white linen, a token of absolute holiness, mark the boundary between the Holy Creator God and the unholy world that sin polluted after he created it. How does the solitary entryway into the area prefigure Jesus Christ?

_____

v9. The sacred anointing oil, made from a unique formula which can be used for no other purpose, is poured onto every object inside the linen boundary. Throughout the Scriptures, oil is a figure for the Holy Spirit. How does the Holy Spirit anoint and sanctify the one who puts his faith in the Messiah?

_____

_____

_____

v12. Aaron and his sons, the priesthood, are ushered in to cleanse themselves and be robed in symbolic garments designed by God. Nothing in their experience or their abilities has prepared them for the work of the priesthood. Rather, the only things that qualify them to serve are things provided by God: their calling and the fact that they are adorned in something supernatural that was given to them.

Who are the priests of the New Testament, and what qualifies them to serve in ministry?

_____

Week Twelve   The Glory of the God Who Came Near

_____

_____

_____

Hint: Revelation 1:5

Now that you are familiar with how the tabernacle was constructed and what it teaches the people of God, wouldn't you like to know what happens in that sacred space during the years after Exodus closes?

Read *Leviticus 16: 1 – 25*. In addition to all the daily sacrifices that are offered up at the Tabernacle, the Day of Atonement is an annual day of sacrifice. On this day and only this day, the High Priest is permitted to enter the Most Holy Place (i.e. Holy of Holies) and see the Ark of Testimony. And once again, even he must go through an elaborate preparation so that he will not be struck dead.

- *v11.* Before intervening on behalf of the sinful nation, he must first take care of his own sin. *What is required of him?*

  _____

- *v12.* He takes a censer filled with incense into the Most Holy Place and smoke quickly fills the chamber. *For what purpose?*

  _____

- *v14.* Merely sacrificing the bull does not atone for his sins. Rather, something must be done with some of the bull's blood. *What?*

  _____

- *v8.* In order to atone for the sins of the nation, two goats are selected.
    - ✓ *v15. What happens to the first goat?*

      _____

    - ✓ *v20.* The second goat is called the "scapegoat." There was no English word for this animal until 1530 when William Tyndale translated the Hebrew Old Testament into English for the very first time. Tyndale made up the word, which continues as a popular English expression for a person who is punished for the offenses of someone else.

    - ✓ What happens to the scapegoat?

      _____

The two goats represent two different processes that are necessary for you and me to be reconciled to God. Theologians actually have two distinct words:
- The sacrificial goat depicts **propitiation**. Because our sins have violated God's eternal justice, He is innately offended. The blood of this goat denotes that our sins must be covered to remove the anger of the Almighty Judge.
- The scapegoat represents **expiation**. This means that God must somehow take care of the personal guilt and shame you and I experience. This goat depicts the way God cleanses us of guilt and personal condemnation.

Exodus 40: 34 – 38. The first nineteen chapters of Exodus are all in preparation for what happens on Mount Sinai in chapters 20 – 24. Once you turn the page to Exodus 25, everything that takes place afterwards is in preparation for this moment in chapter 40. The Tabernacle is now in place and available to instruct the people of Israel in the ways of the God who loves them so much that he personal journeys with them.
- *v34.* Moses has stood in God's presence and beheld his glory on other occasions. Pause and reflect: now that the Tabernacle is complete and functional, why can Moses no longer enter the Holy Place?

If you're stumped, consult Hebrews 8:3-5.

- *v36.* For the next 40 years, Israel will always know when to break camp and travel, and when to remain in camp and be still. What will be their signal?

Personal Application: How does God most commonly direct your life?
- Are there offerings and ministries that you are under orders to perform faithfully on an ongoing basis? What are some of those?

- How does God alert you that something out of the ordinary is in order at a particular time?

Even as I write this, the Holy Spirit has placed this overwhelming burden on me to stop and be still: to meditate on the path to his presence that leads through the path of the cross. *Selah*. Let me encourage you, wherever you are at this moment, to undertake something that I have just experienced in my study.

- Locate *Isaiah 52: 13 – 53: 6* in your Bible.
- Read it slowly, letting each word sink in.
- Now prostrate yourself on the floor in a comfortable place. Extend your arms outward to form a cross.
    - ✓ Allow some time to quietly relax, letting the various joints of your body relax and sink even more closely to the floor.
    - ✓ Select a verse from the passage you just read. It could be a fragment as simple as "He was pierced for our transgressions, he was crushed for our iniquities."
    - ✓ Cycle that statement quietly through your mind again and again.
    - ✓ Try to imagine the disrespect of the arrest, the humiliation of the trial, the violence of the scourging with 39 blows, the bloody agony of the cross. Count the blows as you imagine them. Imagine the sounds of the hammer as you think of the spikes piercing Christ's wrists and legs.
    - ✓ Let thanksgiving to God overflow naturally from your life, either silently or aloud.
    - ✓ Thank God for the way your sins have been covered and your guilt has been cleansed.

Day 4: A Shadow of Things to Come
Read Hebrews 9, & 10
Read these chapters with care, reflecting on the things you have learned about the Law and the Tabernacle. Use your pen or marker to underscore or highlight each phrase or sentence in which Hebrews mentions something being better than or superior to something else.

Hebrews 9: 1 – 10. When the writer mentions the first covenant contained regulations for "an earthly sanctuary," what does this imply?

_____

v2 – 7. Think about a High Priest walking through his assigned steps on the Day of Atonement; passing each of these gleaming, gold accessories now so familiar to you. But ponder this: is this all taking place mostly in bright light, or mostly in shadows and darkness?
    [ ] The bright light of day
    [ ] Darkness, shadows and the dim light of seven oil lamps

What might be the connotation of important things like these being carried out in a place of shadows?

_____

v8. According to this verse, what was the Holy Spirit clearly demonstrating through this? *(Choose only one answer and think about what it means.)*
- [ ] That the way to the Most Holy Place had not yet been revealed
- [ ] That the people walking in darkness have seen a great light
- [ ] That we all walk through the valley of the shadow of death
- [ ] That believers are the light of the world

v9. According to this verse, worship in the Tabernacle was only an illustration of what fact? *(Choose only one answer and pause to let it sink in.)*
- [ ] That God is Spirit and Truth
- [ ] That God is not a God of confusion
- [ ] That faith is walking to the edge of the light and taking one more step
- [ ] That the sacrifices offered at that time could not actually clear the conscience of the one offering them.

v10. What is the clear teaching of this scriptural statement about offerings in the Tabernacle?
- [ ] Man shall not live by bread alone.
- [ ] God gives us our daily bread on a daily basis.
- [ ] These things are just a figurative prelude to the real thing which will be revealed later.
- [ ] Our earthly bodies are just tents which will die and be replaced.

v11 – 14. If the blood of goats were useful at least on the outside, how much more will the blood of Jesus sanctity us inside and out! According to this text, how did Christ accomplish what previous High Priests could never achieve?

_____

_____

_____

v15. Christ has accomplished two things:
- He has become the mediator of a _____ _____
- He has died as a _____ to free us from our sins.

v16. "Testament" is just another term for a will. Before a will can be executed, someone has to _____.

v23-28. Under the Old Covenant, the High Priest had to return with offerings year after year. In the New Covenant, Christ has appeared once and for all to offer one sacrifice, a perfect one. *What is the result of this?*

_____

Hebrews 10:1,2. The Law was not God's ultimate reality, but was simply a _____ of what God would offer in Christ.

v3. All those annual sacrifices in the Old Testament were just annual _____ of our sins, which they could not take away from us.

v8 – 10. Three of the following statements are drawn from this passage. One is not related to this passage at all. <u>Check the three</u> that are paraphrased from these verses.
  [ ] Animal sacrifices and burnt offerings were never appealing to God.
  [ ] God always wanted absolute conformity to the rules.
  [ ] God always wanted holy people dedicated to his purposes.
  [ ] Christ paved the way when he came to do God's will.

v16. This is actually a promise first made in the Old Testament through the prophet Jeremiah.[70] *Which one of the following statements best paraphrases it?*
  [ ] As a man thinketh, so is he.
  [ ] In the New Covenant a man of God will never violate his conscience.
  [ ] The Old Covenant began with outward behavior. The New Covenant will inform the attitudes of the heart in order to change the outward behavior.
  [ ] All people of God should memorize the Ten Commandments.

10: 19 – 21. Remember the backdrop for this text. The High Priest of the Old Covenant must devote time and energy to being "ceremonially clean" before he can enter the Most Holy Place. He must robe himself in specially prescribed garments which he must wear in a particular manner. And even after all of this, there are still bells sewn to the hem of his robe lest God should strike him dead. *Why are these verses so reassuring and so liberating?*

_____

_____

_____

_____

v26. This statement does not infer that followers of Jesus will never sin again. Rather, as verse *28* clarifies, it refers to the larger, foundational sin of saying "No" to God. In other words, people who rejected Moses and the commands of God continued in only one sin: *rejection of God*. The faithful Jews who followed Moses still committed other sins in the days that followed. But they were not condemned because when they first received the Words of God, they embraced them in faith rather than rejecting them.

v31. Some people like to say that God is no longer angry now that the New Testament has been set in place. Read this verse a couple of times and then indicate whether or not you think God still gets angry in the New Testament.
> [ ] No, God's anger and wrath have been assuaged forever.
> [ ] Yes, God still gets angry about sin, and anyone still around for the final judgment will experience his indignation.

Hebrews 10: 19 - 29 is one of several places in which this letter addresses orthodox Jews who have been meeting with the followers of Christ for some time to observe and ask questions. They have participated in worship services and have apparently come within a heart beat of risking everything to publicly confess Christ as Messiah and Lord. But tragically, either the possibility of being disinherited by Jewish families or the larger likelihood of facing violent persecution from Jews and Romans has stopped them in their tracks. It seems that some have suggested they might step back and punt for the moment, supposing they may return and confess Christ later when there's not so much at stake.

These Jewish men and women have been to the Temple. They've heard about the pattern of the Tabernacle from centuries earlier. They have almost certainly offered goats and sheep in sacrifice for their sins. But they have never experienced the peace with God that was promised, because the blood of goats and bulls and the ashes of a heifer serve only to remind them of what they still long for and have yet to discover: *direct access to the God who has drawn near.* The writer of Hebrews exhorts them not to shrink back from the path of the cross in fear, but to boldly call upon Jesus Christ and gladly approach the throne of God!

v39. We are not of those who _____ and are destroyed, but of those who _____ and are saved.

This closing verse of Hebrews 10 looks ahead to the "Faith Hall of Fame" that follows in the next chapter. And it reflects on the history of Israel as narrated in the Exodus. It was not easy for the Hebrew slaves in Egypt to follow a prodigal like Moses out of a land that had grown familiar, and venture unprepared into a dangerous desert.

Q: Why did it require so much courage for disenfranchised people trapped in slavery to take this chance at winning their liberty?

_____

_____

_____

_____

What did God accomplish by calling the Jews to a communal faith in which tribe and family are vital components?

What are some of the treasures they discovered in the desert after they left the gilded corridors of Egypt?

What have you learned about your own faith during these 12 weeks in the desert with Moses?

Share some of the insights into the ministry of the Messiah that you have picked up during this time in the wilderness.

For me, these final paragraphs conclude more than eighteen months exploring Exodus and walking with Moses. Poring carefully over familiar passages and unfamiliar Hebrew words, I have discovered ideas and incidents I had not seen before in my decades of walking with Christ. I have experienced the wonder and excitement that occurs when God pokes around in the fire of a man's life and brings graying embers back to flame again. The tribal element of Exodus has taught me to value my church and friends, my tribe, more deeply than ever. And I have returned to kneel before the cross of Jesus with more gratitude and more awareness of my sin than ever before. A foolish slave, I had sold myself for nothing, so I was not redeemed with money. My freedom required his blood.

Nothing in all of life is beyond the reach of The Ancient of Days. He has all the power of the universe at his disposal. And his son's death on the cross was not an unplanned accident; it was destiny. If God can embrace an ancient instrument of death and incorporate it into a second chance for hundreds of millions, he can transform any event or any human being. So I leave you with a benediction from Ephesians that sounds like it could have been written in old Egypt. "Now to him who is able to do immeasurably more than all we ask or imagine, according to his power that is at work within us, to him be glory in the church and in Christ Jesus throughout all generations forever and ever! Amen!"[71]

ENDNOTES

[1] Deuteronomy 33:19

[2] Hebrews 11: 26

[3] Psalm 42: 1,2

[4] Hebrews 10:35,36

[5] 1 Peter 1:4

[6] Colossians 2:2

[7] Genesis 50:20

[8] 1 Peter 4:12

[9] Hebrews 11:1

[10] The tribe of Levi was given the priesthood rather than a share of the land.

[11] Genesis 12 and 22: 15 - 19

[12] 1 Peter 1:7

[13] Exodus 6:20

[14] 1 Chronicles 4:9; 1 Samuel 4:21

[15] 2 Corinthians 12:10

[16] Acts 7:22

[17] Ephesians 1: 18

[18] Ezekiel 14:21

[19] 2 Chronicles 24:24

[20] Numbers 20:11

[21] 1 Samuel 15:2

[22] Luke 16:25

[23] Daniel 7:14

[24] Hosea 8:7

[25] Genesis 27:12

[26] 1 Peter 5:8

EndNotes

[27] Colossians 1:13

[28] This particular verse mentions only the firstborn, but in Exodus 11:4, Moses promises the Pharaoh that first born sons will die.

[29] See 1 Samuel 1:22; Isaiah 60:19 for examples of each.

[30] Acts 10,11

[31] Sahara Unveiled: A Journey Across the Desert by William Langewiesche; Vintage Books. New York: 1996. Page 263

[32] 1 Samuel 16:7

[33] Hebrews 9:4

[34] Joshua 3: 8,13

[35] Matthew 28: 18 – 20

[36] Malachi 3:10

[37] Matthew 27:51

[38] Matthew 6:9

[39] John 14:13

[40] Luke 21:12

[41] Isaiah 52:7

[42] Matthew 22:37

[43] Genesis 9:6

[44] 1 Samuel 15:1

[45] Matthew 5:9

[46] Surveys suggest that most Christians believe this statement is found in the Bible. Not only is this not a Bible verse, but it's not true either.

[47] Genesis 17:15. God changes the spelling from Sarai to Sarah, changing the meaning as well.

[48] Genesis 12: 10-13

[49] Joshua 2: 4 - 7

[50] 1 Samuel 21: 10 - 15

[51] Proverbs 6:17

[52] Matthew 5: 43-44

[53] Proverbs 30:5

[54] Leviticus 22:28

[55] Deuteronomy 22:6,7

[56] People for Ethical Treatment of Animals

[57] Hebrews 8:5

[58] Numbers 27:21

[59] 2 Chronicles 4:13

[60] Leviticus 16: 11,15

[61] Psalm 7:10; Jeremiah 17:10

[62] For more information read *None of these Diseases* by Drs S.I. McMillen and David E. Stern.

[63] *Keil & Delitzsch*; Peabody, Massachutsetts,1866. Page 465.

[64] Psalm 19: 1 - 3

[65] Exodus 16:34

[66] Numbers 17:10

[67] Exodus 24:5

[68] Exodus 28: 1 - 30

[69] Leviticus 24:2

[70] Jeremiah 31:33

[71] Ephesians 3: 20,21